Borges and the Kabbalah

Borges and the Kabbalah
And other essays on his fiction and poetry

JAIME ALAZRAKI

WITHDRAWN

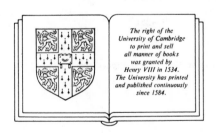

The right of the
University of Cambridge
to print and sell
all manner of books
was granted by
Henry VIII in 1534.
The University has printed
and published continuously
since 1584.

CAMBRIDGE UNIVERSITY PRESS

Cambridge

New York   New Rochelle   Melbourne   Sydney

College - Reserves

PQ
7797
.B635
Z567
1988
c.1

Published by the Press Syndicate of the University of Cambridge
The Pitt Building, Trumpington Street, Cambridge CB2 1RP
32 East 57th Street, New York, NY 10022, USA
10 Stamford Road, Oakleigh, Melbourne 3166, Australia

© Cambridge University Press 1988

First published 1988

Printed in the United States of America

Library of Congress Cataloging-in-Publication Data
Alazraki, Jaime.
Borges and the Kabbalah.
Bibliography: p.
Includes index.
1. Borges, Jorge Luis, 1899–   –Criticism and
interpretation.   I. Title.
PQ7797.B635Z567   1988   868   88-4251

ISBN 0 521 30684 1

British Library Cataloguing in Publication applied for.

Contents

Abbreviations

A *The Aleph and Other Stories 1933–1969* (edited and translated by Norman Thomas di Giovanni in collaboration with the author). New York: E. P. Dutton, 1970.

BIB *The Book of Imaginary Beings* (translated by N. T. di Giovanni in collaboration with the author). New York: Avon Books, 1970.

C *La cifra*. Buenos Aires: Emecé, 1981.

D *Discusión*. Buenos Aires: Emecé, 1964.

DBR *Doctor Brodie's Report* (translated by N. T. di Giovanni in collaboration with the author). New York: E. P. Dutton, 1972.

DT *Dreamtigers* (translated by M. Boyer and H. Morland). Austin: University of Texas Press, 1968.

ES *Elogio de la sombra*. Buenos Aires: Emecé, 1969.

F *Ficciones* (edited by A. Kerrigan). New York: Grove Press, 1962.

GT *The Gold of the Tigers* (translated by Alastair Reid). New York: E. P. Dutton, 1977.

HE *Historia de la eternidad*. Buenos Aires: Emecé, 1961.

HN *Historia de la noche*. Buenos Aires: Emecé, 1977.

HU *Historia universal de la infamia*. Buenos Aires: Emecé, 1962.

I *Inquisiciones*. Buenos Aires: Proa, 1925.

IA *El idioma de los argentinos*. Buenos Aires: Gleizer, 1928.

L *Labyrinths: Selected Stories and Other Writings* (edited by Donald A. Yates and James E. Irby). New York: New Directions, 1964.

MEP *Modern European Poetry* (edited by W. Barnstone et al.). New York: Bantam, 1978.

MH   *La moneda de hierro*. Buenos Aires: Emecé, 1976.

OI   *Other Inquisitions 1937–1952* (translated by Ruth L. C. Simms). New York: Washington Square Press, 1966.

OM   *El otro, el mismo*. Buenos Aires: Emecé, 1969.

OP   *Obra poética*. Buenos Aires: Emecé, 1967.

OT   *El oro de los tigres*. Buenos Aires: Emecé, 1972.

PA   *A Personal Anthology* (edited by A. Kerrigan). New York: Grove Press, 1967.

PD   *In Praise of Darkness* (translated by N. T. di Giovanni in collaboration with the author). New York: E. P. Dutton, 1974.

RP   *La Rosa profunda*. Buenos Aires: Emecé, 1975.

SP   *Selected Poems 1923–1967* (edited by N. T. di Giovanni). Delacorte Press/Seymour Lawrence, 1972.

UH   *A Universal History of Infamy* (translated by N. T. di Giovanni). New York: E. P. Dutton, 1979.

Preface

Why is this book different from all previous books on Borges? In dealing with an author whose critical bibliography has grown to overwhelming proportions, it seems fit to raise the question. Borges not only invites commentary and rumination, he provokes tautology. We all, his readers, search and strive for some unturned stone, for an undiscovered pearl waiting, iridescent – that is, full of new insights – at the bottom of some recondite line, on the reverse of an overlooked ambiguity, in the elusive meaning subtly intimated between the lines. Borges has turned us all into inquisitive Kabbalists. Carried away by this enthralling exercise, we fail to notice the obvious: that the said discovery has already been recorded, and that if we only care to look for it in some concealed corner of the Library, we will find it. There are at least a good half-dozen general introductions to Borges in English alone. I am the author of one of them. Some are more concise than others, some are more detailed and at times prolix, but all aim at giving an overall picture, a comprehensive survey of his writings. I see nothing wrong with that. There is always the possibility of a new twist, of an unexpected nuance in the way of presenting the same stories, poems or essays, but in justifying the place and the necessity for a new collection of essays on Borges' work, I feel compelled to point out the differences underlying this collection vis-à-vis those already in existence.

Although this is not a survey of Borges' writings, it could be described as an introduction to key aspects of Borges' oeuvre. The distinction, far from gratuitous, is worth emphasizing. None of the essays included here were intended as summaries or inventories of previous scholarship. Quite the contrary. Each one grew out of a glaring vacuum in a given area of research. The question of Borges and the Kabbalah, for example. When I published my essays on this topic in 1971 and 1972 respectively,

Rabi's note included in the 1964 mammoth issue of "Cahiers de *l'Herne*" was the only reference available on this fundamental subject. In addition to being written in French, it did not assume the implications, let alone the consequences, of Borges' acquaintance with the Kabbalah in his fiction. I felt that this was an inexcusable gap. My years at the Hebrew University of Jerusalem, between 1958 and 1962, and the study of the Kabbalah I undertook there with Professors Gershom Scholem and J. Tishby gave me the necessary tools to tackle the question of Borges and the Kabbalah. By a happy coincidence, my training in this area coincided with Borges' own sources of information. The next step was to map the presence of those sources in his writings as a preliminary move towards a more challenging end: to establish and study the avenues the Kabbalah opened into his fiction. If the outlook and the methods of the Kabbalah permeated Borges' narratives, what roles do they play and how were they integrated into the fictive fabric? My two essays on this subject seek to answer those questions.

In the next section dealing with his fiction, I addressed myself to one of the most neglected and vexing aspects of study, namely the question of code: the formalistic devices by means of which messages are conveyed. Borges has been repeatedly praised as a master of language. Most contemporary Spanish American writers, from Julio Cortázar to Garcia Márquez, have acknowledged their linguistic debt to Borges. Cortázar best defined the extent and nature of that debt in a 1978 interview: "The great lesson Borges taught us was neither a lesson in themes nor in contents or techniques. It was a lesson in writing, an attitude. The attitude of a man who, when writing a sentence, has very carefully thought not which adjective to add, but which one to suppress. Later on he fell into the trap of using, in a rather displayful way, a single adjective in order to dazzle the reader, thus turning the effective trick into a defect. But originally, Borges attitude towards the written page was the attitude of a Mallarmé: of extreme rigor and precision."[1]

Borges' early critics noticed, likewise, his masterful prose. Amado Alonso put this perception of Borges' style in a lapidary phrase when he wrote in 1935: "Nobody like Borges has created among us a style so style."[2] My book of 1968, and its subsequent new editions of 1974 and 1983 – *La prosa narrativa de J.L. Borges* – was an effort to demonstrate the soundness of that assertion. In the essay on "Borges, or Style as an Invisible Worker" I offer a synopsis of some of my findings. My understanding of style is concerned with language in relation to other levels of literary meaning. Deviance from the norm as the criterion for style analysis has been replaced by the particular vision governing the production of the text. This vision appears embodied in a theme or motif or, in more general terms, at the semantic level of the work, and it is also expressed through other components integrated in that text. Style is measured by its role and participation in the realization of that vision and not merely by its linguistic deviance from a norm. This new criterion enables the analyst to account for elements of style that may be normative – and therefore innocuous according to the old criterion – which are nevertheless relevant in the performance of a stylistic function. We have come full circle to the concept of style postulated earlier by the Russian formalists who emphasized the close correlation between stylistics and thematics in literary studies. V. V. Vinogradov repeatedly insisted upon the internal unity of literary composition and on the systematic nature of a text, in which style is but one wheel more joining the others in the conveyance of literary messages. He underlined "the functional and immanent study of style," meaning style in its relation to a given literary vision as well as to other textual elements. In his study of Gogol's *Overcoat,* Boris Eikhenbaum pointed out that the rhythm of the sentences finds an immediate echo in the analysis of themes. In a later work devoted to the Russian poet Anna Akhmatova, Eikhenbaum studied the frequency of oxymoronic constructions in her poetry and concluded that this stylistic figure becomes also the dominant principle at every level of her work: subject, composition, and of course language.

In my essay on *A Universal History of Infamy,* I tried to show that the use of oxymora in Borges' early narratives responds to his literary vision of infamy as a travestied form of heroism. This parodic approach to his theme engages style as well as other elements of the literary code. Since infamy as theme or motif is not new in Borges' fiction, I begin by defining the peculiar treatment of the theme in this collection. The burlesque approach to his theme is expressed, in stylistic terms, through the use of oxymoron, hypallage, and litotes; and the fact that these stories are summaries of books by other authors has its stylistic counterpart in the use of metonymy, which, like Borges' adopted narrative strategy, condenses the whole in one of its attributes. For the purpose of my analysis, I chose from a multiplicity of stylistic devices those that – following the Jakobsonian concept of the *dominant* – "especify the work and guarantee the integrity of the structure."[3]

In the last essay of this section, I present what could be described as my discourse on method for the study of compositional patterns in Borges' stories. It was first published as the opening chapter of my book *Versiones, inversiones, reversiones* of 1977, a study of mirror as the structural principle underlying Borges' narratives. My point of departure was a comment made by Paul de Man in his pioneering essay "A Modern Master" of 1964, where he wrote: "All his stories have a similar mirror-like structure, although the devices vary with diabolical ingenuity."[4]

Until the publication of my book in 1977, very little was added to de

Man's insightful essay. My piece on "The South" intends to show that structure, far from being an arbitrary skeleton supporting meaning, becomes a configuration of meaning. Juan Dahlmann's dilemma – to fight or not to fight – reaches its true resolution at the symmetrical disposition of the narrative material. Structure – the organization of the fable into a form or signifier – supplies a forceful answer to the problem presented at the level of message or signified. Like mirrors whose images invert and revert the reflected object, structure functions in Borges' stories as a metacommentary which modifies or reinforces a given conflict presented as plot.

The third part is devoted to poetry. In spite of the fact that Borges' poetry far exceeds, in volume as well as in scope, his narrative production, very little has been said, in English at least, of this segment of his work. For several critics Borges is above all a poet. His first book, published in 1923 – *Fervor of Buenos Aires* – was a collection of poems, and so was his last, *The Conjurors* of 1985. He himself has confirmed this assessment: "First and foremost, I think of myself as a reader, then as a poet, then as a prose writer."[5] Now that he is dead and the corpus of his writings is enclosed in the boundaries that finality provides, it it clear that his poetry outweighs his fiction, not only in size – twelve collections of poems as opposed to five volumes of short stories – but also in value. His fiction – as he himself put it – is the work of "a man who has tried to explore the literary possibilities of metaphysics and of religion."[6] His poetry, on the other hand, gives expression to a more personal and intimate human being. As time recedes from his highly intellectualized stories, it also moves towards his more private and confidential poetry. Borges must have felt all along the distance separating one genre from the other. Anticipating the ultimate fate of his own work, he wrote in 1971: "My stories are, in a sense, outside of me. I dream them, shape them, and set them down; after that, once sent out into the world, they belong to others. All that is personal to me, all that my friends good-naturedly tolerate in me – my likes and dislikes, my hobbies, my habits – are to be found in my verse. In the long run, perhaps, I shall stand or fall by my poems."[7]

It took a symposium exclusively devoted to Borges' poetry – held at Dickinson College in 1983 with the presence of Borges himself – to refocus critical attention on his poetry. The volume *Borges the Poet* (1986) resulted from this gathering. My essay "Enumerations as Evocations" was originally read at that conference. It is a study of enumerations as a literary device in Borges' late poetry. It takes into account the Whitmanesque use of this contrivance to then establish Borges' peculiar handling of it. In Whitman's poetry, according to Leo Spitzer, enumerations render that oriental bazaar of our unordered civilization into the powerful Ego, the "I" of the poet who has extricated himself from the chaos. In Borges, on the other hand, enumerations avoid this condition of catalogues to become metonymic contractions, indexes, of previous themes and motifs elaborately sung in earlier poetry.

Between 1969 and 1981 Borges published six full-fledged collections of poetry: *In Praise of Darkness* (1969), *The Gold of the Tigers* (1972), *The Unending Rose* (1975), *The Iron Coin* (1976), *A History of the Night* (1977), and *The Cipher* (1981). Thus he more than surpassed in twelve years his forty-four previous years of poetic output between 1923 (*Fervor of Buenos Aires*) and 1967, when the last edition of his *Poetic Work* was published. Between these two cycles, the changes in his poetry are not limited to the sheer volume of production – sparse and alternating with other genres in the first, intense and almost exclusive in the second – but also include innovations in theme and in form. His blindness is only part of the story (Borges acknowledged that rhythm and meter make the poem a more accessible endeavor for a blind person). With age, Borges became more attracted and attuned to the expressive possibilities of poetry. As he left behind his recalcitrant diffidence and his epic sense of life, his poetry became more introspective and even confessional. One of the most conspicuous changes is precisely this urgent desire for intimacy. If the early Borges understood poetry, in T. S. Eliot's words, "not as a turning loose of emotions, but as an escape from emotions; not as the expression of personality, but as an escape from personality," the later Borges would explore in depth a theme barely mentioned in his previous poetry, that of a man who finally leaves behind his literary persona to confront the drama of selfhood, the ravages of time, and his own poetic performance as death becomes more real than life. These are some of the questions pondered in the chapter on his more recent poetry. I particularly deal here with the effects of these thematic developments on his handling of poetry as language. As a result of a tighter balance between message and code, and due to the persistent reformulation of a few familiar themes and motifs, his poetry has gained in concentration and terseness and has achieved a verbal virtuosity more frequently associated with musical harmony.

The last essay of this group covering his poetry is devoted to mirrors. Not only as a prevailing motif in his poetry – one may say as an obsession – , not only as a mechanism that provides a model for structuring his narratives, but also as the answer of poetry to the conundrum of life and the riddle of identity: "Art should be like that mirror / which reveals to us our own face . . . It is also like the river with no end / that flows and remains . . ."[8] The mirror to which Borges alludes in this and other poems is not the one that "melts away just like a bright silvery mist,"[9] it is not even that other side of mirrors where fantasy and play reside, but the mirror art provides as the residence of the self. And if "it would destroy us to see the shape of our being,"[10] as he wrote in his poem "Oedipus and the Riddle," art provides a mirror that reflects by approximation the awesome enormity of that being. Only as such, mirrors become a metaphor of the revealing powers of poetry.

The fourth and last part of this volume covers broader aspects of his work. When I set out to write the short piece on Borges' essays back in 1969, I was surprised to realize how little had been said on this genre even though Borges' essays were finding their way into discriminating collections such as *Fifty Great Essays* (1964). Several commentators have noticed Borges' paradoxical treatment of this genre, as if fiction and essay were swapping hats. John Updike was the first to underline this reversal of functions when he pointed out that "Borges' stories have the close texture of argument; his critical articles have the suspense and tension of fiction."[11] One year later (1966), the French critic Pierre Macherey restated and tried to explain the same phenomenon: "Instead of tracing the line of the story, Borges indicates its possibility, generally postponed or deferred. This is why his critical essays are fictional even when they are about actual works; and this is also why his stories are told largely for the sake of the explicit self-criticism which they embody."[12] Spurred by these observations, I engaged the question of how his essays are made. Or, to put it differently, by what means do his essays acquire that fictive quality? My next task was to examine the compositional strategy of his essays. Does a given outlook act as a kind of prism filtering the questions under discussion?

The last two chapters deal with two general aspects of Borges' work. The first is a discussion of Borges' impact on contemporary Spanish American fiction. By the time I wrote this essay in 1972, Borges' influence on American letters was being acknowledged as "the Borgesian phase of American fiction," and a full book-length study assessed the extent of that influence on twenty years of American fiction between 1950 and 1970. On the other hand, almost nothing had been written on the debt of Spanish American fiction of the same decades to Borges with the exception of several Latin American writers themselves who had pinpointed here and there what they owe to Borges. My article on this subject was intended as a corrective to that embarrassing omission.

In my last essay on "Borges' Modernism and the New Critical Idiom" I attempted to trace the route opened by Borges' work in the waters of modernism. It is a bit sketchy and should be read as a preliminary step towards a more thorough examination of the subject, but it should also give the reader a clear and accurate picture of Borges' place in and contribution to modernism. From this examination, Borges surfaces as an audacious forger of new analytic notions that have become an important part of the new critical idiom. Borges was a modern writer in spite of himself. His fiction constitutes a sizable territory on the map of modernism, and modern critical theory is – as I tried to show – in debt to him. If Roland Barthes had already written, "all of a sudden, it does not matter to me any longer not to be modern," Borges never acknowledged his own modernity. On the contrary, he insisted on being a professed old-fashioned. Yet, with his death, modernism comes to a full close. Borges' ahistoricism defines a ponderable dimension of it and, at the same time, opens the way to its demise. The translator of Kafka, Joyce, and Michaux was himself a translation of the preoccupations and ideas that animated modernism. Borges' belief that literature – and all forms of intellectualization, for that matter – is above history and apart from reality brought him closer to Jung and away from Freud, closer to Schopenhauer and away from Marx, closer to Valéry and away from Surrealism, closer to Berkeley and away from Kierkegaard and existentialism. He renounced the world and left its disarrays to history. He chose, by contrast, to dwell in the Library as if it were the world. But in Latin America, history was changing life and deeply permeating its literature. One can still hear, in 1986, a latecomer repeating what Borges said in the thirties: "I write using other written texts, rather than by expressing 'reality.' Our reality now *is* other texts. When I read novels now they don't seem to have anything to do with anything. Novels should be aimed at adding to cultural discourse."[13] Some isolated Hispanic American writers may echo Kathy Acker's recycled version of Borges' old belief, but most of them, and the best among them, have absorbed the lessons of modernism and integrated them into their concerns with and commitments to history. They are in debt to Borges, but their allegiance is to postmodernism; they are not the children of the universal and always reasonable Library, but the Latin American sons and daughters of an abused continent in understandable turmoil. Borges was for them a father figure they had to assume and kill at the same time.

Columbia University   J.A.

NOTES

1 Ernesto González Bermejo, *Conversaciones con Cortázar* (Barcelona: Edhasa, 1978), p. 21.
2 Amado Alonso, *Materia y forma en poesia* (Madrid: Gredos, 1960), p. 352.

3 Roman Jakobson, "The Dominant," in *Selected Writings,* 5 vols. (Gravenhage: Mouton, 1962–1982), vol. 3, p. 751.

4 Paul de Man, "A Modern Master," in Jaime Alazraki, ed., *Critical Essays on Jorge Luis Borges* (Boston: G. K. Hall, 1987), p. 59.

5 Jorge Luis Borges, "Foreword" to *Selected Poems 1923–1967,* edited with an introduction and notes by Norman Thomas di Giovanni (Delacorte Press/Seymour Lawrence, 1972), p. xv.

6 *Ibid.*

7 *Ibid.,* pp. xv–xvi.

8 *Ibid.,* p. 143.

9 Lewis Carroll, *Through the Looking-Glass* (New York: The Modern Library), p. 218.

10 Jorge Luis Borges, *op. cit.,* p. 191.

11 John Updike, "The Author as Librarian," in Jaime Alazraki, ed., *op. cit.,* p. 63.

12 Pierre Macherey, "Borges and the Fictive Narrative," in Alazraki, ed., *op. cit.,* p. 80.

13 Kathy Acker, "In the Tradition of Cervantes, Sort of," *The New York Times Book Review,* November 30, 1986, p. 10.

Acknowledgments

"Borges and the Kabbalah" and "Borges and the New Latin American Novel" were published for the first time in *TriQuarterly* (25, Fall 1972); "Kabbalistic Traits in Borges' Narratives" in *Studies in Short Fiction* (VIII, 1, Winter 1971); "Borges, or Style as an Invisible Worker" in *Style* (IX, 3, Summer 1975); "The Making of a Style: *A Universal History of Infamy*" in *Textual Analysis: Some Readers Reading,* ed. Mary Ann Caws (New York: MLA, 1986); "Outside and Inside the Mirror in Borges' Poetry" in *Simply a Man of Letters,* ed. C. Cortínez (Orono: University of Maine, 1982); "Enumerations as Evocations: On the Use of a Device in Borges' Latest Poetry" in *Borges the Poet,* ed. C. Cortínez (Fayetteville: University of Arkansas Press, 1986); "Language as a Musical Organism: Borges' Recent Poetry" in *Review* (New York: Center for Inter-American Relations, no. 28, Jan.–Apr. 1981); and "Oxymoronic Structure in Borges' Essays" in *The Cardinal Points of Borges,* ed. L. Dunham and I. Ivask (Norman: University of Oklahoma Press, 1971). Grateful acknowledgment is made to these journals and university presses for permission to reproduce these essays. I would like also to give my special thanks to Mary Kinzie and Norman Thomas di Giovanni for their meticulous editing of the two essays included in the *TriQuarterly* issue devoted to Borges, and to my friends and colleagues Mary E. Davis and Christopher T. Leland for reading the entire manuscript and making valuable suggestions. Finally, my rather belated thanks to Borges himself for the many hours he spent with me turning his oral lecture on the Kabbalah into a written text.

PART I
Borges and the Kabbalah

1 Introduction

It was in Norman, Oklahoma, during the sessions and breaks of the international symposium on Borges held at the University of Oklahoma in December of 1969, that the idea of studying the impact of the Kabbalah on Borges' writings first took shape. The journal *TriQuarterly* was preparing a full issue devoted to him and when I was approached, I did not hesitate to commit myself to a piece dealing with this subject. It was also in Norman that I first met Borges. Earlier that same year, he had spent ten days in Israel as a guest of the government, and the impressions of this trip were still fresh in his mind. We talked about this visit and his memorable encounter there with Gershom Scholem. While I was a student at the Hebrew University of Jerusalem, from 1958 to 1962, I attended Scholem's course on Jewish mysticism as well as Isaiah Tishby's seminar on the *Zohar*. Borges was the only author writing in Spanish who offered me the unique opportunity of combining my background in the Kabbalah with my professional interest in Spanish literature. I had already published two books on Borges, but the subject of his contacts with the Kabbalah was barely touched upon in those or in any other books. It was only after the Oklahoma symposium – spurred on as I was by my conversation with Borges on this topic and by my commitment to *TriQuarterly* – that I fully embarked on researching the subject. The results appeared in a long article included in *TriQuarterly*, Fall 1972, and in a second piece – "Kabbalistic Traits in Borges' Narratives" – published in the Winter 1971 issue of *Studies in Short Fiction* devoted to the Latin American short story. Although the latter appeared before the former, it represents a derivation from the first, applying the conclusions I reached in my previous examination of Borges' contacts with the Kabbalah to an analysis of his narrative texts. A third article dealing with

Borges' poem "The Golem" appeared in the festschrift honoring the Spanish scholar Joaquin Casalduero, published in Spain in 1972.[1]

In September 1971, I travelled to Argentina on a Guggenheim Fellowship. I saw Borges, who was at the time the director of the National Library, in Buenos Aires and had lunch with him. I asked if he would give me an interview to discuss his long acquaintance with the Kabbalah. He agreed, and gave me an appointment for the next morning. I showed up the following day at the library, equipped with my portable tape recorder and a long list of questions and notes. On that occasion I was to learn, first, of my own inadequacy as an interviewer; and, second, of the difficulties in pinning Borges down to a one-track conversation. He enjoys a branching dialogue in which even the most casual reference to a name, book, place or topic is sufficient reason to ruminate on other subjects. The result is a network of interlocking observations in which each question or remark leads his legendary memory to explore its reservoirs. The same question, asked on different occasions, would never elicit quite the same answer. One could be assured of an unexpected nuance, of a new detail, of a surprising twist. My mistake was – as I look back – attempting a dialogue focused on a single subject. Borges the conversationalist loved to establish unusual links between various authors and ideas, and to leap from one topic to another triggered by the first, as if he were exemplifying his old belief that perhaps all authors are one author, and all texts, one text.

I never brought myself to publish that interview. Borges has made of the interview a new literary genre, and I felt that this one, in spite of some insightful points, didn't warrant its addition to the several dozens – some of them book-length – already published. My own dissatisfaction with the results of my interview led me, however, to hunt down a lecture on the Kabbalah Borges had given at the Sociedad Hebraica Argentina a year earlier, in 1970. I learned that the lecture had been recorded, and was able to borrow the tape. This was a coup, since the lecture included most of the information I was trying to obtain from Borges. It could be considered a recapitulation of his long friendship with the Kabbalah, and although several years later, in 1977, he repeated this lecture in a series of seven talks on various subjects given in Buenos Aires, eventually publishing them in a volume entitled *Siete noches*,[2] I believe that the 1970 version more accurately captures Borges' fascination with his subject. It is a more intimate and focused meditation on the Kabbalah.

When I asked Borges his permission to transcribe his talk for the purpose of publishing it, he replied: "Of course, but since that is only an improvised talk, we'll have to work on it to turn it into a written text." I was, of course, delighted. He then suggested that we meet at the library that afternoon, and after the first session of about two hours, we met for two additional conversations, one of them on a Sunday morning.

That day I awaited him at the entrance of the building, since the library was closed. When the porter saw him approaching, groping with his cane, he opened the door. We worked morning and afternoon to finish the job, with a break for lunch at a Basque restaurant on the corner of Mexico Street where the library is located. Working with Borges was a moving experience. I would read him a paragraph, and he would then repeat the same paragraph to himself. I could see his lips moving voicelessly, sometimes two or three times, until he found a satisfactory formulation which he then dictated to me. Full paragraphs were suppressed, sentences shortened, expanded, rephrased, or reordered; words were changed; names and titles were clarified; blunt colloquialisms were eliminated; and the syntax was tightened. And yet the text preserved the tone and inflections of his voice, which, in turn, I strove to keep in my translation.

After translating Borges' lecture into English, I realized that in my recorded interview there were a few gems omitted in the lecture or in any other published material on the subject. Three important points came to light. The first concerns his discovery of the Kabbalah. Borges intimated that the earliest references to the Kabbalah he came across were in Dante's *Divine Comedy* and in the *Encyclopedia Britannica*. Of the first, he said:

"I found it in Longfellow's translation of the *Divine Comedy* which he undertook during the Civil War to avoid thinking about a war he was too preoccupied with. There is a three-page appendix in that translation that Longfellow took from a book – I believe it was *Rabbinical Literature* – by J.P. Stehelin[3] where there is a discussion of the Hebrew alphabet and of the different meanings and values that the Kabbalists attributed to those letters. And the other reference must have come from the *Britannica*. As a youngster, I used to come here, to the Library, quite frequently, and since I was very shy and didn't dare ask the librarian for books, I would take a volume of the *Britannica*, any volume, from the shelf myself. Since they were readily accessible in the reading room, I did not have to request the assistance of any librarian, so I would take a volume and read it. But the old *Encyclopedia Britannica* was far superior to the more recent editions. It used to be a reading work, and now it has been turned into a reference book. I remember one afternoon, one evening, I felt very happy because I read articles on . . . [pause], wait, on *Druids, Druses,* and then it came – the article on *Dryden.*"

His second comment was a reaction to a reference I had made to Scholem's book *The Kabbalah and Its Symbolism:* "Yes, I have it. I consider Scholem a friend of mine and I think he considers me his friend, although we must have seen each other no more than eight hours in our lifetime . . . But since I have read him and reread him so much . . ." Then I asked him if he had seen Scholem during his second trip to Israel, in 1971, to receive the Jerusalem Prize, and he replied:

> When I was asked in Israel what I wanted to see, I said: Don't ask me what I want to see because I am blind, but if you ask me whom I want to see I'll answer, right away, Scholem. I spent a beautiful afternoon in his house. We met a couple of times. A charming person. He speaks perfect English.

To my question about the possible reasons for his attraction toward the Kabbalah, he answered:

> Dante, referring to Virgil, says *il lungo studio e il grande amore,* I think, my Italian is not to be trusted; in my case, I cannot talk about *a long love,* but I can certainly talk about *a long study* of the Kabbalah, because that study was real. Regarding my inclination toward that study, it has – I think – a double source. To begin with, all things Jewish have always fascinated me and I think this was due to the fact that my maternal grandmother was a Protestant – an Anglican. She knew her Bible, so much so that if somebody quoted a verse, any verse, she would reply: yes, *Job,* such and such chapter and verse, or *Kings,* such and such chapter and verse. So that there was that side. And then, since I have not been able to believe in a personal God, the idea of a vast and impersonal God, the *En-Sof* of the Kabbalah, has always fascinated me. Later on, I have found the same, well, in Spinoza, and in pantheism in general, and also in Schopenhauer, and in Samuel Butler, and in Bernard Shaw's idea of "Life's force," and Bergson's "élan vital." All that responded to the same attraction. There is, in addition, a more circumstantial factor. The first book I read in German, when I was studying German by myself, around 1916, was Meyrink's novel, *Der Golem.* I was sent on the study of German by my reading of Carlyle whom I greatly admired then. (Now I find his style more intimidating than persuasive.) I started by the same foolish thing many people

do, by trying to read Kant's *Critique of Pure Reason* in German, a book not even Germans understand, and which very few people comprehend. Then a friend of mine – what was her name? – she was a baroness from Prague, wait, oh yes, Baroness Forschtüb-ber she told me that a very interesting book had just been published, a fantastic novel entitled *Der Golem* (1916). I had never heard that word before. That was the first book in German I read through – the first book in prose, since I had earlier read Heine's *Lyrisches Intermezzo*.

Almost ten years later, when Borges was at M.I.T. in April 1980, I posed a similar question: What does the Kabbalah mean to you? His answer: "I suppose the Kabbalah means much to me since I think I come of Jewish stock. My mother's name was Acevedo, and another member in her family was Pinedo. Those are Sephardic Jews. But also I find a very interesting idea in the Kabbalah, an idea found also in Carlyle and Leon Bloy. It is the idea that the whole world is merely a system of symbols, that the whole world, including the stars, stood for God's secret writing. That idea is to be found in the Kabbalah, and I think that that may be my chief attraction to it."[4]

To grasp fully the intrinsic affinities between Borges and the Kabbalah, one has only to go over his lecture included in this volume, since what he said there summarizes *his own* essential understanding of the Kabbalah. This understanding, having close links with his own writing, provides a more substantial explanation of his attraction to the world of the Kabbalists. Borges was less impressed by their doctrine, which he felt was Neo-Platonism in Kabbalistic dress, than by the symbols which suggest that doctrine. A similar and deliberate gap is found in his own writings. As much as Borges sought to write fiction with philosophical theories and theological doctrine, he knew all along that the symbols he coined in his tales and poems were by far richer than the ideas that motivated them.

He has often referred to his own stories as "woven symbols" – as metaphors capable of several meanings. He has also spoken of the reader's right to his or her own interpretation of a given text, and of the resulting layers of meaning – often not intended by the writer – added to that text. Literature is thus understood as a multilayered text each writer reads, reinterprets, and rewrites. This conception of literature immediately brings to mind the Kabbalists' perception of the Scripture as an inexhaustible well or as a face enveloped in seventy veils (a number standing for infinity); the bottom can never be reached, the face can never be seen. More recently, Roland Barthes has suggested a literary analogy that bears a striking resemblance to the Kabbalistic model. "The problem of style" – says he – "can only be treated by reference to what I shall refer to as the 'layerdness' (*feuilleté*) of the discourse. If up until now we have looked at the text as a kind of fruit with a kernel, the flesh being the form and the pit being the content, it would be more conducive to see it as an onion, a construction of layers whose body contains, finally, no heart, no kernel, no secret, no irreducible principle, nothing except the infinity of its own envelopes – which envelop nothing other than the unity of its own surfaces."[5]

When Borges says that in his stories "he narrates events as if he did not wholly understand them,"[6] (a device he learned from the Icelandic sagas), he is echoing a strategy adopted by the Kabbalists in their writings. They forged symbols whose ultimate meanings were hinted at but never totally disclosed. "The texts of the Kabbalah" – says Borges in his lecture – "seek the reader's cooperation and were addressed to a reader who did not take them literally but instead strove to discover by himself their hidden meaning." Could the same be said about Borges' short stories? I believe so. It is this Kabbalistic texture in his fiction which warrants, in turn, a Kabbalistic reading of sorts. When asked to comment on a contemporary author he had not read, he replied: "Why should the fact that I was born in this century determine my literary preferences when I have thirty centuries to choose from?" Thus, the notion of novelty gives way to the idea of literature as a timeless text. In spite of the innovations in their understanding of Jewish orthodoxy, the Kabbalists sought very hard to find support for their views and theories in the authority of tradition. Borges underlines this effort in his lecture: "The Kabbalists arrived at a doctrine which was very different from the Jewish orthodoxy, but they did not want to appear as innovators because such condition would have discredited them." Then he goes on to explain that this attitude prevailed in Western literature until the Renaissance: "Today we enjoy knowing that an idea is new, but during the Middle Ages and through the Renaissance the idea of novelty was a displeasing one, and it was thought of as something arbitrary because essential things were already discovered." Writing as a creative act meant imitating the classics, rewriting or reinterpreting what was already written. Following that same line of thought, Borges has insisted, in an almost boastful way, that what he has written had already been written by others. In fact, one can say that his reliance on previous authors, and his conviction of writing as rewriting form the core of his literary credo. He himself has gone so far as to say that it is conceivable that since Homer all metaphors have already been written, and that the contemporary writer's task is to reformulate those old metaphors. In another by now classic text, he has pointed out that "one literature differs from another not so much because of the text as for the manner in which it is read."[7] The Kabbalists would have subscribed to that Borgesian notion: they generated a full library by reading the Scripture anew.

By its Neo-Platonic nature, the Kabbalah was very dear to Borges' attraction to philosophical idealism. There are countless texts in which he posits the old notion that people and the world in which they live are but somebody's dream, that we are mere simulacra of a cosmic consciousness that is thinking us. In his lecture, Borges has pointed out that for "the Kabbalists, we – all the people who inhabit this planet – are only reflections of the archetypal or primordial man, *Adam Kadmon.*" This idea pervades a large portion of his poetry, fiction, and essays. Borges has said that "the generic can be more intense than the concrete and immediate,"[8] and this has been a sort of cornerstone in his fiction: his stories are permeated by the feeling that behind the narrated actions, Platonic notions throb through as the generating force that puts in motion the machinery of plot.

The other essays included here, albeit not directly addressed to the subject of the leading article, are not impervious to its implications, perhaps because – as Harold Bloom has pointed out – "the Kabbalah offers both a model for the process of poetic influence and maps for the problematic pathways of interpretation." I found that several of the pathways charted by Bloom in his book, *Kabbalah and Criticism,* lead Borges to similar conclusions regarding the nature of the literary act. At the center of Bloom's elucidation there stands the principle of *Sefirotic* emanation, which in terms of literary criticism he explains as "the Gnostic formulation that all reading, and all writing, constitute a kind of defensive warfare, that reading is mis-writing and writing is mis-reading."[9] How does this process of poetic influence manifest itself? Bloom answers with the assistance of the sixteenth-century Safed Kabbalist Moses Cordovero, whose theosophic doctrine centers on the configurations of the *Sefiroth.* "The first of the six aspects in any *Sefirath* is its hidden aspect before it is manifested in the preceding *Sefirath.* This is to say, in literary terms, that the initial trope or image in any new poem is closely related to the *hidden presence* of the new poem in its precursor poem."[10] The precursor text – concludes Bloom – is in the new text, not so much in the letter as in the spirit. The old can be detected in the new less in the manifest than in the hidden: "Only weak poems, or the weaker elements in strong poems, immediately echo precursor poems, or directly allude to them. The fundamental phenomena of poetic influence have little to do with the borrowing of images or ideas, with sound patterns, or with other verbal reminders of one poem by another. A poem is a deep misprision of a previous poem when we recognize the later poem as being absent rather than present on the surface of the earlier poem, and yet still being *in* the earlier poem, implicit or hidden *in* it, not yet manifest, and yet *there* . . . Take the descendents of Shelley among the major Victorian and modern poets: Browning, Swinburne, Hardy and Yeats. All four of these strong poets have styles almost totally antithetical to Shelley's style, yet he is the crucial precursor for all of them."[11]

Now this literary inference from the *Sefirotic* theosophy of the Kabbalists bears a remarkable similarity to Borges' own dictum that "each writer creates his own precursors." It appears in his widely cited essay "Kafka and his Precursors," which opens with the following paragraph:

> Once I planned to make a survey of Kafka's precursors. At first I thought he was as singular as the fabulous Phoenix; when I knew him better I thought I recognized his voice, or his habits, in the texts of various literatures and various ages. I shall record a few of them here, in chronological order.[12]

Examples from Zeno, Han Yu, Kierkegaard, Browning, Léon Bloy, and Lord Dunsany follow. In all these "precursors," Borges underlines the fact that "the affinity is not of form but rather of tone," and although his conclusion – "Kafka's idiosyncrasy, in greater or lesser degree, is present in each of these writings, but if Kafka had not written we would not perceive it; that is to say, it would not exist"[13] – slightly departs from Bloom's conclusion, it restates Scholem's observation regarding the "relationships of radiation between the *Sefiroth* and their reciprocal influence," a process, says Scholem, that "is not a one-way influx from cause to effect, but also from effect to cause, dialectically turning the effect into a cause."[14] And, in the same way, Bloom concludes that "Cordovero's theosophical cycle becomes a wheel of images, or tropes, or defenses, by which one text constantly conducts interchange with another."[15] Borges closes his essay with this remark: "The poem 'Fears and Scruples' by Robert Browning is like a prophecy of Kafka's stories, but our reading of Kafka refines and changes our reading of the poem perceptibly. The word 'precursor' is indispensable in the vocabulary of criticism, but one should try to purify it from all connotation of polemic or rivalry. The fact is that each writer creates his precursors. His work modifies our conception of the past, as it will modify the future."[16]

I have tried to apply this Kabbalistic dialectic to Borges' own writings. Thus in the chapter devoted to *A Universal History of Infamy*, I studied his early narrative prose assuming that in each piece included in that collection "Borges' idiosyncrasy is present in greater or lesser degree," but bearing in mind, at the same time, that "if Borges had not written *Ficciones* we would not perceive it, that is to say, it wouldn't exist." The principle of "relationships of radiation" is applied here within the work of a single author.

It will be too prolix to justify whatever Kabbalistic premise was at work in each of the chapters of this volume. What truly matters, I feel, is that aspects of Borges' work such as the mechanics of his prose fiction style, the structuring principle of his short stories, the extent of his influence on contemporary Latin American fiction, the modus operandi of his essays, the new developments of his poetry, and others which heretofore have not received the attention they deserve, are dealt with as layers of a text constantly seeking to be unraveled – "misread" Bloom would say, "reread" says Borges, "read between the lines" suggests the *Zohar*. Ultimately, the hermeneutics of the Kabbalists is not different from any other method for reading a literary text: there is a literal meaning laid at its surface, and there are underlying meanings beneath that outer one. The Kabbalists sought to reach those other levels, urged on by the same endeavor that motivates a student of literature to the business of criticism: to expand our understanding of a given text. It matters not if the Kabbalists strove to read the Holy Text "in accordance with another arrangement of the letters." One is a mystical reading and the other a secular one, but both are attempts at understanding texts beyond their immediacy. In the end, the Kabbalah – not as an esoteric doctrine but as a method for demonstrating its doctrine – is, within its own premises and theosophic purposes, a rigorous method of literary criticism. Borges. conversely, has often posited a literary pantheism that recalls the omniscient text of the Kabbalists. In "The Flower of Coleridge," he quotes Emerson, assuming his voice: "I am very much struck in literature by the appearance that one person wrote all the books . . . there is such equality and identity both of judgment and point of view in the narrative that it is plainly the work of one all-seeing, all-hearing gentleman."[17] If literature as a whole presents a unity similar to the "profound unity of the Word," and if to write is to rewrite that single text, to read can only be the process through which that single text can be interpreted or reinterpreted, as the Kabbalists thought of the Scriptures, infinitely. "Pierre Menard, author of the *Quixote*," is the ultimate metaphor for this conviction: when Menard undertakes to write a contemporary *Quixote* in this century, he rewrites Cervantes' text only to realize that although Cervantes' and his own are identical, Menard's *is almost infinitely richer.*

NOTES

1   " 'El Golem' de J. L. Borges," in *Homenaje a Joaquín Casalduero,* ed. R. P. Sigele and G. Sobejano (Madrid: Gredos, 1972), pp. 9–19.

2   *Siete noches* (Buenos Aires: Fondo de Cultura Económica, 1980).

3   The appendix is indeed included in Longfellow's translation of Dante's *Divine Comedy*, in vol. 3 (*Paradise*), pp. 428–433 (Boston: Houghton, Mifflin and Co., 1886). But in trying to locate Stehelin's two-volume *Rabbinical Literature*, I found that Borges repeated Longfellow's error in attributing the book to Stehelin. Although Stehelin translated the book from German into English and wrote a long preface of over 65 pages, the work, whose exact title is *Rabbinical Writings*, was written by Johann Andreas Eisenmenger. It was originally published in Germany in 1711 and its complete title was *The Traditions of the Jews or the Doctrines and Expositions Contained in the Talmud and Other Rabbinical Writings*. It is a viciously anti-Semitic book. The first page alone states: "Enthusiasm on the one hand, and a Spirit of Domination on the other, are, and have been ever, the Disgraces of the Priests of most Religions: But None are, or have been, more guilty on one side, or more extravagant on the other, than the Rabbins, or Teachers among the Jews. The Rabbinical Domination and Enthusiasm will appear in the following extracts from the best and most celebrated Writings of the Rabbins; a set of men, who, on the foundation of the Oral Law, have erected for themselves an absolute domination over the consciences and understandings of the Jews: and published, for divine and natural truths, the grossest falsehoods and absurdities that ever appeared." In his English translation, Johann Peter Stehelin warns his readers that "Eisenmenger, Professor of Oriental Languages at the University of Heidelberg, published his collection in two large volumes in quarto at Königsberg in order to convince the Jews of their Folly in preferring the Oral to the Written Law, the traditions of men to the precepts of God, the Talmud to the Holy Scripture; he took infinite pains to collect the fables, allegories, absurdities, contradictions, and blasphemies found in the Talmud and other Rabbinical works. As this work was received with great applause in Germany, it was thought proper to give the public an abridged translation. Dr. Eisenmenger's scope was different from mine; his was to ridicule the traditions of the many blasphemies against the Christian religion, mine to prepare the way for their conversion." *The Traditions of the Jews* (London: G. Smith, 1742; 2 vols).

4   *Borges at Eighty*, ed. W. Barnstone (Indiana University Press, 1982), p. 82.

5   Roland Barthes, "Style in Its Image," in *Literary Style: A Symposium,* ed. Seymour Chatman (Oxford University Press, 1971), p. 10.

6   J. L. Borges, *In Praise of Darkness,* Preface. New York, Dutton, 1974.

7   J. L. Borges, *Other Inquisitions, 1937–1952* (New York: Washington Square Press, 1966), p. 173.

8   J. L. Borges, *Historia de la eternidad* (Buenos Aires: Emecé, 1961), p. 21.

9   Harold Bloom, *Kabbalah and Criticism* (New York: Seabury Press, 1975), p. 64.

10 *Ibid.,* p. 66.

11 *Ibid.,* pp. 66–67.

12 J. L. Borges, *Other Inquisitions,* p. 111.

13 *Ibid.,* p. 113.

14 Quoted by H. Bloom, *op.cit.*, p. 70.
15 *Ibid.*, p. 71.
16 J. L. Borges, *Other Inquisitions*, p. 113.
17 *Ibid.*, p. 9.

2 Borges and the Kabbalah

When asked several years ago about his interest in the Kabbalah, Borges replied, "I read a book called *Major Trends in Jewish Mysticism* by Scholem and another book by Trachtenberg on Jewish superstitions.[1] Then I have read all the books on the Kabbalah I have found and all the articles in the encyclopedias and so on. But I have no Hebrew whatever."[2] These remarks, considering the number of interviews Borges has given, come rather late. Except for this single statement, nothing else has been added on the subject since Rabi's essay "Fascination de la Kabbale,"[3] and Rabi's contribution lies in his merely having called attention to Borges' familiarity with Kabbalistic texts. I shall attempt to show how far Borges' acquaintance with the Kabbalah goes beyond the few accidental tracks left in his writings as a result of his readings. Ultimately, as André Maurois puts it, "Borges has read everything" that exists ("and all the books that don't exist," adds John Barth), and it would be unusual not to find in his prose some imprints of the material which, as is the case with the Kabbalah, exerted on his mind such an enthralling fascination.[4]

The impact of the Kabbalah on Borges' work far exceeds the random quotations or allusions the casual reader may find and which, after all, only confirm the interest Borges has conceded. Behind his transparent texts there lies a stylistic intricacy, a certain Kabbalistic texture, a spellbinding characteristic to which Borges finds himself attracted.

To the question, "Have you tried to make your own stories Kabbalistic?" he replied, "Yes, sometimes I have."[5] For the Kabbalists, as one of their classic text shows, "every word of the Torah has six hundred thousand faces – that is, layers of meaning or entrances," and the ostensible aim of the Kabbalah seems to be to reach these profound layers. Borges' writings offer the reader a similar challenge. Most of his narratives do not exhaust themselves at the level of literal meaning – they

14

present an immediate and manifest layer and a more oblique and allusive one. It is the latter which generates in his stories a Kabbalistic aura whose source goes far beyond a fortuitous familiarity of the Kabbalah.

A scrutiny of Borges' Kabbalah library

In "Death and the Compass," Borges examines some books on the Kabbalah from his own library. Echoing Cervantes' device,[6] Borges includes among the volumes of the murdered rabbi's complete works his own essay, "A Vindication of the Kabbalah," collected in the volume *Discusión*. Contrary to what happens in *Don Quixote,* where Cervantes' pastoral novel *La Galatea* receives from the curate a favorable although not excessively generous comment, the reference to Borges' essay in the story goes without any remark at all. However, the mere inclusion of an essay written by the same author who now writes the story produces an effect similar to the one achieved by Cervantes in the famous passage. Essentially it is the effect produced by the theater within the theater, by literature becoming the subject of literature. In this operation, Borges attains a literary magic he himself has poignantly described:

> Why does it make us uneasy to know that the map is within the map and the thousand and one nights are within the book of *A Thousand and One Nights?* Why does it disquiet us to know that *Don Quixote* is a reader of the *Quixote,* and Hamlet is a spectator of *Hamlet?* I believe I have found the answer: those inversions suggest that if the characters in a story can be the readers or spectators, then we, their readers or spectators, can be fictitious. *(OI, 46)*[7]

Among the books that Borges attributes to Rabbi Marcelo Yarmolinsky there figures "a literal translation of the *Sefer Yetsirah.*" The Book of Creation is a brief treatise on cosmologic and cosmogonic matters. It was written between the third and sixth centuries and represents, with the Book *Bahir* (twelfth century), the embryo out of which the bulk of the Kabbalah grew and developed. Its chief subjects are the elements of the world, which are sought in the ten elementary and primordial numbers – Sefiroth – and in the twenty-two letters of the Hebrew alphabet. Together these represent the mysterious forces whose convergence has produced the various combinations observable throughout the whole of creation; they are the *thirty-two secret paths of wisdom,* through which God has created all that exists. In his essay "On the Cult of Books," Borges again refers to the *Sefer Yetsirah.* This time the reference is a long paragraph in which he furnishes some basic information on the book, describes its purpose and method, and brings in a quotation which may or may not be taken directly from the text, since this is the most widely cited passage of the Book of Creation and Borges might well have found it in the books and articles he read on the subject: "Twenty-two fundamental letters: God drew them, engraved them, combined them, weighed them, permuted them, and with them produced everything that is and everything that will be." At any rate, the long reference is an indication that the inclusion of this title in Yarmolinsky's bibliography is as important with regard to the murdered Talmudist as it is with respect to Borges's own interest in the Kabbalah. It shows also, however, that the aura of fantasy created by those enigmatic and often esoteric books springs, rather than from Borges' intention, from the reader's unfamiliarity with these works and authors, although Borges – undoubtedly – is aware of their puzzling impact on the reader.[8] The same holds true for the other books mentioned in the list. Thus the *History of the Hasidic Sect* and the *Biography of the Baal Shem,* attributed to Yarmolinsky, are slightly modified versions of two works by Martin Buber: *The Origin and Meaning of Hasidism*[9] and *The Legend of Baal Shem.*[10] Borges' acquaintance with Buber becomes apparent in the story "The Sect of the Phoenix," where he quotes him, and in the essay "On Chesterton," where he directs the reader to Buber's classic *Tales of the Hasidim.*[11]

The last book mentioned in the list, *A Study of the Philosophy of Robert Fludd,* although not directly concerned with the Kabbalah, is not foreign to its doctrine. Several of Fludd's (1574–1637) postulates are amazingly close to those of the Kabbalah. The English Rosicrucian maintained that the universe proceeds from, and will return to, God; that the act of creation is the separation of the active principle (light) from the passive (darkness) in the bosom of the divine unity (God); and that the universe consists of three worlds; the archetypal (God), the macrocosm (the world), and the microcosm (man). He was a follower of Paracelsus, whose prescriptions for the making of the homunculus bear astonishing similarities to the golem-making formulae of the Kabbalists.[12]

Lönnrot, the "pure logician" of "Death and the Compass," carries these books off to his apartment, "suddenly turning bibliophile and Hebraic scholar" (*A,* 67). Borges could as well have said "Kabbalist," since Lönnrot attempts to solve the mysteries of the seemingly ritualistic murders in the same manner that a Kabbalist deciphers the occult mysteries of the Scripture. The arithmetic value of the dates of the murders and their geometric location on the map become important and revealing. Before Lönnrot can establish these symmetries in time and space, he devotes himself to perusing Yarmolinsky's books. Borges does not miss the chance to unfold his erudition on the subject. Thus, one book revealed to the investigator "the doctrine that God has a secret name in which . . . His ninth attribute, Eternity, may be found – that is to say, the immediate knowledge of everything under the sun that will be, that is, and that was" (*A, 68*). The ninth attribute mentioned in the story takes us to the very core of the Kabbalah's cosmogony – the theory of the *Sefiroth*.

The doctrine of the *Sefiroth*

Borges' first explorations into the subject of the Kabbalah are found in his second collection of essays, *El tamaño de mi esperanza* (The Extent of My Hope), published in 1926. There, in an article entitled "A History of Angels," Borges leaves a testimony to his first readings on the Kabbalah. He mentions two books, Erich Bischoff's *Die Elemente der Kabbalah* (1914) and *Rabbinical Literature* by Stehelin; even more important is the fact that the passage contains the germ of his more mature essay, "A Vindication of the Kabbalah," of 1931. Yet it is in the earlier article, "A History of Angels," where he writes literally about the theory of the *Sefiroth*. Relying on Bischoff and Stehelin, Borges explains that "to each one of the ten *Sefiroth*, or eternal emanations of the godhead, corresponds a region of heaven, one of the names of God, one commandment of the decalogue, a part of the human body, and a class of angels." He adds that Stehelin "links the first ten letters of the Hebrew alphabet to these ten heavenly words. Thus the letter Aleph looks toward the brain, the first commandment, the heaven of fire, the second name 'I Am That I Am,' and the seraphim called Holy Beasts."[13]

Perhaps the most direct bearing the doctrine of the *Sefiroth* has on Borges' work emerges in the story "The Aleph." The theory of the *Sefiroth* postulates that there are two worlds and that both represent God. "First a primary world, the most deeply hidden of all, which remains insensible and unintelligible to all but God, the world of *En-Sof* (Infinite); and secondly, one joined unto the first which makes it possible to know God, the world of attributes."[14] The ninth *Sefirah*, as pointed out by Borges, is the source from which the divine life overflows in the act of mystical procreation. The world of *Sefiroth* is described as a mystical organism, and the most important images used in this connection are those of the tree and of a man. This tree is the unknown and unknowable God, but it is also the skeleton of the universe – it grows throughout the whole of creation and spreads its branches through all its ramifications. All mundane and created things exist only because something of the power of the *Sefiroth* lives and acts in them.[15] This notion of God's externalization is summarized in a passage of the *Zohar* (Book of Splendor): "The process of creation has taken place on two planes, one above and one below, and for this reason the Torah begins with the letter Beth, the numerical value of which is two. The lower occurrence corresponds to the higher; one produced the upper world (of the *Sefiroth*), the other the nether world (of the visible creation)."[16] The pantheistic character of this outlook comes openly to the surface in the Spanish Kabbalist Joseph Gikatila's formula, "He fills everything and He is everything." The theogony of the *Sefiroth* and the cosmogony of creation represent two aspects of the same act. "Creation," says Scholem, "mirrors the inner movement of the divine life. . . . It is nothing but an external development of those forces which are active and alive in God Himself. . . . The life of the Creator pulsates in that of his creatures."[17] The last assertion does not differ, even in its formulation, from Borges' own pantheistic formula, "Every man is an organ put forth by the divinity in order to perceive the world" ("The Theologians," *L*, 124).[18]

The Kabbalistic notion that conceives the Torah as a vast *corpus symbolicum*, representative of that hidden life within God which the theory of the *Sefiroth* attempts to describe, is paraphrased in Léon Bloy's *L'Ame de Napoléon* (as quoted by Borges in his essay "The Mirror of the Enigmas"): "History is an immense liturgical text, where the *i*'s and the periods are not worth less than whole verses or chapters, but the importance of both is undeterminable and is profoundly hidden. . . . Everything is a symbol." Borges' own comments underline the affinity between Bloy and the Kabbalah:

> Bloy . . . did nothing but apply to the whole Creation the method that the Jewish cabalists applied to the Scripture. They thought that a work dictated by the Holy Spirit was an absolute text: a text where the collaboration of chance is calculable at zero.[19] The portentous premise of a book that is impervious to contingency, a book that is a mechanism of infinite purposes, moved them to permute the scriptural words, to sum up the numerical value of the letters, to consider their form, to observe the small letters and the capital letters, to search for acrostics and anagrams. (*OI*, 128)

For the Kabbalists, the letters of the Torah are the mystical body of God, and from this it follows that the Creation is just a reflection or emanation of the Holy text; hence the Midrash "God looked into the Torah and created the world," and the story told in the Mishnah about a scribe (of the Scripture) who, when asked about his occupation, received from his teacher the following advice: "My son, be careful in your work, for it is the work of God; if you omit a single letter, or write a letter too many, you will destroy the whole world."[20] The idea is put in a nutshell in the Kabbalistic axiom, "What is below is above and what is inside is outside,"[21] from which the *Sefer Yatsirah* infers that "on the basis of the lower world we understand the secret law according to which the upper world is governed." The Kabbalist Menahem Recanati adds his own exegesis to the axiom: "All created being, earthly man and all other creatures in this world, exist according to the archetype (*dugma*) of the ten *sefiroth*."[22] The text that best shows the spell of the *Seifroth* on Borges is a passage from his story "The Theologians," in which he gives in a condensed formula the pantheistic essentials of the theory. "In the hermetic books," he says, "it is written that what is down below is equal to what is on high, and what is on high is equal to what is down below; in the *Zohar*, that the higher world is a reflection of the lower" (*L*, 123). From this Borges derives one of his favorite motifs – "every man is two men" – which has ingenious and fertile effects on his narratives.[23]

The legend of the golem

Borges' debt to Gershom Scholem is acknowledged in a couplet from his poem "The Golem": "But all these matters are discussed by Scholem / in a most learned passage of his book" (*SP*, 113). The book is Scholem's *Major Trends in Jewish Mysticism*, undoubtedly the most authoritative work on the subject and a model of scholarship. Borges could not have chosen better. Paradoxically, however – and this is one of the voluntarily involuntary mistakes in which Borges delights – the information for the poem does not arise from the "learned book," *Major Trends*, which hardly devotes a few lines to the question of the golem, but from other sources.[24] Later Borges resourcefully explained in his "Autobiographical Essay" that he twice used Scholem's name in the poem "as the only possible rhyming word" for golem.

The poem represents one of the most felicitous expressions of a main theme in Borges' work – the world as a dream of God. More than in a *topos* of seventeenth-century literature, Borges finds in the religions of India a new foundation for his idealist outlook on reality.[25] Nevertheless, this theme of the world as God's dream is not motivated by only one doctrine, or "perplexity," as Borges calls it. "The Circular Ruins," for example, embodies the Buddhist belief in the world as the dream of Someone, or perhaps no one, but at the same time it casts in the mold of fiction the idealist notion which postulates the hallucinatory character of all reality. Borges' avid erudition, however, does not stop at these two sources. He searches for new formulations of the same basic idea, for new versions of the same metaphor, until he arrives at a brilliantly concise assertion – "Perhaps universal history is the history of the diverse intonation of a few metaphors" ("Pascal's Sphere, *OI*, 6). Therefore, it would be mistaken to point to one source as the motivation of the poem or the story, or to single out one exclusive intonation of a metaphor as the only "perplexity" Borges intends to reinterpret in his fiction. One of the enchanting features of Borges' art is precisely the combination of very diverse constituents, the blending of various intonations into one unified tone. In this process, the metaphors of history are converted into what they essentially are – into metaphors of literature.

Thus the story "The Circular Ruins," which seems to be inspired by Eastern beliefs,[26] is no less imbued with the doctrines of the Kabbalah than the poem "The Golem." Tale and poem are variations of the same theme: a man (a magician in the story, a rabbi in the poem) dreams another man into existence, only later to find that he too, the dreamer, is but a dream. In both instances, the creative powers of man seem to be competing with the creative powers of God. In reconstructing the legend of the golem in the poem, Borges makes use of a long Kabbalistic tradition from which the legend originates. This tradition has its beginnings in an old belief according to which the cosmos was built chiefly from the twenty letters of the Hebrew alphabet as presented in the *Sefer Yetsirah* (Book of Creation). If man can learn how God went about his creation, he too will be able to create human beings. This power is already attributed, at the end of the *Sefer Yetsirah*, to Abraham, who "contemplated, meditated, and beheld, investigated and understood and outlined and dug and combined and formed [i.e. created] and he succeeded."[27] A Midrash from the twelfth century goes even further by stating that "when God created His world, He first created the *Sefer Yetsirah* and looked into it and from it created His world. When He had completed His work, He put it [the *Sefer Yetsirah*] into the Torah [Pentateuch] and showed it to Abraham."[28] The secret is therefore in the Torah, which is not only made up of the names of God, but is, as a whole, the one great Name of God, and yet no one knows its right order, for the sections of the Torah are not given in the right arrangement. If they were, everyone who reads it might create a world, raise the dead, and perform miracles. Therefore the order of the Torah was hidden and is known to God alone.[29] The Kabbalists strove to find that hidden order, and the tradition of the golem goes back as far as the prophet Jeremiah, who busied himself with the *Sefer Yetsirah* until a man was created. For the Hasidim the creation of a golem confirmed man in his likeness to God. Through Jakob Grimm's version of 1808, the legend achieved wide popularity and exerted a special fascination on authors like Gustav Meyrink, Achim von Arnim, and E. T. A. Hoffmann. This is not to say that "The Circular Ruins" is strictly an avatar of the legend, although the poem certainly is, but rather that Borges' familiarity with the legend of the golem has impregnated his story.

The creation of a golem by man is parallel to the creation of Adam by God. As the golem is made from clay or mud, so Adam was made from the matter of the earth, literally from clay. The etymological connection between Adam and earth (Hebrew, ADAM*ah*) is very much stressed in the rabbinical and Talmudic commentaries on Genesis. Furthermore, in the Aggadah (the narrative branch of the Jewish oral law), Adam is designated as *golem,* which means the unformed, amorphous. Adam was said to be golem before the breath of God had touched him; and in a Midrash from the second and third centuries, Adam is described not only as a golem, but as a golem of cosmic size and strength to whom, while he was still in this speechless and inanimate state, God showed all future generations to the end of time. It was only after the Fall that Adam's enormous size, which filled the universe, was reduced to human proportions.[30] "His size [explains Scholem] would seem to signify, in spatial terms, that the power of the whole universe is concentrated in him. He receives his soul only at the end of Creation."[31]

In describing the efforts the magician makes to dream his creature in "The Circular Ruins," Borges interpolates this digression: "In the cosmogonies of the Gnostics, the demiurges mold a red Adam who is unable to stand on his feet; as clumsy and crude and elementary as that Adam of dust was the Adam of dreams wrought by the nights of the magician" (*A,* 59). Here Borges refers to certain Gnostic ideas, originally of Jewish extraction, according to which "the angels of Elohim took some of the best earth and from it formed man."[32] As in the traditional Midrash, this Gnostic Adam did not receive his soul until God and earth joined to make it. The idea that such an act of creation might be repeated by magic or other arts represents the backbone of the Kabbalistic tradition of the golem. It is this idea which one can perceive in Borges' story.

At first glance, the kinship of story and legend is hardly noticeable; "The Circular Ruins" is the story of a magician who sets himself the task of dreaming a man to later project him into reality, but the core of its theme is revealed only in the last paragraph: the dreamer too is but a dream; the creator too is but the imperfect creation of another creator; reality as a whole is but a dream of someone or no one. Thus focused, Borges' story begins to move toward the legend of the golem. Although the magician does not shape his intended son with mud or clay, as in the legend, but dreams him, the goal is still the same – the creation of a man. Yet the magician's dreams are not treated as such – that is, as intangible material – but rather as very concrete clay, as moldable substance: "He realized that, though he may penetrate all the riddles of the higher and lower orders, the task of shaping the senseless and dizzying stuff of dreams is the hardest that a man can attempt." (Recall that "golem" means "unformed matter.") And further on: "He then swore he would forget the populous vision which in the beginning had led him astray, and he sought another method." Before taking up his task again, "he cleansed himself in the waters of the river, worshiped the gods of the planets, uttered the prescribed syllables of an all-powerful name, and slept" (*A*, 58). When Borges writes "the prescribed syllables of an all-powerful name," we may surmise that he is thinking of the *Shem Hamephorash* or Tetragrammaton, which the Kabbalists sought by combining the letters of the Hebrew alphabet. Borges himself has paraphrased the Kabbalistic belief that when the miraculous *Shem Hamephorash* is pronounced over the golem made of clay or mud he must come to life: he "pronounced the Name which is the Key," Borges wrote in the poem "The Golem" (*SP*, 111). In his essay "The Golem" he had also pointed out that golem "was the name given to the man created by combinations of letters."[33] In "The Circular Ruins," the magician succeeds in dreaming a beating heart only after he has uttered "the prescribed syllables of an all-powerful name."

The description of the magician's dream is also reminiscent of the process of transformations (*temuroth*) of the letters as described in *Sefer Yetsirah*. Borges writes: "On the fourteenth night he touched the pulmonary artery with a finger and then the whole heart. . . . Before a year was over he came to the skeleton, the eyelids. The countless strands of hair were perhaps the hardest task of all" (*A*, 58–59). Similarly, in the *Sefer Yetsirah*, the letters of the Hebrew alphabet correspond to different parts of the human organism. Thus the double letters (beth, gimmel, daleth, caf, pei, reish, and taf) produced the seven planets, the seven days, and the seven apertures in man (two eyes, two ears, two nostrils, and one mouth). The twelve simple letters, on the other hand, created the twelve signs of the zodiac and thence the twelve months in time and the twelve "leaders" in man; the latter are those organs which perform functions in the body independent of the outside world – the hands, feet, kidneys, gall, intestines, stomach, liver, pancreas, and spleen (*Sefer Yetsirah*, IV–V). "One prescribed order of the alphabet produces a male being, another a female; a reversal of these orders turns the golem back to dust."[34]

Finally, Borges' magician dreams a complete man, but the dreamed being "could not stand up or speak, nor could he open his eyes." he resorts to the effigy in the destroyed temple, and the multiple god reveals to him that "its earthly name was Fire . . . and that through its magic the phantom of the man's dreams would be wakened to life in such a way that – except for Fire itself and the dreamer – every being in the world would accept him as a man of flesh and blood" (*A*, 59). In the Kabbalistic tradition, too, the act of animation comes with finding the right combination of letters as prescribed in the Book of Creation, an undertaking which normally demands three years of studying the *Sefer Yetsirah,* just as it takes a thousand and one nights for Borges' magician to produce his dreamed son. In both cases, animation comes only after exercising the divine power generated by the "all-powerful name."

Borges suggests in his tale that the dreamed man himself eventually becomes a dreamer and repeats the magic operation, and so will his son, and the son of his son, and so on *ad infinitum.* The golem of the Kabbalists does not reproduce, but it may grow endlessly in size. The only way of controlling this demiurgic growth is by erasing from his forehead the first letter of the word *Emeth* (truth), which makes the word read *meth* (he is dead). Once this is done, he collapses and turns to clay again. As fire can reveal that the magician's created son is a simulacrum, so the dropping of one letter can return the golem to his previous state as dust. Borges goes further by granting the dreamed man all the qualities of human life, thus bringing the golem-maker to a status no different from that of God. In the Kabbalah, on the other hand, the golem remains at a speechless level, a kind of docile Frankenstein,[35] with the exception of one Kabbalistic source – the *Pseudo Saadya,* where the golem is granted soul and speech.

Before sending his created son to another temple, "the magician imbued with total oblivion his disciple's long years of apprenticeship" (*A,* 60) – an idea with deep Kabbalistic roots. The "Midrash on the Creation of the Child" relates that "after its guardian angel has given it a fillip upon the nose, the newborn child forgets all the inifnite knowledge acquired before its birth in the celestial houses of learning."[36] In a parenthesis Borges explains that the oblivion is needed "so that the boy would never know he was a phantom, so that he would think himself a man like all men" (*A,* 60), thus integrating a seemingly bizarre and unconnected idea into the sequential "rationale" of the narrative.

The exegesis of the Midrash comes from Eleazar of Worms (d. 1232?), one of the pillars of German Hasidism: "Why, Eleazar asks, does the child forget? Because, if it did not forget, the course of this world would drive it to madness if it thought about it in the light of what it knew."[37] So no matter how different the two explanations may seem and how unlike their purpose, both share a common ground – the acceptance of a golem-making stage in which the dream and the child knew the mysteries of Creation. To be able to bear this world, the oblivion of that celestial or magical stage becomes inevitable. Scholem has observed that "in the root of the Midrash lies a remarkable variant of the Platonic conception of cognition as recollection, as anamnesis."[38] There is a moment in Borges' tale when the magician is about to recover the effaced awareness of that early stage, as if suddenly the recollection were to yield to a total illumination in which his origins became unveiled: "From time to time," writes Borges, the magician "was troubled by the feeling that all this had already happened." The revelation does not occur, but the hint provides one more clue to what Borges discloses only in the last line: the magician's own condition as phantom.

There is, however, one difference that separates the world-view of the Kabbalah from the outlook presented in "The Circular Ruins." In his story, Borges suggests that every man's reality is a dream and the god who is dreaming us is himself a dream. In the Kabbalah, God makes His creatures according to secret formulas that He alone knows; the first golem He created – *Adam Kadmon* (the primeval Adam) – was a creature of cosmic size and strength, and, furthermore, the first man was God Himself. It is in this light that one may understand the Midrash: "While Adam still lay as a golem before Him who spoke and the world came into being, He showed him all the generations and their wise men, all the generations and their judges and their leaders."[39] The Kabbalists managed to demonstrate this identity between God and Adam by means of *gematria* (isopsephism): they found that the numerical value of yhwh is 45 and so is adam's. As the Torah is but the name of God, Adam is God Himself. Before Adam, God dwelled in the depths of nothingness, and it is this abyss within God that was overcome in the Creation. Borges takes up where the devotion to monotheistic belief reined-in the imagination of the Kabbalists. The Kabbalah goes as far as identifying Adam – God's golem – with God Himself. Beyond this point we are confronted with an infinite abyss of nothingness which is but the primeval and chaotic state of God before the Creation. Borges, on the other hand, echoing old Gnostic beliefs, implies that behind his dreamer there are perhaps innumerable dreamers: his golem-maker is a mere link in a long golem-making chain. He has said it masterfully in the last lines of a memorable sonnet, "Chess":

> The player too is captive of caprice
> (The words are Omar's) on another ground
> Where black nights alternate with whiter days.
>
> God moves the player, he in turn the piece.
> But what god beyond God begins the round
> Of dust and time and sleep and agonies?   (*SP*, 121–23)

The doctrine of the Ibbür

Borges has written, "In the history of philosophy are doctrines, probably false, that exercise an obscure charm on human imagination, [for example] the Platonic and Pythagorean doctrine of the transmigration of the soul through many bodies" (*OI*, 37). Flashes of this doctrine flicker throughout his fiction, converting the revelations of theology into nuances of the fantastic. In several stories and essays, the transmigration of the soul is presented as a possible resolution of incoherent situations or conflicting circumstances.[40] Borges himself has disclosed the sources of this doctrine in "The Approach to al-Mu'tasim," but, as in other instances, here too the motif is a synthesis in which not two but several sources are cohesively blended. In the last paragraph of "The Approach. . . ," Borges supplies the Kabbalistic version of the doctrine of transmigration: "With due humility, I suggest a distant and possible forerunner, the Jerusalem Kabbalistic Isaac Luria, who in the sixteenth century advanced the notion that the soul of an ancestor or a master may, in order to comfort or instruct him, enter into the soul of someone who has suffered misfortune. *Ibbür* is the name given to this variety of metempsychosis" (*A*, 51–52). This Kabbalistic version of the transmigration of the soul enriches the doctrine substantially, adding to it original and highly imaginative elements. Thus, according to Luria (the leading figure of the Safed School), each soul retains its individual existence only until the moment when it has worked out its own spiritual restoration. Souls which have fulfilled the commandments are exempted from the law of transmigration and await, each in its blessed place, their integration into Adam's soul, when the general restitution of all things shall take place. As long as the soul has *not* fulfilled this task, it remains subject to the law of transmigration.

This banishment into the prison of strange forms of existence, into wild beasts, into plants and stones, is regarded as a particularly dreadful form of exile. As to how souls can be released from such an exile, Luria refers to the relationship between certain souls, in accordance with their original place in the undivided soul of Adam, the father of mankind. There are, according to Luria, relationships between souls and even families of souls, which somehow constitute a dynamic whole and react upon one another.[41] These souls have a special aptitude for assisting and supplementing each other's actions. Also, by their piety, they can lift up those members of their group or family who have fallen to a lower plane and can enable them to start on the return journey to higher forms of existence.[42] These are the essentials of the Kabbalah's interpretation of the doctrine which is called *gilgul* or *ibbür*, as Borges refers to it.

Kabbalists of the Lurianic School also held the belief that "everybody carries the secret trace of the transmigration of his soul in the lineament of his forehead and his hands, and in the aura which radiates from his body."[43] I fail to find any traces of chiromancy in Borges' writings, but the idea that a man's soul and its wanderings in search of total fulfillment or, what amounts to the same, that a man's destiny is traced in the lines of his forehead, provides a Kabbalistic clue to one of the most beautiful passages written by Borges: "A man," he says in the epilogue to *Dream-tigers*, "sets himself the task of portraying the world. Through the years he peoples a space with images of provinces, kingdoms, mountains, bays, ships, islands, fishes, rooms, instruments, stars, horses, and people. Shortly before his death, he discovers that that patient labyrinth of lines traces the image of his face" (*DT*, 93).[44] What in the Kabbalah is an ingeniously imaginative thought, in Borges becomes poetry at its best. Yet in the context of the Kabbalah, Borges' text regains the full measure of its implied and perhaps hidden significance. Like God, man creates his own universe, his own labyrinth which, unlike God's, he can penetrate and decipher. Like God, who revealed Himself in the Creation, man reveals himself (his face) in the world he creates (his work). In few writers' work do all the threads of the variegated texture interlock so tightly and firmly as they do in Borges'. This inner unity constitutes another pleasure among the many that Borges' work offers the patient reader.[45]

Reality of the unreal

Another link between Borges and the world of the Kabbalah is the invention of authors and books which do not exist but could. Borges has explained that "The composition of vast books is a laborious and impoverishing extravagance. To go on for five hundred pages developing an idea whose perfect oral exposition is possible in a few minutes! A better course of procedure is to pretend that these books already exist, and then offer a summary, a commentary" (*F*, 15). This effort to abbreviate responds not only to an ideal of verbal economy and density of style, but is also one of the many ways Borges chooses to efface the bounds between what we call the real and the unreal. If life becomes an illusion when presented as a dream somebody is dreaming or as a line of a book somebody is writing, a summary of or commentary upon a nonexistent book produces the opposite effect: the summary or commentary ends by imposing on us the reality of the imagined book. We can see the device at work in the preface to an anthology devoted to Almafuerte and compiled by Borges himself:

> Among the works I have not written and shall not write, but which in some way justify me – though in an illusory or ideal way – there is one that could be titled *Theory of Almafuerte*.

Drafts of it in an early handwriting prove that this hypothetical book has haunted me since 1932. It has, say, some hundred-odd octavo pages; to imagine it as any more extensive would be exorbitant. Nobody should regret its nonexistence or its existence only in that strange motionless world of possible objects. The summary of it that I am now going to give might prove identical to what one remembers over the years of a long book. Furthermore, its state as an unwritten book aptly fits it; the subject under examination is less the letter than the spirit of its author, less the notation than the connotation of his work. The general theory of Almafuerte is preceded by a particular conjecture about Pedro Bonifacio Palacios [Almafuerte], but (I hasten to add) the theory can do without the conjecture.[46]

The same pseudoepigraphic attitude was adopted by the author of the *Zohar*, although motivated by a different purpose. Moses de León came from the world of philosophical enlightenment against which he subsequently conducted an unremitting fight. In his youth we see him brooding over Moses Maimonides' *Guide for the Perplexed,* which he translated into Hebrew in 1264. Somewhat later, de León is turned by his mystical inclinations in the direction of Neo-Platonism, reading extracts from Plotinus' *Enneads,* which in the Middle Ages were commonly known by the title *The Theology of Aristotle.* But at the same time, he was more and more attracted to the mystical side of Judaism, and gradually he came to ponder the mystery of the godhead as it was presented by the Kabbalistic theosophy of his age. Moses de León wrote the *Zohar* in order to stem the growth of the radical rationalistic mood which was widespread among his educated contemporaries. "If I told the people," he is quoted as saying, "that I am the author, they would pay no attention nor spend a farthing on the book, for they would say that these are but the workings of my own imagination." To capture the attention of a small and select circle of Jewish readers, Moses de León sets his book against the background of an imagined Palestine, where the famous Mishnah teacher of the second century A.D., Rabbi Simeon ben Yohai, is seen wandering about with his son Eleazar, his friends and his disciples, and discoursing with them on all manner of things human and divine. To further mislead the reader, Moses de León used Aramaic, the language spoken in Palestine during the second century A.D. Now, of course, it is known that "The Aramaic of the Zohar is a purely artificial affair, a literary language employed by a writer who obviously knew no other Aramaic than that of certain Jewish literary documents, and who fashioned his own style in accordance with definite subjective criteria. The spirit of medieval

Hebrew, specifically the Hebrew of the thirteenth century, is transparent behind the Aramaic facade."[47] And yet Moses de León's literary artifice succeeded; until the overwhelming evidence presented by Gershom Scholem, the question of the *Zohar*'s authorship bore much resemblance to the puzzling problem of Shakespeare's or Homer's identity. Was there one author or were there several? Was the *Zohar* the work of many generations, or a compilation from more than one author, rather than the work of one man? Do its several parts correspond to different strata or periods? Many scholars and students of the *Zohar* still hold the belief that the *Zohar* represents only a final edition of writings composed over a long period; others candidly accept Moses de León's own version – that is, the legendary origin of the book according to which Simeon ben Yohai and his son, sentenced to death by the Romans in the Palestine of the second century A.D., fled to a cave and hid there for thirteen years, in which time the *Zohar* took form.

One of the factors that led to the success of Moses de León's pseudo-epigraphic efforts was his firm consistency in the references and allusions he made to the *Zohar* and its author within the frame of his own works. Borges refers to this equipoise when examining the "enchantments of the *Quixote*": "we are reminded of the Spanish Rabbi Moises de León, who wrote the *Zohar* or *Book of the Splendor* and divulged it as the work of a Palestinian rabbi of the third [*sic*] century" (*OI*, 46). It is at this point that the author of the *Zohar* comes close to some of Borges' own enchantments. Like Borges, who offers to the reader the summary of a novel which exists only in his imagination, Moses de León supplies fantastic references to nonexistent sources. The whole *Zohar* is full of bogus references to imaginary writings which have caused even serious students to postulate the existence of lost sources.[48] In this respect we cannot help recalling that some of Borges' naive readers have also made diligent attempts to obtain "the first detective novel to be written by a native of Bombay City," Mir Bahadur Ali's *The Approach to al-Mu'tasim*, whose summary Borges offers in his story. But Bahadur Ali's novel as well as Moses de León's cited sources exist only in that Borgesian "motionless and strange world of possible objects."

Like Borges, who delights in intermixing fictional characters with real people, in confounding dummy authors with illustrious ones and hypothetical books with existing ones, the author of the *Zohar* has produced an entire library of apocryphal books, and somebody has gone so far as to compile a catalogue of this "library from the upper world" – a tempting idea for a student of Borges. Next to works such as the "Book of Adam," the "Book of Enoch," the "Book of King Solomon," the "Book of Rav Hammuna Sava," and others that Moses de León comments on and profusely quotes – to the perplexity of the reader who knows nothing and can know nothing about them, simply because they exist only in the fancy of the mischievous Kabbalist – we can place Nils Runeberg's *Kristus och Judas* and his major work, *Den hemilge Frälsaren* (with its German translation); Herbert Quain's *The God of the Labyrinth, April March, The Secret Mirror,* and *Statements;* Volume XI of the *First Encyclopedia of Tlön;* the nineteen listed items of Pierre Menard's visible works, not to mention his unfinished masterpiece, *Don Quixote;* and several others that Borges quotes and paraphrases throughout his narratives. Yet these libraries of fictitious books, of nonexistent but possible books, acquire in their respective contexts a reality which makes them as real as those catalogued in, say, the Library of Congress – perhaps more real, since readers of Borges and the *Zohar* know much more about those nonexistent books than they will ever get to know about those millions of volumes in a library as bewildering as the Library of Babel. So what has been said of Moses de León's quotations from his "celestial library" can also be said of Borges' imaginary books: "They are entirely of a piece with the context in which they stand, both in style and terminology, and as a rule they are part of the argument as well."[49] In "Three Versions of Judas," the review of Nils Runeberg's books forms the argument as well as the body of the story.

Often the devices used by Moses de León to attain this effect are similar to those employed by Borges. As in the case of *Theory of Almafuerte,* a book which Borges has not written but of which he gives us a comprehensive summary, Moses de León widely quotes from imaginary books he may have written or may have intended to write. Thus, for example, the long passages quoted by him from the *Book of Enoch,* about which Gershom Scholem says: "There can be no question of his having used an Arabic *Book of Enoch* unknown to us, or anything else of the sort; nor is it necessary to assume that he had himself written such a book before he quoted it, although he may have intended to do so or even have begun writing it; also Moses de León is the first to quote from the 'Testament of Eliezer ben Hyrkanus' which must have been written by the author of the *Zohar* himself."[50]

Style

To these contextual resemblances between Borges' work and the Kabbalah, stylistic similarities can be added. Thus, it has been said of the language of the *Zohar:* "It runs all the way from serene beauty to labored tortuousness, from inflated rhetoric to the most paltry simplicity, and from excessive verbosity to laconic and enigmatic brevity."[51] The reader familiar with Borges' development as a prose writer will immediately recognize in this definition some of the most distinctive traits of Borges' style. His early prose is pompous, strained, and exhibits a too obvious effort to astonish. Borges himself has referred to those years of his earlier volumes of essays in the bluntest terms: "I used to write in a very baroque and tricky way. Out of timidity I used to believe that if I wrote in a simple way people would think that I did not know how to write. I felt then the need to prove that I knew many rare words and that I was able to combine them in a very startling fashion."[52] That inflated and often tortuous style has nothing in common with the restrained, precise, and condensed prose of his short stories and later essays. The Borges of the Ultraist experiments has yielded to a Borges whose terse and pregnant style has all the marks of classic prose.

Oxymoron figures among the fondest stylistic devices used by Borges.[53] This preference has very little to do with rhetorical excesses or baroque mannerism whose intention is "to surprise, to astonish, to dazzle,"[54] nor has Borges' oxymoron any ornamental or embellishing purpose – its use in his prose is definitely expressive and functional. The encounter and reconciliation of two notions which normally contradict or reject each other is, for Borges, a way of expressing at the level of style the paradoxical reality of his fictions. In his stories, frequently, the material of the fable organizes as a huge oxymoron. Style, then, restates and reinforces what is suggested by the theme of the narrative: eternity held in an instant, the chaos of our ordered universe, a dot which contains the universe, a library of illegible books, a pursued pursuer. The author of the *Zohar* also shows a definite predilection for oxymoron and paradox, elements that Scholem defines as a "characteristic peculiarity of his style": " 'It is and is not' signifies, not that something exists, as it were, only partially, but that its existence is of an exquisitely spiritual nature and cannot therefore be properly described."[55] "Properly described," one could add, by means of the normative alternatives offered by language, whose limitations and barriers the Kabbalists, as well as Borges, strive to overcome.

Unveiling the seventy faces of a text

In the *Zohar,* as in Borges' fiction, one also finds the use of an old myth or motif and its subsequent reshaping into a new mode of thought. Moses de León takes the materials from the Aggadah and with them weaves his own fabric. He uses them freely for his own purposes and gives free rein to his imagination in making vital changes, emendations, and reinterpretations of the original. One example of this occurs in

Zohar II, 124a. There, Moses de León converts a brief Talmudic tale which appears sporadically in the treatise of *Pesahim* 3b into a lively story on the same subject. Where the Aggadah already contains mystical elements, these are duly emphasized and occasionally changed into an entirely new myth. A case in point is the mythology of the "great dragon" in *Zohar* II, 35a, which has evolved from the Aggadah on the *Or ha-Ganuz* in the Talmudic treatise of *Hagigah* 12a. Borges' treatment does not differ essentially from Moses de León's. In the recreation of the myth of the Minotaur in the story "The House of Asterion," Borges' purpose is not mere virtuosity. Borges himself has suggested that the idea "of a monster wanting to be killed, needing to be killed"[56] is the fictional reverse or paraphrase of another idea stated in his article "A Comment on August 23, 1944," written during the war. There he said that Hitler would be defeated because he wanted to be defeated: "Hitler is collaborating blindly with the inevitable armies that will annihilate him, as the metal vultures and the dragon (which must not have been unaware that they are monsters) collaborated, mysteriously, with Hercules" (*OI*, 136). Yet Borges' own interpretation of his story does not exhaust its far-reaching implications. I believe it is in this story more than in any other that Borges' labyrinthine outlook has been most fully and richly developed.[57] The old and weary myth has become here an effective medium for bringing forth his own world-view. Like the Kabbalist, Borges creates a new myth out of the old one. He has read into the legend of the Minotaur a new meaning which not only redeems the old myth, but also justifies it. Borges, indeed, fulfills here a task similar to Pierre Menard's in undertaking to write a contemporary *Quixote*. In "Pierre Menard, Author of the *Quixote*," Borges tells us that "Cervantes' text and Menard's are verbally identical, but the second is almost infinitely richer." This is just an exacerbation of the same attitude, of the same concept of literature according to which "one literature differs from another, either before or after it, not so much because of the text as for the manner in which it is read." "If I were able to read any contemporary page," explains Borges to prove his point, ". . . as it would be read in the year 2000, I would know what literature would be like in the year 2000" (*OI*, 164). In a strict sense, Borges' own narratives could be defined – applying this criterion – as different ways of reading the systems of philosophy and the doctrines of theology. "I am," Borges has said about himself, "a man of letters who turns his own perplexities and that respected system of perplexities we call philosophy into the forms of literature."[58] His stories are postures for reading those theories (which have made man what he is), but in the process the claimed "absolute truths" have become myths and marvels, humble intuitions of man's fantasy. Perhaps in this wise and skillful turn of the kaleidoscope lies the revelation of Borges' art. If the essence of this revelation resides in the act of reading the new in an old text, we have simply come to the very point where the Kabbalah begins. These beginnings are described by Borges himself in his essay "The Mirror of the Enigmas":

> The notion that the Sacred Scripture possesses (in addition to its literal meaning) a symbolic one is not irrational and is ancient: it is found in Philo of Alexandria, in the cabalists, in Swedenborg. . . . The portentous premise of a book that is impervious to contingency, a book that is a mechanism of infinite purposes, moved them [the Kabbalists] to permute the scriptural words, to sum up the numerical value of the letters, to consider their form, to observe the small letters and the capital letters, to search for acrostics and anagrams. (*OI,* 125–28)

Now, one should ask what the Kabbalists achieved by means of this mystical hermeneutics. The *Zohar* is undoubtedly the most representative work of many centuries of Kabbalistic exegesis, but it is far from being the only one – there are literally hundreds of such books many of them still in manuscript form. The *Zohar* shares some basic characteristics with most of these books: thus, for instance, its deliberately unsystematic construction, a tendency – rooted in Jewish thought – to avoid logical systematization. Scholem has illustrated the method (or rather the method's lack of method) of the *Zohar* with a very eloquent comparison: "Most of the fundamental ideas found in the *Zohar*," he says, "were expressed only a little later in a systematically constructed treatise, *Maarekheth Ha-Elohuth* (The Order of God), but how dry and lifeless are these bare skeletons of thought compared with the flesh and blood of the *Zohar!*" And he goes on: "In the *Zohar* the most unpretentious verses of Scripture acquire an entirely unexpected meaning. . . . Again and again a hidden and sometimes awful depth opens before our eyes, and we find ourselves confronted with real and profound insight."[59] The foundation of this imaginative wealth and fertility of thought lies in the belief that "the Torah is an inexhaustible well, which no pitcher can ever empty."[60]

Borges proposes a similar premise. When he says that "perhaps universal history is the history of the diverse intonation of a few metaphors," he appears to be postulating the opposite case, since he seemingly underlines the exhaustible character of *human* imagination.[61] But it is only the oblique formulation that creates this impression; actually, Borges is saying exactly the opposite. In the essay "The Metaphor," written in 1952, he offers the reader the prolegomenon of his idea, explaining that

> The first monument of Western literature, the *Iliad,* was composed some three thousand years ago; it seems safe to surmise that during this lapse of time every familiar and necessary affinity (dream-life, sleep-death, the flow of rivers and time, and so forth) has been noted and recorded by someone. This does not mean, of course, that the number of metaphors has been exhausted; the ways of stating or hinting at these hidden sympathies are, in fact, limitless.[62]

Consequently, "perhaps it is a mistake to suppose that metaphors can be invented. The real ones, those that formulate intimate connections between one image and another, have always existed; those we can still invent are the false ones, which are not worth inventing" (*OI,* 47). Taking this one step further, Borges implies that the task of the writer is not to invent new and original works but rather to reinterpret old ones, or – in John Barth's words – "to write original works of literature whose implicit theme is the difficulty, perhaps the unnecessity, of writing original works of literature."[63]

Borges' concept of metaphor (which for him is only a metaphor for literature) does not differ essentially from the *Zohar's* outlook on the Scripture: as the whole world is for the Kabbalists a *corpus symbolicum* (an idea that Borges has repeatedly quoted),[64] so the Torah is conceived, and to interpret it is, consequently, to unveil its "seventy faces" (i.e., infinite levels). Borges has referred to himself as "the man who weaves these symbols" (*A,* 95), and in a different context he has said that "art operates necessarily with symbols";[65] in addition, he has insisted on the idea that universal history is "a Sacred Scripture: one that we decipher and write uncertainly, and in which we also are written" (*OI,* 120), and he has likewise endorsed the belief that "we are the versicles or words or letters of a magic book, and that incessant book is the only thing in the world; or rather, it is the world" (*OI* 120). For the Kabbalists, similarly, God looked at the Torah and created the world. The *Zohar,* like the literature of the Kabbalah at large, is an attempt to penetrate the hidden layers of that holy text; the results are those coined symbols and sometimes elaborated allegories by means of which a new, lucid, and original interpretation of the Scripture has been produced. Borges' narratives and symbols represent a similar attempt, with the difference that the text Borges reads encompasses "the almost infinite world of literature."

It has been asked whether the true interpretation of certain passages of the Scripture may not be found in the *Zohar* and nowhere else; I would like to ask if Borges' symbols – which claim not to be a reflection of the world but rather something added to it – do not imply a new understanding of man's confrontation with the world. Some of these symbols suggest that since man can never find the solution to the gods' labyrinth, he has constructed his own labyrinth; or, in other words, that since the reality of the gods is impenetrable, man has created his own reality. He lives, thus, in a world which is the product of his own fallible architecture. He knows there is another world, "irreversible and iron-bound," which constantly besieges him and forces him to feel the enormity of its presence, and between these two worlds, between these two stories – one imagined by God and the other fancied by man – flows the agonizing history of mankind.

NOTES

1 Borges is referring to Joshua Trachtenberg's *Jewish Magic and Superstition: A Study in Folk Religion* (New York, 1939).
2 See Ronald Christ, "Jorge Luis Borges, an Interview," *The Paris Review*, 40 (Winter–Spring 1967), 162.
3 See Rabi, "Fascination de la Kabbale," *L'Herne, J. L. Borges* (Paris, 1964), pp. 265–71. Since I published this essay back in 1972, several articles and even two brief books on the subject have appeared in Spanish. The latter are: Edna Aizenberg, *El tejedor del Aleph; Biblia, Kábala y judaísmo en Borges* (Madrid: Altalena, 1986) and Saúl Sosnowski, *Borges y la Cábala; la búsqueda del verbo* (Buenos Aires: Hispamérica, 1976).
4 See J. L. Borges, "Una vindicación de la cábala," *Discusión* (Buenos Aires, 1957), pp. 55–60.
5 Christ, *ibid.*, p. 161.
6 As every reader of the *Quixote* knows, in Chapter VI the curate and the barber perform a thorough scrutiny of the library "of our ingenious gentleman." The scrutiny represents a critical examination of romances of chivalry and pastoral novels to whose tradition Cervantes himself contributed *La Galatea*. This book, too, falls into the hands of the scrutinizers who decide to keep it because, the curate says, "that fellow Cervantes and I have been friends these many years, but, to my knowledge, he is better versed in misfortune than he is in verses. His book has a fairly good plot; it starts out well and ends up nowhere." Borges himself has referred to the effects of this "play of mirrors" in his essay "Partial Enchantments of the *Quixote*."
7 I have further discussed the effects of this device in *La prosa narrativa de Jorge Luis Borges* (Madrid, 1968), pp. 87–88.
8 The last sentence was written before the appearance of *The Aleph and Other Stories* (New York, 1970). There Borges provides, for the first time, some enlightening "commentaries" on the background of the short stories collected in that volume. On "Death and the Compass," he says: "No apology

is needed for repeated mention of the Kabbalah, for it provides the reader and the all-too-subtle detective with a false track, and the story is, as most of the names imply, a Jewish one. The Kabbalah also provides an additional sense of mystery" (*A,* 269).

9 Although this book was published in English in 1960, it collects essays published (1927) in Buber's *Die chassidischen Bücher* and his *Der grosse Maggid und seine Nachfolge* (1921).

10 The German edition dates from 1907.

11 There may be other references to Buber that I have overlooked.

12 For further information on this subject, see Scholem's *On the Kabbalah and Its Symbolism* (New York, 1969), pp. 197–98.

13 J. L. Borges, *El tamaño de mi esperanza* (Buenos Aires, 1926), p. 67.

14 Scholem, *Major Trends in Jewish Mysticism* (New York, 1961), p. 208.

15 For comprehensive information on the *Zohar,* see Chapters V–VI in Scholem's *Major Trends.*

16 Scholem, *ibid.,* p. 222.

17 *Ibid.,* pp. 223–24.

18 This is not the place to elaborate on Borges' fertile use of pantheism in his fiction. I have treated this aspect of his work in my book *La prosa narrativa de J. L. Borges,* pp. 60–73. Here it will suffice to observe that the pantheistic notion that frames several of his stories stems from Plotinus, Spinoza, Sufism, Hinduism, Buddhism, and other sources, as well as from the doctrines of the Kabbalah. In some instances, Borges' contacts with the Kabbalah are indirectly established through authors who in one way or another echo Kabbalistic theories. Thus the world of *Sefiroth,* as described above, is found in Francis Bacon's *Advancement of Learning,* but now the theosophic symbols "tree" and "man" are replaced by the image of a book: "God offered us two books," writes Borges quoting Bacon, "so that we would not fall into error. The first, the volume of the Scriptures, reveals His will; the second, the volume of the creatures, reveals His power" (*OI,* 119).

19 The seed of this idea is already found in "A History of Angels," and is literally reproduced in "Una vindicación de la cábala."

20 Quoted by Scholem in *On the Kabbalah,* p. 38.

21 *Ibid.,* p. 122.

22 *Ibid.,* p. 124.

23 In addition to "The Theologians," the motif can be traced in the following stories: "The Shape of the Sword," "Theme of the Traitor and the Hero," "Three Versions of Judas," "Story of the Warrior and the Captive," "The End," "The Life of Tadeo Isidoro Cruz," "The South," and "The Other Death."

24 One of them was undoubtedly Gustav Meyrink's novel *Der Golem,* which young Borges read while still a student in Geneva.

25 A concise exposition of this outlook as conceived by Eastern thought may be found in Borges' essay "Forms of a Legend."

26 I have discussed this in some detail in *La prosa narrativa de Jorge Luis Borges,* pp. 53–59.

27 *Le Sepher Yetsirah,* Texte hébreu intégral, lu et commenté d'après le code

originel de la Cabale par Carlo Suarès (Geneva, 1968), p. 122. I use the English translation as it appears in Gershom Scholem's *On the Kabbalah and Its Symbolism*, p. 169.

28   The Midrash is "Neue Pesikta." Quoted by Scholem, *On the Kabbalah*, pp. 177–78.

29   Scholem, *ibid.*, p. 167.

30   On the subject of the golem, see the chapter "The Idea of the Golem" in Scholem's *On the Kabbalah*, pp. 158–204.

31   *Ibid.*, p. 162.

32   *Ibid.*, p. 164.

33   J. L. Borges, *The Book of Imaginary Beings* (New York, 1969), pp. 112–14.

34   Scholem, *On the Kabbalah*, p. 186.

35   Notice that Mary W. Shelley's creature is also a close descendant of the golem.

36   Scholem, *Major Trends . . .* , p. 92.

37   *Loc. cit.*

38   *Loc cit.*

39   Quoted by Scholem in *On the Kabbalah*, p. 162.

40   Here are a few examples to illustrate Borges' use of the doctrine. To explain the poem "Kubla Khan," dreamed by Coleridge, and the palace Kubla Khan dreamed and then had built, Borges suggests: "The Emperor's soul penetrated Coleridge's, enabling Coleridge to rebuild the destroyed palace in words that would be more lasting than marble and metal" (*OI*, 16). In "The Theologians," one of the sects postulates that "most [men], like Pythagoras, will have to transmigrate through many bodies before attaining their liberation; some, the Proteans, 'in the period of one lifetime are lions, dragons, boars, water and a tree'" (*L*, 123). In "The Shape of the Sword," Borges mentions "'enormous epic poems which sang of the robbing of bulls which in another incarnation were heroes and in others fish and mountains'" (*L*, 68).

41   Cortázar's idea that individual destinies cluster together in *figuras* whose shape and interaction they ignore, just as the stars of a constellation do not know they are part of such a group, may well find in Luria's text a suitable Kabbalistic explanation.

42   Scholem, *Major Trends*, pp. 282–83.

43   *Ibid.*, p. 283.

44   An early formulation of this thought is found in "Ars Poetica," one of Borges' finest poems. The pertinent stanza reads:

> At times in the evenings a face
> Looks at us out of the depths of a mirror;
> Art should be like that mirror
> Which reveals to us our own face.   (*SP*, 143)

45   Like many others in Borges' work, this idea cannot be restricted to one exclusive source. In addition to its bearing on Luria's version of metempsychosis, other connections are disclosed by Borges himself. In his

essay on Oscar Wilde, he has commented on some perspicuous observations left by the author of *De Profundis*. From this posthumous book Borges quotes Wilde's assertion that "there is no man who is not, at each moment, what he has been and what he will be," to explain later in a footnote: "Compare the curious thesis of Leibnitz, which seemed so scandalous to Arnauld: 'The notion that each individual includes *a priori* all the events that will happen to him'" (*OI*, 80). Borges alludes to the letters Leibnitz wrote to Arnauld (in one of which the famous statement was made), and to the negative reaction of the French Jansenist. Here, in the Leibnitz letter, the relationship is more abstract. Borges' memorable page and the Kabbalistic text share the striking image, in addition to the idea of a destiny conceived *a priori*, of a man's destiny traced in the lines of his face.

46 J. L. Borges, *Prosa y poesía de Almafuerte* (Buenos Aires, 1962), p. 6.
47 For a detailed discussion on the subject of the *Zohar's* authorship, see Scholem, *Major Trends*, pp. 156–204.
48 *Ibid.*, p. 174.
49 *Ibid.*, p. 174.
50 *Ibid.*, p. 200.
51 *Ibid.*, p. 163.
52 James E. Irby, "Encuentro con Borges," *Vida universitaria*, Monterey, México (April 12, 1964), p. 14.
53 The reader interested in the use and effects of the oxymoron in Borges' narrative prose may see the subchapter "Oximoron" in *La prosa narrativa de J. L. Borges*, pp. 186–99.
54 E. R. Curtius, *European Literature and the Latin Middle Ages* (New York, 1963), p. 282.
55 Scholem, *Major Trends*, pp. 166–67.
56 See Richard Burgin, *Conversations with Jorge Luis Borges* (New York, 1969), p. 41.
57 See my essay "Tlön y Asterión: metáforas epistemológicas," in *La prosa narrativa de J. L. Borges* (Madrid: Gredos, 1983), pp. 275–301.
58 J. L. Borges, "Foreword" to Ronald Christ, *The Narrow Act: Borges' Art of Allusion* (New York, 1969), p. 9.
59 Scholem, *Major Trends*, p. 158.
60 Scholem, *On the Kabbalah*, p. 60.
61 For a penetrating article on this question, see John Barth's "The Literature of Exhaustion," *Atlantic* (August 1967), pp. 29–34.
62 Jorge Luis Borges, "The Metaphor," in "Up from Ultraism," *New York Review of Books* (August 13, 1970), p. 4.
63 Barth, *ibid.*, p. 31.
64 In a book review in his collection of essays, *Discusión*, p. 164, he says: ". . . for the mystics the concrete world is but a system of symbols."
65 *Discusión*, p. 141.

3   Kabbalistic traits in Borges' narratives

The reader well acquainted with the short stories of Jorge Luis Borges knows that his texts do not exhaust themselves at the level of literal meaning. Like most of his narratives in which one easily distinguishes a denotative plot and a connotative symbol or allegory, his prose also offers an immediate and manifest layer and a more oblique and allusive one. Even the casual reader perceives in his stories an obverse-*fabula* and a reverse-symbol, although he may fail to define the bounds of the former with respect to the latter. On the other hand, in the realm of language, even the alert reader tends to accept the text in its externality, dismissing that interior and elusive side, which may be invisible at first glance but which is no less present and functional than its visible counterpart. One of the wonders of Borges' art is precisely that Kabbalistic feature apparent in many of his narrative texts. This art is Kabbalistic in a sense defined by Borges himself in his essay "A Vindication of the Kabbalah," where he explains that his purpose is to vindicate not the doctrine but "the hermeneutic or cyptographic procedures which lead to it." To elaborate further: "These procedures are the vertical reading of the holy text, the reading called *boustrophedon* (from right to left, one line, from left to right the following one), the methodical substitution of some letters of the alphabet for others, the sum of the numerical value of the letters" (*D*, 55). Borges refers here to "certain techniques of mystical speculation which are popularly supposed to represent the heart and core of Kabbalism," yet, according to Gershom Scholem, "none of these techniques[1] of mystical exegesis can be called Kabbalistic in the strict sense of the word. . . . What really deserves to be called Kabbalism has very little to do with the 'Kabbalistic' practices."[2] However, it is this technical side of Kabbalism that interests us. In essence, it is a question of possible alternatives to the reading of a text. The Kabbalists differentiate between an exoteric interpretation of the Scripture and an esoteric one. In the first case the meaning of the text is literal, but in the second "the Holy Scriptures" – explains a Talmudic mystic – "are like a large house with many, many rooms, and outside each door lies a key – but it is not the right one. To find the right keys that will open the door – that is the great and arduous task."[3] The Kabbalists found that each word of the Torah (Pentateuch) "has six hundred thousand 'faces,' that is, layers of meaning or entrances,"[4] and that "it is made up not only of the names of God but is as a whole the one great Name of God."[5] According to an early Midrash, God "looked into the Torah and created the world, since the cosmos and all nature was already prefigured in the Torah, so that God, looking into the Torah could see it, although to us this aspect of the Torah remains concealed."[6] For Joseph Gikatila, a leading Spanish Kabbalist of the thirteenth century, "the Torah is not itself the name of God but the explication of the Name of God, and the letters are the mystical body of God, while God is the soul of the letters."[7] In order to penetrate to recondite strata of the Holy text, the Kabbalists developed four levels of interpretation: *peshat* or literal meaning, *remez* or allegorical meaning, *derasha* or Talmudic and Aggadic interpretation, and *sod* or anagogic meaning. In addition to these levels of interpretation, they used several techniques of speculation such as *Gematria* or calculation of the numerical value of Hebrew words and the search for connections with other words or phrases of equal value; *Notarikon* or interpretation of the letters of a word as abbreviations of whole sentences; and *Temurah* or interchange of letters according to certain systematic rules. Applying each of these techniques, the possibilities are almost infinite.[8]

To the question "Have you tried to make your own stories Kabbalistic?" Borges has replied, "Yes, sometimes I have."[9] The question as well as the answer are broad and ambiguous enough to encourage speculation. Borges' readiness to be a reader of his own work (through the numerous interviews he has given) has provided rich and valuable information that no student of his work can afford to ignore. In some instances he has furnished possible and alternative clues for the reading of his stories; in others he has suggested new and refreshing interpretations of narratives whose trite understanding was becoming more and more rigid and stereotyped. He has compiled his own anthologies, a conventional undertaking that he has turned into a Kabbalistic reading of his work, not so much because he claims that he would like "to be judged by it [his *Personal Anthology*], and justified or reproved by it" (*PA*, ix), but rather because the preferences change from edition to edition as if Borges were reminding the reader that an author must be judged by his work and not by his opinions of it. So, an author who usually is the absolute creator of his book, cannot be the absolute reader of it. The degree of lucidity varies from author to author, but whatever the acuteness may be "there are many things in an author's work not intended and only partially understood by him."[10] When Borges was asked about the Kabbalistic quality of his writing, he may have thought of the fact that as the literature of the Kabbalah has been defined as "a narrative philosophy,"[11] so his tales have been characterized as "metaphysical fantasies."[12] He may have thought about the idea that the whole world is for the Kabbalists a *corpus symbolicum,* and the definition of himself as "a man who interweaves these symbols" (*PA,* 28). Or he may have simply referred to the belief that as the Torah has for the Kabbalists "seventy faces" (a number standing for infinite), so the symbols he has coined "are capable of many, perhaps incompatible values" (*OI,* 66).

We are not suggesting an application of the method of the Kabbalah to Borges' writings. The Kabbalistic exegesis of the Scripture is motivated by the belief that "a work dictated by the Holy Spirit was an absolute text: a text where the collaboration of chance is calculable to zero" (*OI,* 134). Thus, if the word *light* occurs five times in the story of the first day of Creation, the number is not, cannot, be accidental: it corresponds, as explained in the *Midrash Genesis Rabbah,* to the five books of the Torah. If the Torah begins with the letter Beth, whose numerical value is two, it is because, explains the *Zohar* (The Book of Splendor), "the process of creation has taken place in two planes, one above and one below. . . . The lower occurrence corresponds to the higher; one produced the upper world, and the other the nether world [of the visible creation]" (*Zohar* I, 240b). It is absurd to think that in Borges' writings "every word is capable of becoming a symbol" as is the case of the Scripture for the Jewish mystic, but it is not preposterous at all to treat Borges' texts with a rigor similar to the zeal displayed by the Kabbalists in their reading of the Scripture. After all, the efforts of the Kabbalists to find new layers of meaning in the Biblical text are not essentially different from the endeavors of the critic to establish new possibilities or perspectives of interpretation of the literary text.

There are two more reasons that reinforce our contention: first, the enthralling fascination that the Kabbalah has exerted on Borges' mind; second, the fantastic character of his stories which induces us to estimate some seemingly incoherent words and occurrences as whimsical displays of arbitrary fantasy, thus missing the true impact of those masterfully constructed whimsicalities. An example of this kind of word is the adjective *unanimous* to modify *night* in the first line of the story "The Circular Ruins"; the word is used for its etymological components (*unus animus*)[13] rather than for its normative meaning in order to subtly anticipate what is literally disclosed in the last line of the story: the magician's condition of appearance dreamt by another. An example of the kind of occurrence that may seem to the reader a playful detour of the imagination just to stress the fantastic character of his tale occurs in the story "The Approach to Al-Mu'tasim." The protagonist, a law student in Bombay, finds himself in the center of a civil tumult between Moslems and Hindus; he joins the fray and kills a Hindu. When the police intervene, the student takes flight and makes for the farthest outskirts of town. "He scales the wall of an entangled garden, at the back of which rises a circular tower. . . . Once on the roof, where there is a blackish well in the center, he encounters a squalid man . . . [who]confides in him that his profession is to rob gold teeth from the white-shrouded cadavers which the Parsees leave in this tower" (*F*, 38–39). The encounter of the student with the despoiler of cadavers is an essential link in the sequence of the narrative; the presence, on the other hand, of white shrouded cadavers left in a tower is rather perplexing to the reader unfamiliar with the practices of the Parsees. In the context of Borges' story, though, the detail is far from being a whim meant to astonish. The tower where the student takes shelter is a *dakhma* or Tower of Silence, and in those *dakhmas* Zoroastrians in Persia and India dispose of their dead. The Parsees (Indian Zoroastrians) believe that water, fire, and earth are pure and holy and must be protected, and thus a corpse – the most impure and contaminating object – may not be buried in the earth or cast into a stream, a pool, or the sea, nor may it be destroyed by fire. Instead they place the corpse in towers built for that purpose where the flesh is consumed by vultures. The *dakhma* is a round tower, some twenty feet high, built of stone in the shape of an open cone, with one door near the base, through which the body is carried in. In the center of the tower there is a pit about six feet deep lined with concentric shelves and paved with stones. Once the flesh has been stripped away by vultures, the bones are cast into the central wall where they lie until air, rain, and sun changes them into dust, thereby making them pure again. There are seven Towers of Silence in the vicinity of Bombay.[14]

In the light of this brief description of a *dakhma*, Borges' enigmatic detail gains a completely unexpected function within the narrative. It is no longer a fantastic oddity as the outward appearance seems to imply, but rather a necessary element that fully integrates with the story as a whole. Borges uses all the materials at his disposal to recreate the setting of his tale; he himself has disclosed certain analogies in the first scene of the story with elements from Kipling's "On the City Wall." Yet, the last thing Borges is willing to do is to produce an effect of local color. He has elaborated on this subject in his essay "The Argentine Writer and Tradition":

> Gibbon observes that in the Arabian book *par excellence,* in the Koran, there are no camels; I believe if there were any doubt as to the authenticity of the Koran, this absence of camels would be sufficient to prove it is an Arabian work. It was written by Mohammed, and Mohammed, as an Arab, had no reason to know that camels were especially Arabian; for him they were a part of reality, he had no reason to emphasize them; on the other hand, the first thing a falsifier, a tourist, an Arab nationalist would do is have a surfeit of camels, caravan of camels, on every page; but Mohammed, as Arab, was unconcerned: he knew he could be an Arab without camels. I think we Argentines can emulate Mohammed, can believe in the possibility of being Argentine without abounding in local color. (*L,* 181)

One should remember that Borges' story is written as a summary of the novel *The Approach to Al-Mu'tasim* by the Bombay lawyer Mir Bahadur Ali. As such, he rightly assumes that by just describing the facts as they are, his readers will understand that the encounter of the student with the robber takes place in one of seven *dakhmas* found in the vicinity of Bombay, since – paraphrasing Borges – Bahadur Ali, as a native of Bombay, has no reason to know that *dakhmas* were especially Indian; for him they were part of reality, he had no reason to emphasize them. We know, though, that the summary of the hypothetical novel is an artifice of Borges, but precisely because it is so, Borges has given enough and accurate information – and his description is a true model of minute accuracy[15] – to enable the perceptive reader to realize that he is referring to a *dakhma;* and, at the same time, he has subtly avoided excessive explanation so as not to destroy the magic of the illusion.

In some instances Borges himself provides the clue to the Kabbalistic construction of his narrative. Towards the end of the same story – "The Approach to Al-Mu'tasim" – he suggests an allegorical reading of the "detective novel": "Al-Mu'tasim is the emblem of God, and the punctual itinerary of the hero is in some manner the forward progress of the soul in its mystic ascent" (*F,* 41). The search of the student becomes, thus, a mystical experience no different from the one revealed in the Sufistic poem *Mantiq ut-Tair,* which Borges fully describes in a footnote as the solution to the enigmatic ending of the apocryphal novel. Since its author and its protagonist are Muslim, Sufism is the Islamic form of mysticism that best befits the mystical reverse of the story. Yet other possibilities are suggested as probable sources or clues. Borges mentions among those distant and possible predecessors of Bahadur Ali, the Jerusalem Kabbalist Isaac Luria, "who in the sixteenth century proclaimed that the soul of an ancestor or that of a master might enter the soul of an unfortunate to comfort or instruct him" (*F*, 43). But if we accept Borges' *locus classicus* according to which "each writer creates his own precursor," other predecessors could be added to his list. The story may be read as a Sufistic experience, as an expression of Kabbalistic *Ibbür*, and also as a narrative translation of Hindu Ātman. As in Ferid ed-Din Attar's poem where the Simurg is God and all men are the Simurg, in *Mundaka* Upanishad "all things proceed from Brahman as sparks from a fire, and all things return to him as rivers to the sea – Ātman (the eternal soul) is the means by which one obtains Brahman";[16] thus, Brahman is Ātman and Ātman is Brahman.[17] It could be argued that once one mystic system is presented, the others are essentially implied in it. In our case Hindu Ātman, Sufism (a form of mysticism that has been defined as "Vedanta in Muslim dress")[18] and the *Ibbür* of the Kabbalah are different manifestations of a same attempt: to feel the presence of the Godhead in such a way that God becomes the center and the circumference or, as the *Brihadaranyaka* Upanishad puts it, "the hub and felly of the wheel of which the individual souls are the spokes."[19]

Yet, it is this well-wrought ambiguity in Borges' stories that often generates their density of meaning. The apparent ambiguity is produced by the conjunction of several intuitions, by the overlapping of several motivations and sources that, like thin layers, were masterfully pressed into one tight and limpid fabric. One can simply enjoy the product in its outward result, or one can attempt to strip off those layers in order to comprehend fully the hidden richness embedded in the whole. When the reader recognizes in the wanderings of the Bombay student a form of the mystic ascent of the soul, the detective novel gains in breadth; when, later in the story, Borges discloses that his tale can be read as an echo of the Sufistic poem, one can sense that a new dimension has been added to the narrative. By providing new perspectives for reading the story, Borges has become – without leaving the bounds of the narration – his own critic: he offers to the reader new ways of understanding the story and additional clues for further enjoying it. Yet Borges has by no means singled out all the strands braided together in his tale.

We have seen that the Hindu notion of Ātman may as well be implied in the Bombay student's search, to be more precise, in the moment when the student finally "arrives at a gallery at the rear of which there is a door hung with a cheap and copiously beaded mat curtain, behind which a great radiance emanates. The student claps his hands once, twice, and asks for Al-Mu'tasim. A man's voice – the incredible voice of Al-Mu'tasim – urges him to come in. The student draws back the curtain and steps forward. The novel ends" (*F,* 41). The previous adventures throughout India become, thus, only steps leading towards this Atmanic fulfillment. Borges has also anticipated the critic by disclosing "certain analogies" in the first scene of the novel with elements from Kipling's story "On the City Walls," but he has said nothing about the "possible" analogies with the motif of the searcher knocking at the door of a house where the mystic union is about to occur. The motif, notwithstanding, as presented by Borges in the passage we have troubled to quote in its entirety, is found in the first part of the Sufi collection of mystical parables, *Masnawi,* of the Persian poet Jalal-ud-din Rumi. Here, a man knocks on the door of his friend. The latter asks, "Who is it?" He answers, "I." The friend sends him away. For a whole year the sorrow of separation burns in him; then he comes again and knocks once more. To the question of his friend, "Who is it?" he replies, "Thou." And at once gains entrance to the room in which there is not room for two "I's," that of God and that of man.[20] Martin Buber has found a parallel to this motif in a Hasidic tale that obviously shows traces of Sufi influence. In the Jewish version, the element of a man (friend of Rabbi Aaron of Karlin) knocking at his friend's door is also present. "Who are you?" asked a voice from within, and, certain that his friend would recognize him by his voice, he answered, "I." No reply came, and the door did not open even though he knocked again and again. Finally he cried, "Aaron, why do you not open for me?" Then he heard from within, "Who is it who presumes to say 'I,' as it is fitting for God alone to do!" He said in his heart, "I see then that I have not yet finished learning."[21]

In the context of this old mystic motif, Borges' rather vague and mysterious passage regains the quasi-geometric cohesiveness characteristic of most of his narratives. The detailed explanation supplied by Borges as a footnote at the end of the story only confirms what is subtly alluded to at the conclusion of the student's peregrination. The full description of Ferid ed-Din Attar's poem operates at an outward level: it tells the reader, in a literal manner, that at the moment the student is confronted with the "splendor" coming from the inside, he realizes that he, too – as the birds of the poem with respect to the Simurg – is Al-Mu'tasim. The variation of the motif of Jalal-ud-din Rumi's parable implied in the last ambiguous link of the narration tells the same, but with the Borgesian finesse that converts an apparent insignificant detail into the magic key of the story. The exoteric and esoteric levels of meaning thus coalesce in a text that has the texture of a Kabbalistic cryptogram.

Although one can find these Kabbalistic traits throughout most of his narratives, it is only natural that they are particularly stressed in stories with some degree of mystic coloring. "The Zahir," "The Aleph," and "The God's Script" are in the same line with "The Approach to Al-Mu'tasim." In three of them, Borges intends, as it were, to show that "there is no fact, however insignificant, that does not involve universal history and the infinite concatenation of cause and effect . . . the visible world is implicit in every phenomenon" (*L,* 163). To achieve this, Borges coins three symbols and presents them as depositories of a microcosmic totality that as such is no different from the Godhead that holds in Himself all that is, was, and will be. The three symbols have deep roots in three different religions. At the outset of the first story, the Zahir is presented as "an ordinary coin" whose worth is twenty centavos. By the middle, Borges explains, "Zahir in Arabic means 'notorious,' 'visible'; in this sense it is one of the ninety-nine names of God." The information comes from the *Koran,* where (Surah, LV, 3) it is written that Zahir – the evident, the manifest – "is one of the ninety-nine attributes of God; He is the First and the Last, the Visible and the Occult." The coin is no longer a fortuitous object and becomes a form of mystic illumination. At the end of the tale, the narrator concludes: "In order to lose themselves in God, the Sufis recite their own names, or the ninety-nine divine names, until they become meaningless. I long to travel that path. Perhaps I shall conclude by wearing away the Zahir simply through thinking of it again and again. Perhaps behind the coin I shall find God."

What in "The Zahir" is presented only as a possibility, actually takes place in "The God's Script": "There occurred the union with the divinity, with the universe (I do not know whether these two words differ in meaning)." A magician, secluded in the darkness of a prison (it goes without saying that for the mystic the body is a dark prison that he strives to transcend), searches for the magical sentence that the god wrote on the first day of Creation "with the power to ward off" the devastation and ruin bound to happen at the end of time. In the prison, he devotes himself to the task of deciphering that secret sentence. Here it should be recalled that for the Kabbalists the Creation is but the result of multiple combinations of the twenty-two letters of the Hebrew alphabet. In the *Sefer Yetsirah (Book of Creation),* we read: "Twenty-two letter-elements: He outlined them, hewed them out, weighed them, combined them, and exchanged them, and through them created the soul of all creation and everything else that was ever created" (II, 2). The combination of the letters from which the Creation sprang was put into the Torah (the Pentateuch) but, explains a Midrash on Job 28:13, "No one knows its right order, for the sections of the Torah are not given in the right arrangement. If they were, everyone who reads in it might create a world, raise the dead, and perform miracles. Therefore the order of the Torah was hidden and is known to God alone."[22] The tradition of a magical and divine script that Borges recreates in his tale is also a Christian motif: in the Gospel it is said that Christ is the word that will save men from the horrors of the end of all times.

The revelation of the god's script comes finally in a vision of "an exceedingly high Wheel, which was not before my eyes, nor behind me, nor to the sides, but every place at one time" (*L*, 172). Here, Borges resorts to a symbol from Hinduism, the *Bhavacakra* (Wheel of Life), which represents the different spheres of existence where the infinite concatenation of causes and effects operates. References to the Wheel and its explicit significance are found in two fundamental texts of Hinduism. In the *Bhagavad-Gita* we read, "Thus was the Wheel (*cakram*) set in motion, and that man lives indeed in vain who in a sinful life of pleasures helps not in its revolutions" (III:16). In *Svetasvatara* Upanishad, the notion of the Wheel (of Brahman, of Creation, of Life, as it is often translated) is further developed:

> We understand him as a wheel with one fell, with a triple tyre, sixteen ends, fifty spokes, twenty counter-spokes, and six sets of eight (I:4). . . . This is the great wheel (*cakram*) of Brahman, giving life and livelihood to all, subsists in all: in it the swan of the soul is hither and thither tossed (I:6).

The vision of the Wheel, as seen by Tzinacán, is introduced in Borges' story with the following words: "That Wheel was made of water, but also of fire, and it was (although the edge could be seen) infinite. Interlinked, all things that are, were and shall be, formed it, and I was one of the fibers of that total fabric. . . . There lay the causes and the effects and it sufficed me to see that Wheel in order to understand it all, without end" (*L*, 172). This description seems to be an echo or paraphrase of Chapter XI of the *Bhagavad Gita*, a book that Borges familiarly quotes in his essay "Note on Walt Whitman." There he evinces an acquaintance with the *Gita* that goes beyond the casual reading of the book. Even the image of "the infinite fibers of a total fabric" is of Vedantic lineage: "one rope of innumerable strands" says *Svetasvatara* Upanishad, referring to Hindu Wheel.

The *Gita* is the major devotional book of Hinduism. It is an episode of India's great epic, the *Mahābhārata*. Its main story is the war between two branches of the Kaurava family. The *Gita* consists of a long dialogue between Arjuna and Krishna, a local prince who volunteered to act as Arjuna's charioteer; but Krishna was not merely a prince – he was God incarnate, the great God Vishnu. Arjuna sees many of his kinsmen and friends in the ranks of the opposing army and refuses to fight, declaring that he would rather die than kill those he loves. To convince him that he must fight, Krishna is not content merely to use arguments already familiar to him, his caste-duty as a warrior, for instance. He sees fit rather to reveal to him the structure of the universe as it really is, and in which Arjuna is just a pawn moved by the hand of an all-powerful God whose will no man or god can resist or thwart. "The ostensible purpose of the *Gita* is to persuade Arjuna to fight; but the bulk of the poem is not concerned with the respective merits of war and peace, but with the deepest things of man and God."[23]

Chapter XI constitutes the climax of the *Gita*. In it, Krishna reveals Himself in all His terrifying majesty. Arjuna, not content with the account of Krishna's powers of which he had heard, asks to see Him. Krishna grants his request and gives him "a celestial eye" with which he may behold his transfiguration. The rest of the chapter is an account of the tremendous vision: we see the universe in all its variety as Krishna's body, all its multiplicity converging onto One. Arjuna then describes what he sees: the entire world is rushing headlong into Krishna's mouths. It is at this point that Tzinacan's account of his vision in "The God's Script" bears striking similarities to Arjuna's in the *Gita*. In both cases a universal totality is presented within the unlimited limits of a microcosmic image. Borges' text reads:

> I saw the universe and I saw the intimate designs of the universe. I saw the origins narrated in the Book of the Common. I saw the mountains that rose out of the water, I saw the first men of wood, the cisterns that turned against the men, the dogs that ravaged their faces. I saw the faceless god concealed behind the other gods. I saw infinite processes that formed one single felicity and, understanding all, I was able also to understand the script of the tiger. (*L*, 172–173)

In both Borges' story and the *Gita,* the godhead and the universe are referred to as synonyms. We have seen earlier that Tzinacan fails to distinguish between the divinity and the universe: "I do not know if these words are different," he says. Krishna, before giving Arjuna the "celestial eye," tells him, "See now the whole universe with all things that move and move not, and whatever thy soul may yearn to see. See it all as One in me" (XI:7). As Tzinacan's vision is not the result of mystical meditations and ecstasy but a kind of miraculous apparition, so the union (or *yoga* as it is often called in the *Gita*) with the One is not mystically reached by Arjuna – it is rather granted to him as a token of Krishna's omnipotence.

Arjuna's vision is also described in terms similar to those that introduced Tzinacan's vision. Borges presents the Wheel as "made of water but also of fire." And in verse 28 Arjuna describes his vision, "As roaring torrents of *water* rush forward into the ocean, so do these heroes of our mortal world rush into thy *flaming* mouths" (*ibid.*, 28). For the *Gita* the flames of Arjuna's mouths burning the world up are a representation of Time, which at the end of a worldaeon will devour all the worlds. We know that for Borges, too, Time is a consuming fire and a sweeping river, but – as he adds – "I am the fire . . . , I am the river" (*OI*, 197). Likewise, in verse 32, Krishna reveals Himself as Time, "I am all-powerful Time which destroys all things." The same imagery, though, conveys different meanings: in the *Gita*, it underlines Krishna's condition as absolute master of all; in Borges' text, it suggests that man is at the same time the master and the victim of his fate.

Yet the closest parallel between the two texts occurs in the description of the theophany itself. Neither the *Gita* nor Borges is willing to substitute the fullness of the vision for an emblem or symbol as the mystic does in a similar situation. Borges names some of the most memorable symbols in the history of mysticism: a blazing light, a sword, a rose, a bird, a sphere, an angel, and adds, "Perhaps the gods would not be against my finding an equivalent image, but then this report would be contaminated with literature, with falsehood" (*PA*, 149) The challenge (for the writer) lies in confronting the reader with the same shocking vision experienced by the seer, in reconstructing with words an infinite diversity that transcends words. The alternative left to the poet is the creation of a literary illusion, of a linguistic reality that becomes a reality in itself. In the description of his vision, Arjuna uses – as Tzinacán – the same anaphoric subject-verb that underscores the overwhelming feeling of perplexity. It is also a way of reinforcing the illusion of a genuine translation: What I am describing is indeed what I see – there seems to be the understated intention:

> I see in thee all the gods, O my God; and the infinity of the
> beings of thy creation. I see god Brahma on his throne of lotus,

and all the seers and serpents of light. . . . I see the splendour of
an infinite beauty which illumines the whole universe. It is thee!
with thy crown and sceptre and circle. How difficult thou art to
see! But I see thee: as fire, as the sun, blinding, incomprehensi-
ble. . . . I see thee without beginning, middle, or end. . . . I see
thine eyes as the sun and the moon. And I see thy face as a sacred
fire that gives light and life to the whole universe. . . .

. . . .

The Rudras of destruction, the Vasus of fire, the Sadhyas of
prayers, the Adityas of the sun; the lesser gods Visve-Devas, the
two Asvins charioteers of heaven, the Maruts of winds and
storms, the Ushmapas spirits of ancestors; the celestial choirs of
Gandharvas, the Yakshas keepers of wealth, the demons of hell
and the Siddhas who on earth reached perfection: they all behold
thee with awe and wonder.
Gazing upon thy mighty form with its myriad mouths, eyes,
arms, thighs, feet, bellies, and sharp, gruesome tusks, the
worlds all shudder in affright, – how much more I! (*Gita,* XI)

The technique of chaotic enumeration is also evident in both accounts
of the theophany. The most obvious difference between the two,
though, is the secular character of Tzinacán's vision as compared to the
divine nature of Krishna's transfiguration. In the *Gita,* the universe is
described in terms of the tremendous sight of God; conversely, in
Borges' text, God is described in terms of the infinite multiplicity of the
universe, hence Borges' remark, ". . . the divinity, the universe, I do
not know whether these two words differ in meaning."

Borges repeats the experience in "The Aleph." The seer now is Borges
himself as the narrator of the story, and the mystic symbol is the Aleph,
as before the Zahir and the Wheel. This time, he chooses a letter, the first
letter of the Hebrew alphabet, and we ask why. Borges' postscript is
only half of the answer.[24] For the Kabbalah the divine language is the
very substance of reality: the Creation is just the result of the infinite
combinations of these twenty-two letters. For the Spanish Kabbalist of
the thirteenth century, Abraham Abulafia, "every letter represents a
whole world to the mystic who abandons himself to its contemplation."[25] It is the contemplation of a letter – the Aleph – that Borges
describes in the last part of his story, a letter which soon becomes a vision
of the whole world. A disciple of Abulafia describes a mystical experience in which he saw the letters of God's Name, permuted and combined, taking on the shape of great mountains, the form of a polished

mirror shining, as it were, from inside.[26] In the *Sefer Yetsirah* (Book of Creation) the letters *aleph, mem,* and *shin* are called mothers. They are not only the three mothers from which the other letters of the alphabet are formed, but they are also symbolical figures for the three primordial elements: the mute *mem* is the symbol of the water in which the mute fish live; the hissing *shin* (or *sin*) corresponds to the hissing fire; the airy *aleph* represents the air. The first emanation from God was the *ruach* (air) that produced fire, which, in its turn, formed the genesis of water (*Sefer Yetsirah,* III). So, the *aleph* constitutes for the Kabbalah the source of all articulate sound; it is regarded as the spiritual root of all other letters.

Borges describes the Aleph as "a small iridescent sphere, of almost intolerable brilliance. . . . Its diameter must have been about two or three centimeters, but Cosmic Space was in it, without diminution of size" (*AP,* 150). Here too the vision is presented in the best tradition of the Kabbalah. An old Midrash of the thirteenth century refers to God as having concentrated His *Shekhinah,* his divine presence, at the place of the Cherubim, as though His whole power were concentrated and contracted in a single point. The sixteenth-century Kabbalist of the Safed School, Isaac Luria, developed this idea in the doctrine of the *Tsimtsum* (concentration or contraction). Luria explains that "sparks of the *Shekhinah* are scattered in all worlds and there is no sphere of existence, including organic and inorganic nature, that is not full of holy sparks which are mixed up with the *kelipoth* (material world) and need to be separated and lifted up."[27] The Aleph is revealed in Borges' story in a cellar of a house that is about to be demolished so that a restaurant can be built there. Borges seems to be repeating Moses Cordovero's pantheistic formula: Where you stand, there stand all the worlds.

The description of the Aleph is a variation of the vision of the Wheel. Now the images are less apocalyptic and more personal because the narrator is not a magician of the pyramid of Qaholom, but Borges himself. In them, one can see, as through a kaleidoscope, the most essential fragments of the two Borgeses: the one of Androgué and Fray Bentos, and the other concerned with mirrors, tigers, and labyrinths.[28]

These few examples are indicative of the pregnant quality of Borges' art. The Kabbalistic texture of his narrative adds to their manifold complexity and to their richness of meaning. Borges challenges the reader to activate all his resources, to become himself a Kabbalist. He seems to be saying: If man, powerless to solve the labyrinths of the gods, is left with the choice of weaving and deciphering his own, let us – at least – devise them as close as possible to the divine model, let us write a secular text in the manner that the holy one was fashioned. A second understated motivation comes to our mind: If "universal history is the history of the diverse intonation of a few metaphors" and "true metaphors have always existed," the most a writer can do is to reinterpret them, to find new intonations of those few ones that have always existed. Borges' unhesitant use of old myths, motifs, *topoi,* and even metaphors in the literal sense, is perhaps a form of suggesting that the task of literature lies not in the hunt after the new, in being original (as conventionally understood) but rather in finding new forms of perceiving the old, in being creative with respect to the already created literature. What renders the old, new, the unoriginal, original is, thus, the ability to read the old texts afresh. Like the Kabbalah, which has generated a whole literature out of the Scripture, Borges implies – in praxis – that to write new literature is to read the old one anew. He has said it poignantly: "If I were able to read any contemporary page – this one, for example – as it would be read in the year 2000, I would know what literature would be like in the year 2000" (*OI,* 173).

NOTES

1 A comprehensive reference to those techniques can be found in Gershom Scholem's *Major Trends in Jewish Mysticism* (New York: Schocken, 1946), p. 100. For more detailed information, see the article "Gematria" by S. A. Horodezky in *Encyclopaedia Judaica,* 170–179, and the same entry by Caspar Levias in *The Jewish Encyclopedia,* 589–592.

2 Gershom Scholem, *Major Trends, loc. cit.*

3 Quoted by Gershom Scholem in *On the Kabbalah and Its Symbolism* (New York: Schocken, 1965), p. 12.

4 *Ibid.,* p. 13.

5 *Ibid.,* p. 39.

6 *Ibid.,* p. 40.

7 *Ibid.,* p. 44.

8 See Caspar Levias' article on "Gematria."

9 Ronald Christ, "J. L. Borges: An Interview," *The Paris Review,* XL (Winter–Spring 1967), 161.

10 J. L. Borges, "Foreword" to Ana María Barrenechea's *Borges the Labyrinth Maker* (New York University Press, 1965), p. vii.

11 Gershom Scholem, *On the Kabbalah,* p. 87.

12 Adolfo Bioy Casares, "Prologo" to *Antología de la literatura fantástica* (Buenos Aires, 1965), p. 12.

13 I am using a remark made by James E. Irby in his "Introduction" to *Labyrinths: Selected Stories and other Writings* (New York: New Directions, 1962), p. xxi. Another example of this kind of elusive allusion is the verb *to revive* in the story "The Other Death." The intricate question of the two deaths of Pedro Demián with their puzzling incoherences is already solved in the

second sentence of the tale. The two contradictory deaths occur at the same time, but while the first happens in actuality, the second takes place only in Damián's delirium, when in his dying bed he *revived* the battle of 1904. In that imaginary battle he died as a brave man. The word is a definite clue to the whole story, since *revived* means here that he recalled the battle and that he also lived the battle anew, as is implied in the etymological sense of the word *revivere*, to live again.

14 For further reference, see S. Vernon McCasland, Grace E. Cairns, and David C. Yu, *Religions of the World* (New York: Random House, 1969), chapter on "Zoroastrianism," pp. 127–149.

15 Even the apparently insignificant detail of a thief robbing the gold teeth of the cadavers left in the tower is far from being a fortuitous contingency. The Parsees are one of the best educated and prosperous communities of India. The huge Tata industrial empire bears the name of one of India's most famous Parsi families. So, the robber knew exactly what he was doing in the *dakhma*.

16 R. C. Zaehner, *Hindu and Muslim Mysticism* (London: University of London, 1960), p. 52, especially the chapter "God and Brahman."

17 Rudolf Otto, *Mysticism East and West: A Comparative Analysis of the Nature of Mysticism* (New York: Collier Books, 1962), p. 97. See the chapter "Atman and Soul."

18 R. C. Zaehner, pp. 86–109.

19 *Ibid.,* p. 40.

20 Quoted by Martin Buber in *The Origin and Meaning of Hasidim* (New York: Horizon Press, 1960), p. 222. See the chapter "The Place of Hasidism in the History of Religion."

21 *Ibid.,* pp. 221–222.

22 Gershom Scholem, *On the Kabbalah,* p. 167.

23 R. C. Zaehner, *The Bhagavad-Gita,* with a commentary based on the original sources (Oxford: Oxford University Press, 1969), p. 6.

24 There, he says: "As is well known, the Aleph is the first letter of the Hebrew alphabet. Its use for the strange sphere in my story may not be accidental. For the Kabbalah, that letter stands for the *En-sof,* the pure and boundless godhead; it is also said that it takes the shape of a man pointing to both heaven and earth, in order to show that the lower world is the map and mirror of the higher; for Cantor's *Mengenlehre,* it is the symbol of transfinite numbers, of which any part is as great as the whole." [*The Aleph and Other Stories* (New York: Dutton, 1970), p. 29]

25 Quoted by G. Scholem in *Major Trends,* p. 134.

26 *Ibid.,* pp. 151–155.

27 *Ibid.,* p. 280.

28 About the autobiographical character of many of his stories, Borges has said, "I have felt my stories so deeply that I have told them, well, using strange symbols so that people might not find out that they were all more or less autobiographical. The stories were about myself, my personal experiences"

(R. Christ, p. 155). In "The Aleph," the passage devoted to the National Prize for Literature, for which Borges-narrator's book *The Cards of the Cardsharp* did not get a single vote is, as everybody knows, an oblique reference to the Municipal Prize for Literature, which was not awarded to Borges in 1941, the year he published *The Garden of Forking Paths.*

4 Appendix to Part I: "The Kabbalah," by Jorge Luis Borges

I begin by confessing my ignorance of the Hebrew language and my perplexity over the various books I have read and consulted on the Kabbalah. I have perused Erich Bischoff's two-volume set suggested to me by the Spanish painter and mystic Xul Solar – a troublesome task I would not recommend to anybody. I also read Scholem's work *Major Trends in Jewish Mysticism,* and a study by an English writer Stehelin, who, according to Scholem, managed to intuit the doctrine's core. I then went through a thick volume, entitled *La kaballe* (1947), written by a Frenchman Henri Sérouya, and articles on the subject in several encyclopedias. In addition, I have examined translations of the *Sefer Yetsirah* (Book of Creation) and the *Zohar* (Book of Splendor). From these readings, I came to suspect that the classical texts of the Kabbalah did not intend to make statements or give arguments but rather to suggest and inspire. They chose myths or metaphors over reasoning. Perhaps, they felt like Irenaeus who said that to put a book in the hands of an ignoramus is like putting a sword in the hands of a child. Such a concept coincides with the Buddhist image of the fist that lets drop only a few of the innumerable seeds it holds. The *Zohar,* for example, was not written to expound a doctrine but rather to intimate one. There is also a book by Joshua Trachtenberg, *Jewish Magic and Superstition,* that abounds in references to the Kabbalah. In 1969, during my stay in Israel, Scholem gave me a copy of his *On the Kabbalah and Its Symbolism* which I am still reading. The word symbolism seems important to me. It refers, as I pointed out, to a deliberate effort not to present truths in abstract terms but rather to hint at them by means of symbols and metaphors. The ancient texts of the Kabbalah sought to engage the reader's cooperation and were addressed to a reader who did not take them literally but instead tried to discover by himself their hidden doctrine. This makes the study of the Kabbalah a complex undertaking.

In the language of the mystics, as in any other language, words presupposed a shared experience. If I use the word *red,* for instance, I have to assume that you know that color. Other words, on the other hand, refer to intimate experiences that can only be suggested through metaphors. Saint John of the Cross's poems and other poems of a mystic nature have to resort to erotic images to signify the divine. The same happens with symbols such as the wine and the rose of the Sufis.

To speak on the Kabbalah presupposes the understanding of two facts. The first, which has drawn the attention of many scholars, is the method employed by the Kabbalists. At first glance that method may seem senseless. I believe, however, that it is possible to justify it by adopting a rigorous approach. Let us imagine a text, any text, the columns of a newspaper for example. Here the purpose is to communicate true or false facts in an intelligible way. Now let us take a poetic text. In this case there are other intervening factors: the number of syllables, stresses or rhyme have been determined by the writer. Mallarmé said that only verse exists since prose results from sheer careless writing; the moment we begin to write paying attention to the rhythm of a paragraph, we are versifying, regardless of whether we are writing prose or verse. When Flaubert wrote his prose, for instance, he was versifying since he paid careful attention to sound. The name of Robert Louis Stevenson also comes to mind. For him, the art of verse consisted in anticipating an expectation and then satisfying it. If we start reading a sonnet we can already foresee the sonnet's music. The art of prose is more complex. It consists in building an expectation and then thwarting it, but in a pleasant and unexpected way. This view would explain why in all literatures verse appeared earlier than prose. Once we have written or composed one verse, since the composition of a verse can precede its writing, we possess a unit. This unit could be found through rhyme, through stress, through alliteration, through parallelism, as in the Bible, or through whatever other device that provides a pattern to be repeated. Prose, on the other hand, precludes the repetition of its units. It requires units which are not totally dissimilar and, at the same time, fit in with one another. This leads us to the conclusion that every human text possesses an element of chance, something that has not been foreseen. In the case of a poet or a rigorous prose writer much has been foreseen, but there are still elements left to chance. Let us now imagine an infinite intelligence that condescends to literature: such would be the case of the Holy Scripture. Those who wrote the Old or the New Testament were amanuenses of the Spirit who premeditated everything. Now we come to the question of chance. If an infinite intelligence condescends to literature, if an infinite intelligence dictates a text, we can safely assume that in this text nothing has been left to chance, everything has a meaning: the letters, their number, the fact that the text begins with the letter *a* or the letter *b*. And so, each Biblical verse contains an infinite number of purposes. This reminds me of the Irish mystic Scotus Erigena, who said that all verses in the Bible were capable of an infinite number of interpretations and compared them to the iridescent plumage of a peacock. There were also rabbis who believed that each Biblical verse had been written for each one of its readers. It was assumed that God's intelligence is infinite. It encompasses past, present and future, the entire bibliography of each of us, and the precise moment in which we read the Bible. Each verse has been premeditated for each of an almost infinite number of readers.

Dante thought that in the Bible each line could be subject to four possible interpretations. In *L'epistola a Cangrande della Scala,* he said that the *Divine Comedy* could also be read in four different ways. It would be naive to suppose that Dante believed that Hell, Purgatory, and Heaven resemble, exactly, what he described. He wrote, as one of his contemporaries put it, to portray, in Hell, the culprit's life, in Purgatory, the repenter's life, and in Heaven, the life of the blessed. The examples he adduced – the lovers in Canto V, for instance – were presented as archetypes since he didn't dare to pass judgment on individuals. But let's go back to the Kabbalah.

The Kabbalah presupposes that the Bible, particularly the first five books, is a divine text. If this text is the product of a divine intelligence, it can tolerate nothing accidental, absolutely nothing, not even the number nor the shape of the letters. The Kabbalists lacked a historical perception and did not believe that language preceded writing. They stated explicitly that the existence of the letters preceded language. In the first verses of the Scriptures we can already witness the power of words: "And God said, 'Let there be light'; and there was light." It is assumed that the word *light* He uttered was not a fortuitous word, but one in which the essence of light was in some way ciphered. Thus the world was created by means of words. All this is far removed from what linguists tell us about words, but it helps us understand the Kabbalists' mind. They studied each single verse, its initial letter, its number of letters, the fact that some numbers were duplicated, and so forth. From these inquiries into the Holy text, they inferred their doctrine. Everything has been premeditated, and therefore everything can and must be studied. They thus conceived various methods for reading the Biblical text. They considered, for example, the ordering of the letters and the possibility of reading them – in addition to their normal way from right to left – from left to right, what the Greeks called *boustrophedon*. They also watched what happens when one or more letters were skipped and calculated the numerical value of the Hebrew words, calling this technique *Gematria*, and so on and so forth. These are some of the foundations of the Kabbalistic method, a method that we don't have to accept but which is not senseless if we understand the Kabbalists' premises. Let's now touch on the subject of their doctrine.

The word Kabbalah means, if the texts I have read don't mislead me, something like "received" or "the received tradition," and this etymology sends us to a fact far distant from us. Today, we enjoy knowing that an idea is new. The notion of novelty is not an unpleasant one, but during the Middle Ages, let us say during the eleventh or twelfth century, and even during the Renaissance, the idea of novelty was a displeasing one. It was thought of as something arbitrary because essential things were already discovered. The Kabbalists arrived at a doctrine which was very different from the Jewish orthodoxy, but they did not want to appear as innovators because such a condition would have discredited them. I am now trying to find an example that may seem unrelated to my subject – a literary example from seventeenth-century Spain – but which is not really. I think that in one of his *Soledades*, Góngora speaks of a shipwreck victim who has been "vomited by the waves." This image was reproved by the critics. Góngora's apologists, however, argued that the image shouldn't shock anybody since in the *Aeneid* there was a similar passage. The defending argument then would today be construed as an accusation of plagiarism. In the seventeenth century, any line from Virgil was indisputable, and condemning him would have amounted to blasphemy. "The vomited shipwreck victim" was, consequently, invulnerable.

The concept of authority prevailed then, but today that is no longer the case. The notion of a tradition, orally transmitted from Paradise on, was promulgated by the first Kabbalists in the Middle Ages. It was understood that Adam was the first Kabbalist and that he passed his wisdom on to his children, and they to their children, and so on until present times. Furthermore, since Adam had learned those mysteries in Paradise, and since he was filled with divine light, the doctrine had to be exact. According to Scholem, the Kabbalah was born in Spain with the *Zohar*, but if Moses de León, its author, had said that he wrote it, nobody would have paid any attention to him. He was forced to attribute the book to a second-century Palestinian rabbi and to talk about ancient manuscripts which he refused to produce.

With time, the teachings of the Kabbalah were spread over the world and found new interpretations. Such interpretations have been reduced to a few basic ideas in which Neo-Platonic and Gnostic influences are apparent. It is reasonable to think that Gnostics and Neo-Platonists were not ignored by the first Kabbalists who opted, naturally, for seeking and finding Jewish sources in the Bible and reading it in that peculiar way I have mentioned: counting the letters, attributing to each one a numerical value, and a virtue, and turning them into various symbols. I have found a similar tendency among contemporary German writers. In Spengler's *The Decline of the West,* for example, I have been surprised by the number of references to Goethe. The author was obviously pleasing a German taste that delights in the belief that everything has already been thought over by Goethe. A quotation from Goethe is tantamount to a quotation from the Holy Ghost. Perhaps the same happens with other classics in other nations. Similarly, the Kabbalists thought that their doctrines of Neoplatonic or Gnostic origins were already in the Scripture. I have discussed this question with Scholem who, perhaps through sheer courtesy, approved this conjecture that the doctrine preceded the method. Yet, once the doctrine was accepted, it either led to mystical experiences or, conversely, these mystical experiences led to the formulation of the doctrine. The method was adopted so that the doctrine would remain within the confines of Jewish tradition. Let us now examine the doctrine.

Its core is the *En-Sof,* a name used for the Godhead. I do not know whether there is any relationship between this word and the Greek name for wisdom (*sophos*). This Godhead challenges definition, very much like the Buddhist Nirvana. We begin, therefore, with an indeterminable divinity to whom we cannot ascribe any attribute, about whom we cannot even say "It" is wise, because to be wise is to know something, and to know implies a distinction between what is known and the knower, and this distinction ends up cancelling the infinite nature of the latter. If that were the case, this Godhead would be imperfect because it would not be infinite; we would have, on the one hand, the divinity, and, on the other, that divinity's knowledge, one subject and one object. Neither is it legitimate to say that this divinity wants something, since if it wants something it is because it lacks something. Besides, all these verbs – *to create, to love, to hate, to think,* and even *to be* – become too personal for a godhead since they are, ultimately, all too human. There is from the beginning – although to speak of *beginning* implies already a temporal limitation – from eternity, a godhead, the *En-Sof.* This divinity rejects any affirmation; we cannot say that the *En-Sof is* or *was* or *will be,* because this will amount to limiting him. The condition of *being* corresponds to our human world, and the divine nature ought to be different. Neither can we speak of his goodness or his wisdom, because this would be the same as speaking of his wickedness or his ignorance, since they are all human attributes. The *En-Sof* rejects any qualifier, even a metaphoric one. I think that it is also forbidden to say that *he is* or *he is not,* because it would be too precise. The Godhead is impervious to words and cannot create anything, because the act of creation reduces him to a human intelligence that first plans something and then carries it out. The Kabbalists and the Gnostics resorted to a word which did not qualify the Godhead too far (albeit all words do) and that word is *emanation*. They reasoned that from the unreachable divinity, ten *Sefiroth,* ten intelligences, ten angels emanated. Such beings are emanations of the *En-Sof,* but their essence is not different. There are Kabbalistic texts in which this is clearly explained. It is like a light coming from a lamp, and yet that light is not different from the lamp. It is as if those ten emanations – the first being the "Crown" and the last the "Kingdom" – were inherent in the *En-Sof.* Here we can recall medieval scholasticism which maintained that the soul is composed of memory, reason and will, yet the three are faculties of the soul and not separate entities. The same could be said of the *Sefiroth* since they are facets of an indivisible being. Worlds emanate from those emanations, and those worlds last as long as the sparks thrown off from a furnace do.

And so we come to the sixth day of Creation – the day man was created. That man is the archetypal being, *Adam Kadmon* or the primordial man, and he is composed of the ten *Sefiroth.* The attributes of rigor are on the right side, the attributes of mercy, on the left side, the attributes of justice, in the middle, and so on, comprising an entire body, including masculine and feminine features. That primordial Man is a sort of microcosm, since everything that exists in the world has been condensed in him. This doctrine has been echoed throughout time. During the Middle Ages, for example, it was believed by Christians that animals had been created, like the creatures from the fables, with a moral purpose: ants and bees were created to teach us to work, eagles to teach us to elevate our thoughts like their flight, lions to serve as a paragon of majesty, and so on.

In the nineteenth century, a writer like De Quincey stated flatly that we must not seek any scientific learning in the Bible since its purpose is to stimulate man's faculties – not to teach him anything. Thus, when God spoke of the six days of Creation, He was metaphorically referring to six periods of indefinite time. Concerning the information given in the Bible about the Creation, that information was bound to be, according to De Quincey, by necessity, false, since otherwise God would be revealing to us something we must find out by ourselves. The universe should, consequently, be understood as a scientific stimulus to man. A French writer, Leon Bloy, whose work is so related to the Kabbalah, came to doubt the existence of the celestial spheres. He said that the heaven and stars we see are only reflections of our soul. He believed in the soul, not in the truths of astronomy or natural history. He was, in a certain way, close to the Kabbalists. We, all the people who inhabit this planet, are only reflections of the archetypal or primordial man. Scholem quotes a Kabbalist who maintained that to speak of God's right arm as metaphorical language is false. The only real arm, the only real heart, he concludes, are God's arm and God's heart, ours are metaphorical. The true world is that of the archetypes which, naturally, leads us to Plato.

That is, in conclusion, a universe created by emanations, and not by the deliberate act of a divinity. This curious doctrine brings us to Milton. Denis Saurat found a Kabbalistic idea that Milton studied and then placed in the center of his *Paradise Lost:* the notion of a God creating a world not by direct action but by his absence. To understand this notion we need to think of dreams. While we are awake, we are more or less aware of ourselves, of our acts and thoughts. In our sleep, however, our thinking takes a different form, a dramatic form, and we forget about ourselves, we forget that the characters and figures in our dreams are our emanations, and those emanations have their own, independent life. Doctor Johnson told Boswell about one of his dreams. He told him that in the dream somebody asked him something, and he was left perplexed by the question and couldn't answer it. Then the stranger gave him a correct answer, an answer he thought was correct. Only upon awakening, did he understand that the stranger was himself, or his projection, and that the answer was his own answer. Schopenhauer says that possibly the same happens to us in reality: we are but projections of a cosmic Will. This would lead us to solipsism, to the idea of one single being who is each of us and who dreams the entire universe and its history.

I had, not long ago, a dream that later I used in a story. I met a man dressed in black who had one of his hands hidden. That hand troubled me. I recognized the man and told him: "You are so and so." And he answered me: "Yes, but I have changed a lot." While he was talking, I saw him changing, and I felt that he had changed in a terrible way. Then he showed me his hand: it was a claw. I had invented the dream, or the dream had emanated from me, and the dreadful surprise that the hand was a claw, an inhuman claw, a crow's or vulture's claw, was prepared by me and yet I was frightened.

The God of the Kabbalists created the world by his absence. When we sleep, we withdraw from our conscious state to enter into the lives and dramas of the characters of our dreams; in reality, we are alone sleeping in the darkness of a bedroom. Similarly, God withdraws from the world and the world begins to live by itself; that is the part of the world we know and in which we dwell, that part constitutes the world of history, that part is us in this very moment. God has abandoned us, but we continue living as creatures of his dream.

There is another Kabbalistic doctrine common to the Pythagoreans – reincarnation. Many Kabbalists believed in it, and they attached to it a moral end. I read, for instance, in one anthology of Kabbalistic texts, that a murderer's soul becomes water, water condemned to run just as the blood of the man he had killed ran. The soul of an egoist becomes a stone, a blind, deaf stone, reduced to its own silence and its own solitude. All this would sound totally alien to the first Hebrews. There is another singular belief that is owed, I think, to the Kabbalist from Jerusalem, Isaac Luria. It refers to the soul of a teacher or an elder which enters our soul and becomes part of it when we need its help. This soul helps us as long as we need it, and then withdraws. This dwelling of one soul in another has been compared, by means of a powerful metaphor, to a woman who holds in her womb the flesh and the spirit of her child.

I have only been able to sketch a few tenets of the Kabbalah. I am not even sure of having interpreted them correctly. The book I would like to recommend to you again and again is Gershom Scholem's *Major Trends in Jewish Mysticism.* This is the clearest work I have read on the subject. Everything is explained there, not only stated but reasoned through and justified. Scholem goes beyond the great myths and the cosmic metaphors. Of the many books I have read on the Kabbalah, this is the only one that is written in an intimate manner. The others impress me as having been written by outsiders; they overwhelm us with outlines, subdivisions and illustrations, but they aim not at explaining, only at dazzling. They tell us about the number of *Sefiroth,* they compare three *Sefiroth* with the three figures of the Trinity – the Father, Son and Holy Ghost – to tell us that they are one and three at the same time; they include diagrams showing the celestial man, and each *Sefirah* occupying a different place in that celestial organism, yet all this is declared but not explained. Scholem, on the other hand, has composed his book from within. Something similar was achieved by Martin Buber in his book on Hasidism, although I suspect that he was less interested in the Kabbalah than in the sect of the Hasidim. I have also read history books of Jewish philosophy where there is no reference whatever to the Kabbalah, as if it were a form of heterodoxy alien to Jewish thought. I do hope that you would eventually undertake the study of the Kabbalah, and that it won't take you long to discover the many mistakes I have surely made in the course of this talk.

Translated by J. A.

PART II
Fiction

5 Structure as meaning in "The South"

Quand j'ai écrit "Le Sud", je venais de lire Henry James et de découvrir qu'on peut raconter deux ou trois histoires en même temps. Ma nouvelle est donc ambiguë. On peut la lire au premier degré. Mais aussi considérer qu'il s'agit d'un rêve, celui d'un homme qui meurt à l'hôpital et aurait préféré mourir sur le pavé, l'arme à la main. Ou celui de Borges qui préférerait mourir comme son grandpère le général, à cheval, plutôt que dans son lit – ou encore que l'homme est tué par son rêve, cette idée du Sud, de la Pampa, qui l'avait conduit là.

– Borges, *L'Express,* May 1977

Is there a structuring principle underlying Borges' short fiction? How are his stories made, and to what degree is it possible to derive from them a narrative code? How do his narratives *signify?* In other words, how are the literary signs organized and what meanings or functions do they propose, beyond their explicit content? Borges' work has repeatedly and perhaps excessively been examined at the level of its content, as a denotative language no different from that of the press. If, as Hjelmslev says, literature is a semiotic system whose means of expression is another semiotic system – language – it must be concluded that in a literary text there is, first, a linguistic function, a vehicle common to language and to literature that explains that "all the words with which a Garcilaso sonnet is written, appear *verbatim* in any dictionary of the Spanish language," as Cortazar has remarked. But it must also be recognized that in the literary discourse the linguistic sign becomes a signifier with functions or signifieds absent in the system of signs of language. The literary sign absorbs the linguistic sign in order to convert it into a new signifier whose signified transcends the orbit of language. The *"fiction* of literary language seeks not to clear up the meaning of a word but to reconstruct the rules and norms of elaboration of that meaning."[1] The literary text "un-

65

folds in some way in order to add to its own explicit or literal significa-
tion, or denotation, a supplementary power of connotation that enriches
it with one or several secondary meanings."[2] Literature is "a domain of a
translinguistic or metalinguistic nature that comprises techniques of sig-
nification situated not next to language, but above or inside it."[3] Gerard
Genette explains this effect of oversignification in literature with an example from classical rhetoric:

> In the synecdoche *sail-ship* there is a signifier, *sail,* and there is
> an object (or concept) signified, *the ship:* that's the denotation.
> But since the word *sail* has substituted the noun *ship,* the rela-
> tionship (signification) that unifies the signifier with the signified
> constitutes a figure. This figure, in turn, designates clearly,
> within the rhetorical code, a poetic state of the discourse. The
> figure functions, then, as the signifier of a new signified – poetry
> – over a second semantic plane, that of the rhetorical connota-
> tion. The inherent quality of connotation is, in fact, its capacity
> to establish itself above (or underneath) the first signification,
> but in an unconnected fashion, using the first meaning as a
> means of designating a second concept.[4]

This second concept, inserted in the first, would then be the object of
literary studies or at least of one type of study, since a text becomes
literature when it produces poetic functions which organize themselves
in a coherent system of signs, when it transforms natural language into a
second language, when it abandons the denotation of the linguistic code
and gives way to connotation to create with it its own expressive code.
This transformation constitutes an operation by means of which the
writer interrogates the world. The function of the critic would then be to
examine this operation, since if for a writer literature is "a first language
or language-object, criticism is a discourse about a discourse, a second
language or metalanguage."[5]

Being a reader as well as a critic of his own work, Borges was the first
to suggest that his story "The South" "could be read as a direct narration
of fictional facts and also as something else" (*F,* 105). Asked about this
second way, he answered:

> Everything that happens after Dahlmann leaves the hospital
> could be interpreted as his own hallucination when he is about to
> die of septicemia, as a fantastic vision of how he would have
> chosen to die. Hence the slight correspondences between the
> two halves of the story; the volume of *One Thousand and One
> Nights,* that appears in both parts; the horse-carriage that first

takes him to the hospital and then to the railroad station; the resemblance between the tavern's owner and a hospital worker; the touch Dahlmann feels on his forehead when wounded and the touch of the bread-crumb thrown by the "compadrito" to provoke him.[6]

This interpretation suggested by Borges himself escapes the denotative or literal level. At that level, Borges wrote a linear story in which Dahlmann recovers in the hospital and travels to his ranch to convalesce. It is in the make-up of the story that a second meaning is implied. The text has been organized in such a way that the first signifier is forced to fold over onto itself and generate a second signifier capable of new poetic functions. This organization consists of an introduction and two parts. In the first part, the protagonist is introduced and the conflict is presented: in the clash between his two lines of descent, we are told, Juan Dahlmann chose the line of his romantic ancestor, the one with a romantic death. It should be noticed that the Argentina of the 1930s is not the romantic country of Francisco Flores, and that Juan Dahlmann, librarian, reader of *Martín Fierro* and of the *One Thousand and One Nights,* leads a life closer to that of his Germanic ancestor than to that of his *criollo* grandfather. His circumstances are Argentine, but his name is the same as that of the evangelical minister, and so is his faith in culture. This element of the conflict appears in the introduction. Juan Dahlmann is a symbol of his country's fate: the conflict between his two lineages is an expression of Sarmiento's formula "civilization and barbarism." Dahlmann chooses the first of these alternatives, but the country will force him to face the second. The first link of the story is thus a compendium of the story as a whole.

The autobiographical character of this story is obvious. Juan Dahlmann is a mask of Borges, of a Borges who chooses, like his ancestor Laprida, books, but who knows that the deep reality of his other lineage is pierced by violence – a violence he abhors and whose futility he has repeatedly underlined, but which he recognizes as "an apocryphal past, at the same time stoic and orgiastic, in which any Argentine has defied and fought to finally fall silently in an obscure knife-fight."[7] There is a second factor of a psychological nature. Grandchild and great-grandchild of colonels, offspring of heroes of the wars of independence, Borges has expressed in several poems his admiration for those military ancestors who shaped Argentine history. Secluded in a humble library, Borges has given in, more than once, to a nostalgic fascination for that past he views as epic. In his *Autobiographical Essay* he has said: "On both sides of my family I have military forebears; this may count for my yearning after that epic destiny which my gods denied me, no doubt wisely."[8] Borges returns to that epic universe of his ancestors seeking neither a futile violence that he condemns nor an empty bravery that he insistently calls "useless," but a virtue that our time, predominantly individualistic, has forgotten. It is no accident that Bernard Shaw was one of his favorite writers. In him, Borges finds an alternative of liberation to the anxiety of modern man, and through Shaw he defines the meaning of that virtue he admires in his ancestors:

> Bernard Shaw is an author to whom I keep returning. . . . He has epic significance, and is the only writer of our time who has imagined and presented heroes to his readers. On the whole, modern writers tend to reveal men's weaknesses, and seem to delight in their unhappiness; in Shaw's case, however, we have characters like Major Barbara or Caesar, who are heroic and whom one can admire. Contemporary literature since Dostoievski – and even earlier, since Byron – seems to delight in man's guilt and weaknesses. In Shaw's work the greatest human virtues are extolled. For example, that a man can forget his own fate, that a man may not value his own happiness, that he may say like our Almafuerte: "I am not interested in my own life," because he is interested in something beyond personal circumstances.[9]

In his heroic forefathers, Borges seeks to rescue that virtue: an epic sense of life, values that transcend the narrow limits of our individual selves and propose a stoic dimension that liberates life from its existential bounds. To the values of the novel – centered in the destiny of the self – Borges opposes the axiology of the epic: acts of courage that prove that people are capable of transcending their own egos in defense of humanistic ideals and elevated tasks. Violence is thus understood as a cathartic agent. The destruction of a life is not a gratuitous act, nor a macho's boastful display of guts. A hero – reasons Borges – defends a cause (a virtue, a destiny, a duty) whose value far exceeds that of his own life. In the duel between Juan Dahlmann and the boisterous *compadrito* who forces him to fight, Dahlmann succumbs as victim of a violence he has not chosen and of which he does not feel part, but in the final analysis the decision to fight is Dahlmann's. When Dahlmann bends over to pick up the knife thrown to him by "the old ecstatic gaucho in whom *he* saw a cipher of the South," he understands that he will be able to defend his injured dignity with the only language his provoker knows: the knife. The *compadrito* fights motivated by laws of honor which Borges has unequivocally condemned as a form of barbarism. Dahlmann's motivation is quite different. Dahlmann defends a moral value – his injured dignity – with his life. From this act one must conclude that for Dahlmann – for that Dahlmann who is dreaming his death in an innocuous hospital bed where he indeed is dying of "physical miseries" – dignity is dearer than the life that holds it. Viewed from this set of values, it is understandable that Dahlmann chose to pick up the knife that "would justify his killing." Between his death and the loss of his honor, Dahlmann chooses death.

But this choice is framed within a dream. When he is about to die of septicemia, prostrate in a hospital bed, Dahlmann confesses to himself that "if he had been able to choose, *then,* or to dream his death, this would have been the death he would have chosen or dreamt."[10] The adverb (*then*) is important on two accounts. First, because it points to the circumstances under which that violent death was chosen. Second, because it refers to a literary dream that restores an Argentine myth: "a lowly knife fight dreamed by Hernández in the 1860's."[11] Dahlmann's dream represents, in a way, the dream of all Argentines. It is just an avatar of that fight in which "a gaucho lifts a black off his feet with his knife, throws him down like a sack of bones, sees him agonize and die, crouches down to clean his blade, unties his horse, and mounts slowly so he will not be thought to be running away."[12] Hernández's dream – Borges adds – "returns infinitely." The whole of Argentine history is ciphered in that dream that time has turned into a "part of the memory of all." Before dying, Dahlmann returns to that dream he knows he is part of. He chooses the dream of his *criollo* lineage, but only when nearing death. Dahlmann's life, devoted to books, has been an effort to correct the violence of that lineage. But as an Argentine vulnerable to the "imperatives of courage and honor," Dahlmann is forced to return to that "dream" of one man which is part of the memory of all, he is compelled to go back to that myth that defines the essence of his violent condition.

Borges' story presents with deliberate ambiguity the futility of that dream, and at the same time its paradoxical inevitability. There is not a single and logical meaning, and yet Borges has articulated his story with impeccable logic. The laws of that logic go beyond syllogism. Its coherence stems from the text itself and from a very Borgesian worldview, but this world-view is contained as a whole in the narrative. The text, in its etymological sense of texture, tissue, structure, contains the answers to its seeming incongruities: How does one explain the fact that Dahlmann, who has devoted his life to books, would agree to a "useless" fight that amounts to his own destruction? Borges' answer is formulated through the organization of the narrative. By dividing the story into two halves – the accident and the trip to the South – and by suggesting that the second half, connected to the first by subtle symmetries, is a dream that the protagonist dreams before dying in the hospital, Borges faces the question of the credibility of the knife fight by turning it into a dream. By doing this, he gives the fight a precise meaning: this fight – Borges seems to imply – exists only as a dream, and that dream is no different from the one dreamed by Hernández in *Martín Fierro*. Because it is "part of the memory of all," we return to this dream infinitely as to a collective unconscious which intrinsically defines Argentines, as to a mirror that, more than reflecting a façade, gives back the image of *the other,* a violent face waiting to tear the surface with a knife. For the image of *the other* to appear, Borges takes his character to the South – the last stronghold of courage, the last sanctuary of that religion of gauchos and compadres – and to dispel all doubt about his condition of dream, or, what amounts to the same thing, of expression of an intimate collective unconscious, Borges structures the story like a mirror in which the second half is a symmetrical reflection of the first. This structure suggests that the second half is a dream and that in this dream, Dahlmann would fulfill the duties of courage. He will carry them out as any Argentine for whom Hernández's fight is the cipher of his own destiny would, and for whom the purpose of the tango is "to give Argentines the conviction of having been brave, of having complied with the requisites of courage and honor."[13]

In the poem "Junín," Borges, the poetic speaker, searches for *the other* in the battle of his forebears. Like Juan Dahlmann, he also seeks to rescue that mythical being which defines him in his most essential condition:

> I am myself but I am also *the other*
> The man who died, the man whose blood and name
> Are mine: a stranger here, yet with a fame
> He won keeping Indian spears at bay,
> I come back to this Junín I have never seen,
> To your Junín, grandfather Borges.[14]

The poem shows a greater degree of explicitness than the story. In this imaginary return to the "epic Junín," Borges recreates in more abstract terms the trip of Juan Dahlmann to the South. It could be argued that the historical battle is not a knife fight in a humble country tavern, and that while the first is an indisputable epic event, the knife fight is merely an expression of showy courage. But for Borges, there is a common denominator between the battle and the duel: in both acts there prevails a cult of courage that turns the duel into an epic act, and the battle into an expression of personal bravado. Speaking about the civil war that followed Argentina's war of independence, Borges has said of the *caudillos*:

"Fighting a war was not for them the coherent execution of a plan but a game of manliness."[15] And referring, in *Evaristo Carriego*, to the knife fight between Wenceslao and the *Santafesino*, he alludes to this duel as "the epic of Wenceslao," adding that the episode has "a clearly epic and even knightly character,"[16] which is not to say that the wars of independence and the duels of the knife fighters have for him the same value. If there is any doubt regarding Borges' aversion towards this type of vain violence, it will suffice to refer to his more recent short story "Rosendo Juarez" to dispel it. At the same time, this kind of aversion does not exclude his admiration for the violent side of a knife fight. Otherwise, his preference and pleasure for knife-fight stories could not be understood. Nor could it be understood that in order to explain the etymology of the word *virtue* he wrote: "*Virtus,* which in Latin means courage derives from *vir,* which means man."[17] Or that, in order to demonstrate that the tango and the milonga seek to express "the conviction that fighting can be a feast,"[18] he resorted in his book, *Evaristo Carriego,* to the major epic poems of European literature (the *Iliad,* the *Beowulf,* the *Chanson de Roland* and *Orlando*). If we add that courage, which could also be an epic trait found in a knife fight, is the virtue most worshipped by Argentines as an act or as a dream, Borges' evocation of Junín and Dahlmann's dream assume an unequivocal meaning.

As a linear story, "The South" leaves the impression of an arbitrary act and a gratuitous gesture. But if Borges had said in the text that Dahlmann's trip to the South *was a dream* of the patient who was dying in a hospital, the fight would have lost much of its effectiveness, and the text itself would not have had the tension and the precision that it has. "Since everything could happen in dreams – we would have reasoned – the fight impresses us as any other arbitrary act." Borges' solution lies in preserving the linear narrative at the level of the denotation and in correcting it at the level of connotation through the structure of his text. This double solution is a technical achievement, but it also represents the counterpart – at the level of the signifier – of the duality of meanings that, like a double-edged weapon, the trip to the South suggests. Through the linear reading of the story, Borges condemns the fight as an act of vanity – vanity in the *compadrito*'s provocation, vanity in Dahlmann's acceptance, vanity in a blind act that subscribes to and celebrates barbarism. From this point of view, Dahlmann does not choose his death: he fatalistically succumbs to the law of the knife. Through the reading suggested by the structure of the story, on the other hand, the fight reorganizes itself as a dream. Before dying in his hospital bed, Dahlmann dreams a death in consonance with that of his forebears. This dream is an encounter with *the other,* with the blood of his grandfather killed by the Indians of Catriel; it is an encounter with the epic sense of a fight in which one chooses to die to prove a virtue more important than life. Dahlmann's dream is also an encounter with his past, it is a last journey to that history that exhausts itself in "a lowly knife fight," a last effort to enter into that "dream of one man that is part of the memory of all," the fight narrated in *Martín Fierro*.

It could be argued that the two meanings are contradictory; that violence cannot be reproved and, at the same time, celebrated; that a knife fight cannot be an epic act and, at the same time, empty bravado. But, like most of Borges' work, "The South" plays with contradictory meanings that resolve themselves in ambiguous paradoxes. Like the tango and the milonga that are reminiscent of "a stoic and orgiastic past," the fight that Dahlmann dreams is an excess and a deprivation, a destruction and a form of fulfillment, a negation and an act of affirmation. Borges' answers are not causal: they assimilate, like an oxymoron, two terms that seemingly contradict and reject each other. In a way, "The South" is a story that holds two stories, and each of them suggests a contradictory version of the meaning of Dahlmann's fight. But in order to suggest a second meaning, it was necessary to interpolate in the story a second signifier incorporated into the first one. The narrative presents difficulties that the poem ignores. In "Junín," the first line says straightforwardly: "I am myself but I am also the other, the man who died." To convey a similar idea in the story, Borges constructs a mirror structure: the second half of the story reflects the image of *the other* that Juan Dahlmann seeks to be, and in order to preserve the verisimilitude of the story – a librarian suddenly turned into a knife fighter – that *other* surfaces, as if in a dream, from the agonies of a dying librarian.

Borges has warned that "the verbs *to live* and *to dream,* according to the Idealist doctrine, are strictly synonyms."[19] He has also said that "literature is a controlled dream."[20] Through literature, through literature's dream, Borges "returns to Junín where he had never been"; he is "a vague person and also the man who stopped the spears in the desert." Dahlmann also will rescue his *other* through a dream and, like Pedro Damian in "The Other Death," he will die two deaths. Most of Borges' stories offer this double level, a false bottom of sorts; the second of these levels, like a mirror, returns the image of the first, but inverted. Like Borges, who recognized himself as a divided personality in the short prose piece "Borges and I," Juan Dahlmann is that frail librarian fascinated by the marvels of books, and that violent *other* whose final fulfillment happens in a knife-fight dream.

In many ways, "The South" is the inverted version of a poem from *San Martin Copybook* (1929), entitled "Isidoro Acevedo." Borges' maternal grandfather, Acevedo was not a military man, but "he fought in the battles at Cepeda and Pavón." In the poem, Borges sets out "to rescue his last day," or, more accurately, "an essential dream" of the last day of his life: "For in the same way that other men write verse / my grand-father elaborated a dream." In this young Borges, the formula "literature = dreams" already appears as an equation of interchangeable terms. Here, as in Dahlmann's last dream in the poem, Borges will fulfill the epic destiny of his grandfather in an apocryphal dream. This fictitious dream of a heroic death, when Acevedo is actually dying of a pulmonary disease in his bedroom, will be, however, his true death, "the death that he [like Dahlmann] would have chosen or dreamed, if he had been able to choose or to dream his death." The story and the poem are motivated by the same effort: to force destiny to correct itself, to make it comply with the requisites of courage, to be part of that memory in which, con-sciously or unconsciously, all Argentines recognize themselves. This is the dream that Borges makes his grandfather dream.

> While a lung ailment ate away at him
> And hallucinatory fevers distorted the face of the day,
> He assembled the burning documents of his memory
> For the forging of his dream.
> . . . .
> His dream was of two armies
> Entering the shadow of battle;
> He enumerated the commands, the colors, the units.
> "Now the officers are reviewing their battle plans,"
> He said in a voice you could hear,
> And in order to see them he tried sitting up.
> . . . .
> He made a final levy,
> Rallying the thousands of faces that a man knows without
> Really knowing at the end of his years:
> Bearded faces now growing dim in daguerreotypes;
> Faces that lived and died next to his own at the battles
> Of Puente Alsina and Cepeda.
>
> In the visionary defense of his country that his faith
> Hungered for (and not that his fever imposed),
> He plundered his days
> And rounded up an army of Buenos Aires ghosts
> So as to get himself killed in the fighting.
>
> That was how, in a bedroom that looked onto the garden,
> He died out of devotion for his city.[21]

In this dream that Borges weaves, like a mask of his grandfather, death gives expression to an intimate will, to a strong necessity to exalt that epic side that Borges admires in Shaw's characters. Man's epic sense of life finds in death its ultimate challenge. Acevedo, killed by a pulmonary disease, and Dahlmann, killed by septicemia, refute that heroic side of life in which they believed. Such an innocuous death negates that stoic past of their heroic ancestors, an epic past to which Borges relentlessly returns and with which he identifies. It also negates the substance that makes up the gaucho or the *compadre* or any Argentine for whom courage is still the highest virtue. In order to correct those fortuitous deaths unworthy of his heroic sense of life, and in order to comply with the requisites of courage, Borges resorts to dreams or to their homologue, literature. Freud thought of dreams as the blurred fulfillment of desires and needs intimately repressed (or postponed), and Jung's contribution to the theory of dreams was his idea of a collective unconscious and its reverberations in archetypal dreams, in myths that express not the individual but the species. Borges' intent is to rescue that collective dream that is part of the memory of all. He compels Juan Dahlmann, Isidoro Acevedo, Pedro Damián and even Martín Fierro himself, in his story "The End," to dream it.

In "The South," as in "The Other Death," "The End," and in the poem "Isidoro Acevedo," there are two deaths, and those two deaths embody two different signifieds expressed also through two different signifiers. The first signifier finds its expression linearly; the second is coined through the structure, through those two symmetrical halves of the story that induce us to read the second part as a dream. The story leaves a perplexing aftertaste because the two signifieds proposed by those two signifiers are contradictory. On the one hand, courage is presented as a useless virtue that forces Dahlmann to a death no less useless; on the other, courage is presented as Dahlmann's last attempt to return to a stoic past. His death makes possible the fulfillment of a dream in which Dahlmann meets the epic past of his grandfather who died a romantic death.

These two opposite sides of courage are intertwined in the story as an oxymoron through which Borges expresses his two-fold and contradictory view of courage. For Borges as an individual and a book lover, courage is useless, a token of barbarism, a primitive state fitting a nation of shepherds and riders who do not understand urban civilization. For Borges as a member of a national group that sees in bravery the most precious of virtues, and as a descendant of heroes who wove a good stretch of the history of his country, courage is a yearning, an intimate epic necessity, a romantic death-wish that expresses itself in an apocryphal dream, a dream that is part of the memory of all. As a conscious reflection, as an act of lucidity, Borges rejects and condemns courage; voicing the dictates of a collective unconscious that glorifies bravery,

Borges sees courage as a myth he knows himself to be part of, as a myth that fulfills the dark depths of his blood. Borges' literary accomplishment in "The South" lies in having given expression to that ambivalent vision, in having turned the first signifier (the linear narrative) into another signifier (the second narrative suggested through the structure), and finally in having chosen the plane of the linear or causal narration to express his lucid version of courage, while at the same time permitting his mythical or unconscious version of courage to be expressed, as it were, underneath the text, through the structure of the story or, what amounts to the same thing, through an implied dream.

NOTES

1   Roland Barthes, *Essais critiques* (Paris: Seuil, 1964), p. 306.
2   Gerard Genette, *Figures* (Paris: Seuil, 1966), p. 213.
3   *Ibid.*
4   *Ibid.*, p. 215.
5   Roland Barthes, *op.cit.*, p. 304.
6   J. Irby, N. Murat and C. Peralta, *Encuentro con Borges* (Buenos Aires: Galerna, 1968), p. 34. Borges' interpretation of his own story has prompted a rather long and fertile controversy. Allen W. Phillips was the first to deal with this aspect of "The South" in his article " 'El Sur' de Borges" (*Revista Hispánica Moderna*, vol. XXIX, no. 2, April 1963, pp. 140–147). I discussed his interpretation and suggested a different reading of the story in *La prosa narrativa de J. L. Borges* (Madrid: Gredos, 2nd ed. 1984), chapter IX (pp. 122–137). Subsequent articles by Z. Gertel (" 'El Sur' de Borges: búsqueda de identidad en el laberinto," *Nueva Narrativa Hispanoamericana*, I, 2, Sept. 1971, pp. 35–55), Robert M. Scari ("Aspectos realista-tradicionales del arte narrativo de Borges," *Hispania*, LVII, 4, Dec. 1974, pp. 899–907), and particularly John B. Hall ("Borges' 'El Sur': A Garden of Forking Paths?" *Iberoromania*, Göttingen, no. 3, neue folge, 1975, pp. 71–77) have contributed new views and enriched the discussion of this story.
7   Jorge Luis Borges, *Evaristo Carriego* (Buenos Aires: Emecé, 1955), p. 149.
8   J. L. Borges, "An Autobiographical Essay," in *The Aleph and Other Stories 1933–1969* (New York, Dutton, 1970), p. 208.
9   Rita Guibert, *Seven Voices* (New York: Vintage, 1973), pp. 97–98.
10 Jorge Luis Borges, *Ficciones* (New York: Grove, 1962), p. 174.
11 J. L. Borges, "Martín Fierro," in *Dreamtigers* (University of Texas, 1964), p. 40.
12 *Ibid.*
13 J. L. Borges, *Evaristo Carriego*, p. 149.
14 J. L. Borges, *Selected Poems 1923–1967* (Delacorte Press/Seymour Lawrence, 1972), p. 211.
15 J. L. Borges, *Evaristo Carriego*, p. 124.

16   *Ibid.*, p. 154.
17   *Ibid.*, p. 146.
18   *Ibid.*, p. 147.
19   J. L. Borges, *El Aleph*, p. 113.
20   J. L. Borges, *Other Inquisitions*, p. 72.
21   J. L. Borges, *Selected Poems 1923–1967*, pp. 53–56.

6 Borges, or style as an invisible worker

As early as 1965, John Updike wrote a lengthy essay on Jorge Luis Borges' fiction in which he underlines "the absolute conciseness of his style."[1] He also commented on the potential effects Borges' writings may have an American fiction: "The question is, I think, whether or not Borges' lifework, arriving in a lump now, can serve, in its gravely considered oddity, as any kind of clue to the way out of the dead end narcissism and downright trashiness of present American fiction."[2] Two years later, John Barth celebrated Borges as "one of the 'old masters' of twentieth-century fiction," and he added: "His artistic victory, if you like, is that he confronts an intellectual dead end and employs it against itself to accomplish new human work."[3] To define this phenomenon, Barth coined the concept "literature of exhaustion." In his book *City of Words: American Fiction 1950–1970*, Tony Tanner devotes the first chapter to surveying the strong impact that Nabokov and Borges have had on contemporary American fiction.[4] Finally, Morris Dickstein describes one segment of American fiction written in the last few years as "the Borgesian phase."[5] As much as these and other writers stress Borges' "terse, laconic, and economic style,"[6] much of his virtuosity is muted by the contextual body of English literature against which the American reader is forced to read Borges in translation. Within a Spanish context, on the other hand, the innovative accomplishments of Borges' prose acquire truly revolutionary stature.

In order to realize fully the extent of this linguistic revolution, one must be aware of the fact that until Borges Latin America lacked a literary language of its own. Argentine or Mexican prose writers resorted to a Spanish benumbed by centuries of stagnant *casticismo* (the Spanish version of linguistic purism). They wrote in a language which, even when dealing with the most regional subjects, denied their own

cultural and national reality. Between the language used in their daily
lives and the one written in their fiction there was a gap of dependence
and servitude: dependence on a language inflated with rhetoric, and servitude towards a literary tradition which even Spaniards found, at the
turn of the century, obsolete and provincial.[7] Prose writers in Latin
America were imitating, with a few exceptions, dead models, lifeless
"mummies with Hispanic bandages" in Cortázar's words. Borges
launched the most devastating revision of the limitations and handicaps
confronting the Argentine writer. After the seventeenth century, the
language was locked in academies, asphyxiated by sermons, drowned in
obscurantist dictionaries, insulated from the intellectual and literary
forces shaping the rest of Europe's culture. The Latin American writer
was attempting the impossible: to create living organisms with dead
cells. In 1927, in an essay entitled "El idioma de los argentinos" (The
Argentines' Language), Borges sketched the nature of the language the
Latin American writer was striving to recast as his expressive tool: "We
would prefer" – he wrote – "a pliant and hopeful Spanish, which would
be in harmony with our own landscape and our own ways and our
professed faith."[8] In sum, a language rooted in what was real for the
Latin American consciousness, a language whose code would no longer
be alien to the reader's sensitivity and imagination. To accomplish this,
Borges undertook to study and diagnose the ailments which incapaci-
tated Spanish and prevented it from being the effective literary instrument he sought. A great deal of the first three volumes of essays he
published between 1925 and 1928, and a good part of the subsequent
collections, particularly *Discusión* and *Other Inquisitions,* are devoted to
this pursuit.

In his early essays he developed a new concept of style, moving from
traditional ornamentation and artistry to functionality and invisibility,
thus setting an alternative for most Latin American fiction writers who
came after him.[9] Yet, it was not until he began to write his first stories in
1935 that his formula "total effectiveness and total invisibility should be
the twin aims of any style" was applied to his own writings. Up to that
point, Borges' prose suffered from the very disease he was trying so hard
to cure – ostentation, verbosity, floridness – traits which defined the
Spanish version of literary style. Young Borges, compelled to exhibit the
hallmarks of what was traditionally held as "good writing" if he wanted
to prove that indeed he had mastered the tricks and countertricks of the
craft, was later to acknowledge the necessity of playing the conven-
tionalized game as a preliminary step to rid himself of its excesses:

> I began writing in a very self-conscious, baroque style. It was
> probably due to youthful timidity. The young often suspect that

their plots and poems aren't very interesting, so they try to conceal them or elaborate on them by other means. When I began to write I tried to adopt the style of classical Spanish seventeenth-century writers, such as Quevedo or Saavedra Fajardo. Then I reflected that it was my duty as an Argentine to write as an Argentine. I bought a dictionary of Argentinisms, and managed to become so Argentine in my style and vocabulary that people couldn't understand me and I couldn't even remember very well myself what the words meant. Words passed directly from the dictionary to my manuscript without corresponding to any experience. Now, after a great many years, I believe that it's best to write with a very simple vocabulary, and concentrate on the person whom certain modern poets are apt to forget entirely: the reader.[10]

This period of apprenticeship took the form of contracting all the diseases that plagued Spanish prose in an effort to become immunized against them. Before changing the rules of the game, Borges had to play all the way according to those old rules. His adamant refusal to allow the reprinting of his first three books of essays, written in that showy baroque style, constitutes his own condemnation of the stylistic gymnastics of his first epoch. By 1927 he had written "The Argentines' Language," a seminal essay dealing with his outlook on language. There he argued against what he called "the Spanish superstition of style": against ornate synonymy, the cult of the dictionary, acoustic pirouettes, syntactic juggling, and, in sum, against a squandered language euphonically dazzling but expressively superfluous. In a culture that had abused literary language up to the point of sterilization, Borges' call for linguistic restraint and austerity was a sort of antidote to "the verbal parade of defunct bodies and gesticulating ghosts."[11] Thus, his appeal first of all for "total invisibility" of style was the most forceful way of saying that verbal acrobatics in itself meant nothing and that a style which delights in its own visibility is a fraud.

The second stylistic notion postulated by Borges was "total effectiveness," that is, the capacity of style to convey with a minimum of signs the intended thought, idea, or perception. Borges distinguishes two ways of assuming reality: that of the classical writer and that of the romantic writer.[12] The first (Voltaire, Swift, Cervantes) does not attempt to represent "the first raw feelings of reality" but merely to register "their final elaboration into ideas. . . . The many events to which he alludes were compounded of highly charged individual experiences, perceptions, and reactions. These may be inferred from the narrative but are not in it. . . . Reality as the romantics present it" – on the other hand –

"is for the most part thrust on the reader, their stock in trade being overstatement and half truths."[13] Borges concludes: "The classic writer trusts language; he believes in the sufficient value of each of its symbols." To those who chose the effusiveness of the romantic mode, Borges replied with Occam's razor: "Entities are not to be multiplied without necessity."[14]

Spanish literature suffered from a deficit of thought and human experience which resulted in a linguistic inflation and an external concept of style. Spanish American writers were prejudiced by the same bias. Reputable Argentine authors such as Lugones and Paul Groussac blamed Cervantes for his poor and colorless style. For Lugones, style was Cervantes' weakness; for Groussac, a good half of the *Quijote* was, with reference to form, weak and careless, and Cervantes' rivals were right when they condemned "his after-dinner prose as a humble language."[15] When Borges defended Cervantes he was defending his own view of style: "After-dinner prose" – he writes – "conversational and not declamatory prose is Cervantes' and he did not need a different one. I suppose that the same observation will also be fair with regard to Dostoyevsky, or Montaigne or Samuel Butler. . . . It suffices to check a few paragraphs from the *Quijote* to sense that Cervantes was not a stylist (at least in the present acoustic-decorative meaning of the word) and that he was too concerned with Quijote's and Sancho's destinies to allow himself to be distracted by his own voice."[16] Borges hastened to add that he was not encouraging improvisation and clumsiness in writing, but that "the voluntary omission of two or three minor niceties – ocular and auditory distractions – proves that the passion for the chosen theme prevails in the writer."[17]

The fiction writers who preceded Borges, those who followed the esthetics of Spanish American *modernismo,* did exactly the opposite. For them theme was a pretext for building a world of sensory impressions, artistic transpositions, and verbal rhythms where all things were valued for their esthetic potential and their capacity to generate beauty. Their novels and short stories were written in a prose full of color and melody, and the themes of those narratives were either deluged by the bright colors or deafened by the vibrant rhythms of the prose. Borges was attempting to correct this imbalance by restoring the equilibrium between message and code. His point was that the effectiveness of the code cannot be measured independently from the urgency of the message and that the performance of the code is intrinsically related to the necessities of the message: Cervantes' prose may not be elegant, lavish or euphonic, but his novel "did not need that." Borges never used the word *functional* to describe his idea of style, but obviously this concept was the core of his contention: as the anatomy of an organ is determined by the function it performs, so is style. There are no set rules as to what should or should not be the stylistic texture of a narrative or a poem: metaphor can work effectively in one text but it can become obstructive or gratuitous in another. Metaphor in itself, like any other stylistic device, doesn't guarantee a thing by the sheer virtue of its use. Language is the medium of literary messages, but the transformation of language into a literary message implies a selection through which the message is encoded with those signs which most effectively convey to the decoder its intended message. It is this selection which determines the good, or bad, functioning of any style. Linguists have pointed out the arbitrary nature of the linguistic signs: there is no kinship whatsoever, with obvious exceptions, between signified and signifier. Not so in literature which, in Hjelmeslev's definition, is a semiotic system whose means of expression is another semiotic system – language. Since in literature the messages depend on how effectively they have been encoded, it follows that style, as the way the writer handles the linguistic code, should be examined in relation to the messages it conveys. Or, in Jakobson's words, the study of literature from a linguistic viewpoint "is likely to explore all possible problems of relation between discourse and the 'universe of discourse': *what* of this universe is verbalized by a given discourse and *how* is it verbalized."[18] Borges was perhaps the first among Spanish American writers to point out this relation between the *what* and the *how* of a literary discourse, and his redefinition of style was an effort to restore the broken balance between form and matter, not at the expense of the former but by finding the natural breadth of that matter which the writer attempts to shape.[19]

It was not until 1933 that Broges began writing prose fiction by rewriting old stories. In the preface to the first edition of *A Universal History of Infamy* he characterized these adaptations as "exercises of narrative prose" and acknowledged that they "derived from my rereading of R. L. Stevenson and Chesterton and even from the films of von Sternberg." In the note to the second edition of the same volume, not published until 1954, from the perspective of almost twenty years of fiction writing Borges recognized "the baroque character" of this early prose and made the following remark: "These pages are the irresponsible game of a shy young man who dared not write stories and so amused himself by falsifying and distorting the tales of others. From these ambiguous exercises, he went on to the labored composition of a straightforward story – 'Streetcorner Man'."[20] Yet, in spite of Borges' insistence on its baroque nature, these "ambiguous exercises" of fiction writing had all the essential traits of his later and more mature style. Amado Alonso wrote in 1935 a fine review of the collection and pointed out that the stories were written in a "masterly prose." Alonso, surveying some of Borges' excellences of style, greeted "Streetcorner Man" as "a master-piece."[21] In the next fifteen years Borges wrote the bulk of his fiction (*Ficciones,* 1944, and *El Aleph,* 1949). Some of the guidelines he defined in the late twenties as the desiderata for an efficacious and unobtrusive style were masterfully put to work in the prose of those two collections.

To illustrate the mechanics of this style, I have chosen the opening paragraph from one of his stories. It is from "The Life of Tadeo Isidoro Cruz"; it could have been from any other:

> On the sixth of February, 1829, a troop of gaucho militia, har-ried all day by Lavalle on their march north to join the army under the command of López, made a halt some nine or ten miles from Pergamino at a ranch whose name they did not know. Along about dawn, one of the men had a haunting night-mare and, in the dim shadows of a shed where he lay sleeping, his confused outcry woke the woman who shared his bed. No-body ever knew what he dreamed, for around four o'clock that afternoon the gauchos were routed by a detachment of Suárez' cavalry in a chase that went on for over twenty miles and ended, in thickening twilight, in tall swamp grasses, where the man died in a ditch, his skull split by a saber that had seen service in the Peruvian and Brazilian wars. The woman's name was Isidora Cruz. The son born to her was given the name Tadeo Isidoro.[22]

The texture of the paragraph brings to mind the factual style of a history book or the rigorous construction of a philosophical treatise. This stat-utory appearance has prompted Keith Botsford to say: "Borges' prose is a prose of statements and definitions; it is not a prose of description or ambiguity. . . . Brief, clear, and dense, it seems almost legal in in-tent. . . . Nothing is superfluous; all is limpid. The overall effect is as though one were reading in a science or philosophy, where exact mean-ing is all."[23] But, as Botsford himself notices, "this is half the illusion; the other half is what Borges evokes beyond his statements, what he alludes to,"[24] and Botsford cites three examples of Borges' allusive style to show the secret reverses of his prose, the unexpected surprises inserted in a seemingly neutral prose. Actually, those surprises function like any stylistic device in transgressing a norm. But in Borges' prose the lin-guistic artifices are to his style what the machinery of toothed wheels is to a watch: we only see its face and the numbers and the hands moving, and that's all we need to read the time, but the accuracy of the movement is determined by the quality and precision of those invisible pieces inside the case.

In the text we chose, the phrase "in thickening twilight, in tall swamp grass" is the translation of three words in the original, a noun, a modifier and an adverb (*pajonales ya lóbregos*). I am not dealing with the merits of the translation; what interests me is the connotative side of the original Spanish lost, perhaps inevitably, in the English translation. *Lóbrego* (thickening twilight) means in Spanish dark but also the feeling of gloominess generated by darkness. At a normative level, *lóbrego* is rarely used for dark, as in English *tenebrous* is not used for dark alone but for expressing the dreary side of darkness. Yet Borges is employing *lóbrego* in its more literal meaning of dark. He does that by adding the adverb *ya* (already), which points to the advanced course of the day, thus forcing the word *lóbrego* to return to his etymological meaning. Why then bother with *lóbrego?* In his early books of essays Borges wrote on the pleasure of going back to the etymology of certain words whose original meaning had been eroded by time and usage.[25] In his early writings he delighted in playing with this "primordial meaning" of particular words. It is safe to suspect that a few of those early linguistic habits permeate his late prose, not as sheer effusion but as a means of molding the subjects of his stories more effectively. In our example, the adjective points to the time of day – twilight – but also anticipates, as an ominous echo within the text, the gloomy event which is to take place towards the end of the same sentence: the killing of the fugitive. Also the translation of *pajonales* as "tall swamp grasses" may be correct from the standpoint of the dictionary, but the connotations contained in the original are again lost; not only because the other fugitive, Martín Fierro, is later in the story going to take shelter in a *pajonal* (which is translated this time as "a growth of tall reeds"), but mainly because the Spanish word is packed with compressed layers of connotative meaning for the Argentine reader. Borges himself digresses in the story to tell us that the episode of his tale "belongs to a famous poem," and towards the end of the story, again commenting on his own text, he admits: "An obvious reason keeps me from describing the fight that followed." The poem is the book by José Hernández, *Martín Fierro,* and the reason for the omission is that the fight is fully described in the same poem. Borges has written literature about a work of literature but his rendition of the episode narrated by Hernández is, like Menard's Quijote in relation to Cervantes', "almost infinitely richer." Borges is going to explain the significance of an act seemingly arbitrary in the poem by means of a stylistic twist. In his story, Borges tells us that Fierro, pursued by soldiers, "had taken shelter in a growth of tall reeds" (*se había guarecido en un pajonal*), but in Hernández's poem, it is Cruz, and not Fierro, who took shelter in a growth of tall reeds (*me guarecí en los pajales,* says Cruz in the poem). The importance of the inversion lies in the fact that the dénouement of the story has already been formulated at a much subtler level, at the level of the signifiers: through the skillful handling of the word *pajonales/pajales* the connotative level of the code has stated what is going to become explicit at the denotative level of the message at the end of the story: "Cruz understood that the other man was himself."

"Gaucho militia" is possibly the most accurate translation for *montoneros* since it explains with the help of a regional word (gaucho) what a montonero was, but here again several nuances implied in the original are lost. The *montonera* (gaucho militia) was a sort of institution which served the Argentine army during the fight for independence and which eventually became a kind of military police at the service of local caudillos during the Argentine civil war, this being the time framing the narrative. In a story dealing with gauchos, Borges uses the word *gauchos* only once in a very inconspicuous way. In our paragraph *gauchos* appears as the "English version" of *montoneros* in the original. His preference for *montoneros* is an effort of precision and restraint: it points to a chapter of Argentine history and it avoids any distractive trace of local color. There are a few other words of this kind in the same paragraph (*estancia, galpón, zanja*), as well as several others throughout the story, which do not seek any display of localism for its own sake; they respond rather to Borges' search for a Spanish "which would be in harmony with our own landscape and our own ways."

Yet the most puzzling detail in the entire paragraph is the reference to the "haunting nightmare." Borges tells us that the man's "confused outcry woke the woman who shared his bed," and he adds in a rather whimsical way: "Nobody ever knew what he dreamed." If this is the case, why was the dream mentioned? When I ask my students about this mysterious dream, one favorite answer is that the nightmare is perhaps a premonition of the fatal destiny of the dreamer. The difficulty with this answer is that it challenges verification. It is a reasonable guess but just as valid as any other. If one considers that the story paraphrases an episode of a book which in an Argentine context "has come to mean all things to all men" according to Borges; that in the collection entitled *Dreamtigers* (*El hacedor*) he has included a short piece under the name "Martín Fierro"; and that finally, in addition to a few essays, Borges has written a 62 page pamphlet on Hernández's poem, it becomes clear that Borges regards *Martín Fierro* as the most accomplished work of literature produced in his country, and he has said so in several places.[26] I'd like to focus on the short piece from *Dreamtigers*. There Borges offers an ultra condensed synopsis of Argentine history in order to derive from it the meaning of its core. That meaning is conveyed through a passage from *Martín Fierro* which Borges presents in the following way:

> In a hotel room in the 1860s, a man dreamed about a fight. A gaucho lifts a Negro off his feet with his knife, throws him down like a sack of bones, sees him agonize and die, crouches down to clean his blade, unties his horse, and mounts slowly so he will not be thought to be running away. This, which once was, is again infinitely: the splendid armies are gone, and a lowly knife fight remains. The dream of one man is part of the memory of all.[27]

Is there any relationship between the gaucho's nightmare in our paragraph and this dream? It is true that Borges often uses the verbs *to write* and *to dream* as synonyms,[28] and that the reference to the man in a hotel room in the 1860's is an allusion to José Hernández who is believed to have conceived and begun writing Martín Fierro in a hotel room to overcome the weariness of his political flight, but the idea of a dream which "is part of the memory of all" also expresses a myth, a collective unconscious whose archetype is the knife fight narrated by Hernández. Like the Jungian concept of the archetype which "indicates the existence of definite forms in the psyche which seem to be present always and everywhere,"[29] the episode told by Borges "belongs to a poem which has come to mean all things to all men." For Argentines, according to Borges, courage reaches the height of a cult in whose fulfillment they reconize the kernel of their destiny. Borges has devoted a good part of his work to this Argentine destiny and the story "The Life of Tadeo Isidoro Cruz" is but an avatar of the subject. His view is that the essence from which all Argentine history evolves is that dream of a knife fight. It is only consistent with this outlook to conclude that the unrevealed dream of the fugitive is the dream which "is part of the memory of all," a dream which contains his destiny as a lone wolf and that of his son who is going to discover it, as in a revelation, in a knife fight. This revelation, absent in Hernández's poem, was Borges' motivation for rewriting the story and it is already implied in the first paragraph as an untold dream, as a challenging clue so typical of Borges' narratives, and as an anticipation of what the story as a whole purports to express.

Finally it should be noticed that the dreamer of the story dies in a ditch, "his skull split by a saber of the Peruvian and Brazilian wars." Metonymy is often found in Borges' prose;[30] here it is not only a condensed way of expressing what forces Suárez's cavalry represent, but it is also a restatement of the traditional struggle between civilization and barbarism which since Sarmiento's days has been accepted as the main principle governing

Argentine history. In the short piece "Martín Fierro," Borges replaced the wars of Peru and Brazil with the battles that epitomized those wars: Ayacucho in Peru and Ituzaingó in Brazil, but the idea is the same in both texts: "these things (glorious armies and heroic battles) are as if they had never been." It is the knife fight, it is the violence of barbarism which forever returns and decides the course of Argentine history. Because, as Laprida – the man who presided over the Congress that declared Argentine independence in 1816 – says before being killed by a gaucho militia in one of the most memorable poems written by Borges: "The gauchos have won, the barbarians have won . . . / I see at last that I am face to face / With my South American destiny."[31] Here we have again Hernández' dream expressing the deepest reality of Argentine history. The saber of the Peruvian and Brazilian wars split the gaucho's skull, won temporarily over barbarism, but what remains is his "haunting nightmare" – an inescapable destiny to be a lone wolf which his son would fully understand and embrace when, at the end of the story, "he threw down his soldier's kepi . . . and began fighting against his own soldiers, shoulder to shoulder with Martín Fierro, the deserter."

To sum up: the compressed metonymy, the undisclosed dream, the ambiguous use of a modifier in its etymological meaning as well as in its more normative sense, and the preference for two nouns (*pajonales* and *montoneros*) full of historical and literary reverberations for the Argentine reader are but a few examples, occurring in the same paragraph, of Borges' handling of style. They illustrate his endeavor to write in a skillful yet unobtrusive style. Since his beginnings as a prose writer in the twenties he has made a 180 degree turn. Following the dominant inertia within Spanish literary tradition, he started writing as a mannerist who "prefers the artificial and affected to the natural, and wants to surprise, to astonish, to dazzle."[32] Borges knew that this mannerism inherent in the Spanish language was a superstition, but in a literature where mannerism was the norm, this evil was the inescapable virtue a writer sought to display. If theoretically he overcame this superstition as early as 1927, the process of cleansing the cosmetics from his prose was slow and painstaking. He sought and achieved the other extreme – an invisible style. The examined paragraph shows that this invisibility is far from meaning absence of style. It is, quite the contrary, an effort to spare the reader from the intricacies of a linguistic machinery too precise and too masterfully crafted to need any display beyond the limpid surface of its own accomplishment and effectiveness. Borges himself has offered an updated discourse on method with regard to his own style: "The reader" – he said – "ought never to feel that the writer is skillful. A writer ought to be skillful, but in an unobtrusive way. When things are extremely well done, they seem inevitable as well as easy. If you are aware of a sense of effort, it means failure on the writer's part. Nor do I want to imply that a writer must be spontaneous, because that would mean he hit on the right word straightaway, which is very unlikely. When a piece of work is finished it ought to seem spontaneous, even though it may really be full of secret artifices and modest (not conceited) ingenuity."[33]

NOTES

1 John Updike, "The Author as Librarian," *The New Yorker*, October 30, 1965, p. 223.
2 *Ibid.*
3 John Barth, "The Literature of Exhaustion," *The Atlantic Monthly*, 220, no. 2 (1967), 31.
4 Tony Tanner, *City of Words: American Fiction 1950–1970* (New York: Harper and Row, 1971), p. 33.
5 Morris Dickstein, *The New York Times Book Review*, April 26, 1970, p. 1.
6 John Barth, *op. cit.*, p. 34.
7 Referring to this problem, Amado Alonso, one of the most brilliant critics in Spanish literature, wrote: "Since the seventeenth century our prose has not witnessed a single attempt of innovation. Rubén Darío was right in decrying the flatness in the prose of all of our writers. For centuries our literary language was not a changing force which each writer should have contributed to develop; it was a single-number uniform which fitted all sizes." From *Materia y forma en poesía* (Madrid: Gredos, 1960), p. 239.
8 J. L. Borges, *El idioma de los argentinos* (Buenos Aires: Gleizer, 1928), pp. 182–83. The essay whose title gives the name to the entire collection was first published in *Anales del Instituto Popular de Conferencias*, Buenos Aires, vol. 13, 1927.
9 For the influence of Borges on contemporary Latin American fiction, see Chapter 12 of this volume.
10 Rita Guibert, *Seven Voices* (New York: Vintage, 1973), p. 100. The following is an example of this mannerist prose taken from one of his early essays: "Ni de mañana ni en la diurnidad ni en la noche vemos de veras la ciudad. La mañana es una prepotencia de azul, un asombro veloz y numeroso atravesando el cielo, un cristalear y un despilfarro manirroto de sol amontonándose en las plazas, quebrando con ficticia lapidación los espejos y bajando por los aljibes insinuaciones largas de luz. El día es campo de nuestros empeños o de nuestra desidia, y en su tablero de siempre sólo ellos caben. La noche es el milagro trunco: la culminación de los macilentos faroles y el tiempo en que la objetividad palpable se hace menos insolente y menos macisa" (*I*, 79).
11 J. L. Borges, *op. cit.*, p. 172.
12 See his essay "La postulación de la realidad" in *Discusión* (Buenos Aires: Emecé, 1957), pp. 67–74. English translation: "The Assumption of Reality"

(by N. T. di Giovanni in collaboration with the author) published in *Tri-Quarterly*, no. 25 (Fall 1972), pp. 194–99.

13 *Ibid.*

14 J. L. Borges, "Sobre la descripción literaria," uncollected essay published in *Sur*, No. 97, (Oct. 1942), pp. 100–01.

15 Quoted by Borges in "La superstición ética del lector," *Discusión* (Buenos Aires: Emecé, 1957), pp. 45–50.

16 *Ibid.*, p. 47 (the translation is mine).

17 *Ibid.*, pp. 48–49.

18 Roman Jakobson, "Linguistics and Poetics," in *Style in Language*, ed. Thomas A. Sebeok (Cambridge, Mass.: M.I.T. Press, 1960), p. 351.

19 To prove his point Borges went beyond general and sweeping statements. He entered thoroughly into the anatomy of a text by carefully dissecting its linguistic cells, by examining closely its mechanics and by disassembling the various parts that assure its effective or ineffective functioning. Borges, who was not unaware of stylistics, wrote perceptive and lucid exercises of style analysis. Since Gracián, no Spanish writer was as keenly concerned with the intricacies of language as a literary tool as this early Borges was. Long before Jakobson showed us the poetic function underlying the linguistic structure of a political slogan ("I like Ike"), Borges was attempting a similar undertaking by describing the linguistic "attractions and rejections" operating in the text of a simple *milonga* (Argentine popular song).

20 J. L. Borges, *Historia universal de la infamia* (Buenos Aires: Emecé, 1954), p. 10. English translation of the preface by N. T. di Giovanni, *TriQuarterly*, op. cit., pp. 203–4.

21 Amado Alonso, "Borges, narrador," *Materia y forma*, p. 350. See also Chapter 7 of this volume.

22 J. L. Borges, *The Aleph and Other Stories, 1933–1969*, tr. N. T. di Giovanni in collaboration with the author (New York: Dutton, 1970), p. 81.

23 Keith Botsford, "The Writings of Jorge Luis Borges," *The Atlantic Monthly*, 219 (Jan., 1967), p. 101.

24 *Ibid.*

25 See the essay "El idioma infinito" in *El tamaño de mi esperanza* (Buenos Aires: Proa, 1926), pp. 37–42. I have also devoted to this aspect of Borges' prose a lengthy footnote in *La prosa narrativa de J. L. Borges* (Madrid: Gredos, 1968), pp. 189–190.

26 See his essay "The Argentine Writer and Tradition," *L*, 177–85.

27 *DT*, 40.

28 In his essay on Hawthorne, Borges writes: "Jung the Swiss, in charming and doubtless accurate volumes, compares literary inventions to oneiric inventions, literature to dreams." *OI*, 49. In the Preface to *Doctor Brodie's Report*, he reiterates: "After all, writing is nothing more than a guided dream." *DBR*, 11.

29 C. G. Jung, "The Concept of the Collective Unconscious," *The Portable Jung* (New York: Viking Press, 1971), p. 60.

30 For a detailed study on the use of metonymy in Borges' prose fiction, see chapter V (second part) of my book *La prosa narrativa de J. L. Borges,* pp. 200–25, also pp. 176–79.

31 J. L. Borges, "Conjectural Poem" (tr. N. T. di Giovanni), included in *SP,* 82–5.

32 Ernest Robert Curtius, *European Literature and the Latin Middle Ages* (New York, 1963), p. 282.

33 Rita Guibert, *op. cit.,* p. 111.

7 The making of a style: *A Universal History of Infamy*

It would be an overstatement to say that *A Universal History of Infamy,* published in 1935, contained, even in an embryonic state, the mature fiction of the author of *Ficciones* (1944) and *The Aleph* (1949). The truth is, though, that the early collection prefigures the later Borges. One can safely approach those stories through the notion of the precursor as understood by Borges himself in his memorable – and by now axiomatic – essay "Kafka and His Precursors." In each of the texts included in the collection of infamy "Borges's idiosyncrasy is present in greater or lesser degree, but if Borges had not written *Ficciones* we would not perceive it; that is to say, it wouldn't exist."[1] And if it is true that "each writer *creates his precursors,*" it is equally true – I suggest – that his later work "modifies our conception" of his earlier work (*OI*, 113). The pieces that compose this first collection anticipate *Ficciones,* but our reading of *Ficciones* refines and changes perceptibly our reading of his first narrative endeavors. To go back to the Borges of 1935 after the successive Borgeses of 1944 (*Ficciones*), 1949 (*El Aleph*), 1960 (*Dreamtiger*), 1970 (*Doctor Brodie's Report*), and 1975 (*The Book of Sand*) is to recognize his voice when that voice was still a sort of sketch or first draft, to read him as he couldn't have been read when those "exercises of narrative prose" (*UH*, 13) appeared almost fifty years ago. This is the type of reading we are about to undertake.

Infamy as theme

The first and most evident trait underlying this type of reading occurs at the level of theme. Infamy as a subject does not disappear in Borges' subsequent collections. It is present in various degrees in several of his later stories. "Emma Zumz" is the story of a self-inflicted rape and

90

a vindictive murder to avenge an infamous injustice. The spy Yu Tsun, in "The Garden of Forking Paths," kills the venerable sinologist who solved the enigma of his ancestor just to signal to his chief in Berlin the needed information about the new British artillery park. "The Shape of the Sword" is the story of an informer or, rather, of the mark of his infamy. So is "Three Versions of Judas," where we are told that "God became man up to the point of infamy" (*L,* 99). Other forms of infamy are recorded in "The Lottery in Babylon," "The Approach to al-Mu'tasim" (which the narrator describes as a "kind of contest of infamies" [*F,* 401]), "Theme of the Traitor and the Hero," "The Secret Miracle," "The Theologians," "Deutsches Requiem," "Ibn Hakkan al-Bokhari, Dead in His Labyrinth," "The Dead Man," "The Waiting," and "The Man in the Threshold." This gallery of spies, traitors, murderers, kidnappers, informers, rapists, killers, torturers, thieves, stranglers, despoilers of corpses, and so on suffices to prove that Borges' fascination with infamy transcends his *Universal History* and pervades his later collections. But "variegated infamy," as he refers to it in one story, enters *Ficciones* and *The Aleph* in a way different from that of the early collection. The subject seems to be the same, but the tone and the manner are not. Borges approached infamy in the first collection as a kind of fine art reminiscent of De Quincey's definition of "murder in fiction," that is to say, devoid of value judgment or ethical implications.

As the detective story purports to be an intellectual operation – an exercise of the intelligence without any moralistic connotations – the story of infamy in Borges' first collection seeks to amuse and astonish. If detective fiction appeals to the intellect and the imagination, these exercises with infamy are intended to entertain by suspending our beliefs in good and evil, by turning despicable acts into laughable fits, by drawing a caricature out of civil horror and abhorrence. Hence the words of the prologue: "The man who forged this book was utterly unhappy but entertained himself writing it; I hope that a fraction of that pleasure may reach the reader" (*UH,* 12).

The approach to infamy in the later collections is different. By mixing justice, heroism, holiness, shame, ideals, faith, and, in short, virtue with infamy, Borges restates Plotinus's old notion: "Everything is everywhere, anything is all things, the sun is all the stars and the sun" (*Enneads* 5.8.4; quoted in *OI,* 73). "The world," says the narrator of "The Immortal," "is a system of precise compensations" (*L,* 115). To explain further:

> In an infinite period of time, all things happen to all men. . . .
> Just as in games of chance the odd and even numbers tend to-

ward equilibrium, so also wit and folly cancel out and correct each other. . . . I know of those who have done evil so that in future centuries good would result. (*L*, 114)

This pantheistic understanding of good and evil permeating his later fiction presents striking similarities with the Kabbalistic notion of the "breaking of the Vessels" as formulated by Isaac Luria. These Vessels contain the divine light or cosmic seed from which the visible world resulted. But the shells (*Kelipot*) of those Vessels carried in them the forces of evil that existed already before their break. When the Vessels broke, comparable to the breakthrough of birth, the divine light diffused together with the powers of evil released from the scattered fragments. "In this way the good elements of the divine order came to be mixed with the vicious ones."[2] This Kabbalistic understanding of the coexistence of good and evil, of virtue and infamy, is echoed in Borges' short prose piece "*Paradiso, XXXI, 108*," where Diodorus Siculus tells the story of "a god, broken and scattered abroad. . . . We lost His features, as we may lose a magic number, as one loses an image in a kaleidoscope, forever" (*DT*, 43).

Borges' keen interest in infamy is present in the later stories but without the tongue-in-cheek characteristic of the first collection. The letter is present, but the spirit has changed. Infamy is no longer a show of sheer burlesque, but one more character in a much broader fictional drama.

In search of a style

But the stories of infamy are important in Borges' development as a writer, less as theme than as form. It is in this latter account that *Universal History* represents a real breakthrough. When Borges wrote the stories of infamy, he definitely left behind the contorted baroque style of his *ultraist* (avant-garde) years. As early as 1927, in his book *El idioma de los argentinos*, he harshly criticized "the ornaments, lavishness and pretended wealth" of the Spanish language as forms of fraud, and he saw in "its perfect synonymity and its profuse verbal parade" a dead language, a display of ghosts and mummies. In that same essay, he proposed a goal that was the very opposite of that showy, expressionless, and affected style: "Total invisibility and total effectiveness" (*IA*, 158). In the prologue to the second edition of the stories of infamy of 1954, he renewed that attack, now free of the controversial circumstances of 1927 and also free of his own youthful insecurities: "I should define as baroque that style which borders on its own caricature. . . . Baroque is the final stage of any given art, when it parades and squanders its own means of expression." And regarding his own tales of infamy, he added: "The very title of these pages flaunts their baroque character" (*UH*, 11). The prose of *Universal History*, however, is far from suffering from that baroque ill of his youth. In those "falsified and distorted" stories, as he calls them, Borges found his voice, the style of the mature writer. Amado Alonso was the first to record that change, in a note published the same year the book appeared:

> This book surpasses the previous ones, by the same author, in its prose. It is a masterful prose in a strictly literary sense and not by its sumptuous tricks of pluperfect and its ostentatious language. . . . The ideas find always a rigorous form and words are addressed to their target. Economy and condensation. Borges achieves here a style of high quality. I mean a true style, and not an impeccable grammar and a profuse vocabulary: a style which is not a rhetorical exercise. Words and sentences are pregnant with meaning. His youthful phraseology and vocabulary which used to bestow to his prose a bumpy and squeaky course, have almost completely disappeared.[3]

Alonso also pointed out, in that early note, several features of that prose: "its precision and conciseness," "its careful perfection and exactness," and, as a summary, "its accomplished stylistic level." Those stylistic features he noticed in the early collection of 1935 would become the attributes of Borges' later prose.

Let us now examine those attributes in *Universal History*, from the perspective elicited by his later prose. Some of them are readily visible to the alert eye; others require a more meticulous analysis. I will just mention the first ones, but I'll elaborate on the second type. Here is a list of narrative devices and stylistic traits from the early prose of *Universal History* that also appear in the later prose of *Ficciones* and *The Aleph*:

1. The story as a rereading and a summary of another story, either an imaginary text or an actual one or both. The list of sources given at the end of the collection on infamy attests to this practice, which Borges formulated in 1951 in his essay on Bernard Shaw: "One literature differs from another not so much because of the text as of the manner in which it is read" (*OI*, 173).
2. An ostensible preference for the use of adjectives, anaphora, and enumerations.
3. The return to the lost or unused etymological meaning of some words ("conmovido palacio" refers to the Latin *commoveo* [79];

"nos ilustró la condición de Rosendo" points to *illustrare* 'to clarify' [96]).

4. The narrator's commentaries on his own text or metatexts (37, 73–74).
5. A declaration of sources at the beginning of the story (53).
6. The frequent use of parenthetical commentary in the middle of a sentence with various functions.
7. Transposition of neutral verbs into transitive verbs and vice versa (18).
8. Bivalent adjectives of a physical and abstract nature modifying the same noun.
9. A series of nominal phrases governed by the same verb.
10. Use of rhetorical notions to describe a character.
11. The frame story as a frequent narrative technique.

I will now examine in greater detail a few dominant stylistic features that stand out in *Universal History*.

Metaphor and metonymy

I begin with metaphor because of its paradoxical absence in the prose of *Universal History*. For an author who during his ultraist years defined metaphor as an "essential element," who admired and greeted the eighteenth-century baroque author Torres Villarroel as "a brother" of the writers of his generation and celebrated him for this love for metaphor, the absence of metaphor in the prose of 1935 is perplexing, to say the least. His early books of essays and poetry are plagued by metaphor and simile. This overabundance of images in his early writings was responsible, to a great extent, for the mannerist and downright euphuistic style of *Inquisitions, El tamano de mi esperanza,* and the first volumes of poetry. By 1935, Borges had contracted all the linguistic ills he had criticized in his essay of 1927. He reasoned, like Averroes: "The only persons incapable of sin are those who have already committed it and repented" (*L*, 153). He didn't have to prove any more – as he put it later – that "he knew many rare words and could combine them in a startling and showy way."[4] By 1935, he was able to purge from his prose the metaphorical excesses of his youth. When images appear in the tales of infamy, they have the same restraint and classic finality as those sparingly present in his later prose. This one, for instance, from "Kotsuké no Suké": "Una *nube* de arqueros y de esgrimistas custodiaba su palanquín" (*HU*, 76), so tempered that it disappears in the English translation as "A *crowd* of archers and swordsmen" (*UH*, 71), but Borges must have liked the image since it recurs in "The Circular Ruins" as "*nubes de alumnos* taciturnos" (60), translated as *"clouds* of silent students" (*L,* 146). The metaphor pointed, of course, to the motley and in-motion quality of the crowd.

With few exceptions, the prose of *Universal History* avoids figures of similarity. The absence of such figures strongly contrasts with the heavy use of metonymy and synecdoche. Borges' preference for contiguity is of one piece with his marked penchant for brevity and synopsis in the sense that, just as a summary is an effort toward conciseness and focalization, so is metonymy. Saying "casas de farol colorado" 'houses showing red lanterns' (*HU,* 54) is a way of describing the bordellos through one of their many aspects, but it is also a form of summarizing in one attribute the totality of the object. The choice of one attribute over others is not and cannot be accidental: it seeks to condense the whole in the part that best suits the purposes and effectiveness of the story; this is precisely the strategy Borges adopts in his stories of infamy and those that followed, when he chooses to offer a summary of the books indicated at the end of the volume as the sources of his narratives.

Other instances of metonymy reappear in the stories of *Universal History.* Thus the metonymic construction "The man who would become known to *terror and glory* as Billy the Kid" (*UH,* 61) is fairly common in the later stories. The metonymy "un alcohol pendenciero" ("quarreling alcohol") from the same story on Billy the Kid reappears in the story "The Dead Man." Here Borges did what he pointed out regarding the word for "threat" in Old English, which meant "crowd" but was used to mean a crowd's effect, "the threatening crowd." In both translations, the figure has vanished: in the story of infamy, it is rendered as "men drink a liquor that warms them for a fight" (*UH,* 63); in "The Dead Man," "beben un alcohol pendenciero" becomes "the men fall into quarreling over their liquor" (*A,* 65). Finally, the metonymy that so dazzled Amado Alonso in "Street-Corner Man": "Later there were blows at the door, *and a big voice called"* ("Al rato llamaron a la puerta con autoridad, *un golpe y una voz"* [*HU,* 97]); "He looked exactly like his voice" ("El hombre era parecido a la voz" [*HU,* 97] is repeated in "Funes the Memorious": "His voice was speaking in Latin; his voice was articulating a speech" (*L,* 62). And, once again, slightly modified, in "Emma Zunz": "The face looked at her with amazement and anger, the mouth of the face swore at her in Spanish and Yiddish" (*L,* 136).

Oxymoron

Another figure of style frequently used in his later prose and abundant in the stories of infamy is oxymoron. The title of the collection offers a first example. Borges must have felt the epigrammatic twist in linking "infamy" to "universal history," since he commented in the prologue of 1954 that "the very title of these pages flaunts their baroque character." It is hyperbolically baroque, but the paradoxical nature of the link, which opposes a negative element to a positive one, generates the same tension and incongruity that crisscross the entire collection. Notice that, with one exception, all the stories of the first part have similarly oxymoronic titles: "The Dread Redeemer," "The Implausible Impostor," "The Lady Pirate," "The Purveyor of Iniquities," "The Disinterested Killer," "The Uncivil Master of Etiquette." These titles anticipate the adopted treatment: not the reproving or moralistic side of infamy but its splendidly humorous and parodic vein. One single instance encapsulates this approach. In "The Purveyor of Iniquities," we are told about heroes who are "insignificant or splendid" (*UH*, 56), that is, men who achieve their heroic stature through their insignificance. The world of these heroes is not epic but infamous; as the same text puts it: "Heroes from police files, heroes reeking of tobacco, smoke and alcohol . . ., heroes afflicted with shameful diseases, tooth decay, respiratory or kidney problems" (*UH*, 56). These infamous heroes owe their reality less to their crimes than to the travestying account that records those crimes. The frequent use of oxymora in this prose comes, therefore, as no surprise.

In a natural way, as if style were already dictated by the adopted narrative strategy, Borges speaks of "the *guilty and magnificent* existence of the *nefarious redeemer* Lazarus Morell" (20), of "the incomparable villain," of "bestial hopes" (*UH*, 21), of "white-haired scoundrels and successful murderers" (*UH*, 22). A bullet, a knife, or a blow is a means "*to free* the runaway slave from sight, hearing, touch, day, infamy, time, his benefactors, pity, the air, dogs, the world, hope, sweat and himself" (*UH*, 25). The tone is clearly sardonic, bordering on caricature. In the first eight stories of infamy, the number of oxymora climbs to forty.[5] In addition, there are three paragraphs whose organization is also oxymoronic. Their number alone indicates the dominant presence of an artifice that expresses at the level of style what the story does at the level of theme or narrative vision.

Hypallage

Like oxymoron, hypallage is frequently used in the stories of infamy. Hypallage, or "exchange," is a change in the relation of words whereby a word, instead of agreeing with the word it logically qualifies, is made to agree grammatically with another word. The normative sentence "Bartolomé de las Casas, taking great pity on the *laborious Indians* who were languishing in the hells of Antillean gold mines" (*UH,* 19) becomes the first sentence of the collection's first story: "Bartolomé de las Casas, taking great pity on the Indians who were languishing in the *laborious hells* of the Antillean gold mines" (*UH,* 19). The logical relation – in semantic terms – is "laborious Indians" and not "laborious hells," but while the first is stylistically neutral, the second carries an expressive intention absent in the first: the emphasis is now on the hells to which the Indians are condemned. Notice that "hells" is here a metaphor for the "Kingdom of Heavens" the Indians were promised. But, in addition to that merely stylistic function, hypallage, like oxymoron, defines Borges' approach to the theme of infamy – an approach not in logical terms, in which case we would be facing a moral issue, but in imaginative terms that are the only ones literature cares for: that is, grammatical terms.

In another place, Borges defines literature as a "syntactic fact."[6] He has also said that all literature is made up of tricks or artifices. Here those imaginative terms lie less in the events proper than in the tone or rather in the intonation with which those old stories are retold. The stories are about infamy, but the tone of the narrative is nonchalant and parodic, since they deal with infamous people disguised as heroes. Hence the epic overtones and gestures the narration often assumes, makes us laugh because it is a heroism of carnival, a festival of masks, inversions, and displacements. There are twenty-seven examples of hypallage in the first eight stories of infamy. Some of them are literally repeated in his later prose. The "imperious cigar" (*L,* 77) of Inspector Treviranus in "Death and the Compass" had been "the thoughtful cigars" (*L,* 27) smoked by Lazarus Morell. The "numerous bed" (translated as "populous couch" [*L,* 24]) that Ts'ui Pên renounced in order to compose *The Garden of Forking Path* has its forerunner in the "numerous bed" (now translated as "the plural bed" [*L,* 63]) that Brigham Young did not renounce in the story on Billy the Kid. The "happy war" in "Deutsches Requiem" (translated as "successful war" [*L,* 145]) and the "balazo anhelado" or "desired shot" (translated as "a long-desired bullet" [*L,* 75]) that entered the breast of the traitor and hero derived from "the happy detonation" (translated as "lucky blast" [*UH,* 64]) that converts Bill Harrigan into Billy the Kid.[7]

These three elements of style (metonymy, oxymoron, and hypallage) appear in the stories of infamy as well as in the later ones. They constitute active ingredients in the texture and functions of Borges' prose. There is, however, a difference in the proportion: they are considerably more frequent – as their counting indicates – in the first ones. The new themes and motifs of the later stories have also resulted in a change in the ludicrous tone and intent characteristic of the early stories, and the sly style that reinforced the grotesque quality of the themes has also suffered a readjustment. The proclivity toward caricature in the early prose has yielded to a more balanced style: the number of those three figures – and particularly of the last two (oxymoron and hypallage) – is now much lower, and for a good reason. In the stories of infamy, those figures contributed to the same dislocations advanced by the themes: infamous heroes. The stories of *Ficciones* and *The Aleph*, however, are addressed to those "games with time and infinity" that require from the same devices different functions.[8] Despite these differences, the early and the later styles share some distinguishing marks of Borges' best prose. In addition to a deliberate effort to overcome the baroque style of his early writings and the use of those three stylistic devices, the prose of a *Universal History of Infamy* anticipates a few pearls that are repeated – verbatim or nearly so – in the subsequent collections. Here are a few memorable samples:

1. "The Shape of the Sword" opens with the sentence "A rancorous scar crossed his face" (*L*, 67). Almost the same is said about Kira Kôtsuké: "A scar crossed his forehead" (translated as "His forehead still bore a scar" [*UH*, 74]). The narrator of the first story says further on: "With that half moon I *rubricated* [translated as "carved" or "sealed"] on his face forever a moon of blood" (*UH*, 71); the narrator of the story of infamy uses the same images: "De la Torre drew his sword and aimed a blow at the master's head. Kôtsuké ran away, his forehead *rubricated* [translated as "barely marked"] with a faint thread of blood" (*UH*, 70).

2. The declaration of the heresiarchs from Uqbar recalled by Bioy in "Tlön, Uqbar, Orbis Tertius" – "Mirrors and fatherhood are abominable because they multiply and extend the universe" (*L*, 4) – appears for the first time in the cosmogony of "The Masked Dyer": "The world we live in is a mistake, a clumsy parody. Mirrors and fatherhood are abominable because they multiply and confirm it" (*UH*, 84).

3. Otálora in "The Dead Man" thinks that "just as the men of certain countries worship and feel the call of the sea, we yearn for the boundless plains that ring under the horse's hooves" (*A*, 95); Billy the Kid, too, in his flight west, feels that "the nearness of the elementary earth quickens the heart like the nearness of the sea" (*UH*, 63).

4. Like Tadeo Isidoro Cruz, who one night "saw his own face"

and "understood that the other man was himself" (*A,* 83, 85), Yakub, in "The Mirror of Ink," was able to see that face (the Man with Mask) in the mirror of ink "and understood it was his own" (*UH,* 128).

5. Finally, it should be noticed that the magic lantern, or "Fanusi Jiyal," in "The Mirror of Ink" is a preview of the epiphany glimpsed through the iridescent sphere called the "Aleph" in the story so entitled.

Litotes

Since the stories of infamy are parodic in nature and intent, they employ two devices peculiar to caricature: exaggeration by augmentation and exaggeration by diminution, or overstatement and understatement. In rhetoric, those two devices are called hyperbole and litotes. Because Borges' approach to infamy is not based on moralistic principles, it preserves an imaginative distance aimed at producing irony and at times sarcasm that at the level of style results in hyperbole at the positive pole and litotes at the negative one. Examples of the first from *Universal History:*

1. "Morell contemplated a *continental response, –* a response in *which crime would be exalted to the point of redemption and History*" (*UH,* 27).
2. "Over *this whole country,* another image – that of Billy the Kid, the hard rider firm on his horse, the young man of the harsh pistol shots that *bewildered the desert* sending out *invisible bullets which (like magic) kill at a distance*" (*UH,* 61).
3. Of the Mexican Belisario Villagrán, from the same story, it is said that "*he was overfilled with a gargantuan sombrero*" (translated as "endowed with an immense sombrero" from "abunda en un desaforado sombrero"). But in the previous sentence, the narrator explains, "Someone has come in – a burly Mexican, with *the face of an old Indian woman*" (*UH,* 64).

The hyperbolic description of the Mexican's hat contrasts with the description of his inoffensive face. Hyperbole next to litotes acts like the obverse and the reverse of the same operation: to exaggerate by inflating or by deflating. In both cases, the effect is irony, but while in the first it borders on humor and laughter, in the second the irony is more subtle and at the same time caustic, since the face of an old Indian woman is the face of a killer.

To describe the pirates' excesses and wretchedness in "The Lady Pirate," the narrator says with a beguiling poker face: "Their object is not benevolent; they are not and never were the true friends of the seafarer" (*UH*, 45), after which a violent tirade of hyperboles describes the same activity. To describe the bloody cruelty of the Emperor Kia-king in the same story, he tells us: "Never forget that clemency is an attribute of the Emperor" (*UH*, 46). Other examples:

1. "For each troublemaker *he calmed down*," for "he killed" ("he quelled" is a better translation but loses the artifice [*UH*, 54]).
2. Monk Eastman's gangs of murderers are referred to as "recreative societies" (translated as "sporting clubs" [*UH*, 57]).
3. The encounter between two groups of gangsters that left "four corpses, seven critically wounded men and one dead pigeon" (*UH*, 56) is later alluded to as "the indiscreet battle of Rivington Street" (*UH*, 57).
4. The recalcitrant racism of Billy the Kid is referred to as "the pride of being white" (*UH*, 62).
5. Billy the Kid's enthusiasm for cowboy melodramas is described in the sentence "he was not indifferent to cowboy plays" (*UH*, 62).
6. Suké's refusal to perform hara-kiri is presented as "Suké refused to suppress himself as a gentleman" (translated as "Suké refused to perform hara-kiri" [UH, 56]).
7. Kyoto, the ancient capital of the empire, the heart of Japanese culture and the center of her history, is described as "a city unmatched in all the empire for its autumn colors" (*UH*, 72).
8. Hakim the Masked's unquenchable sexuality, which "114 blind women did their best to satisfy," is referred to as "the needs of his divine body" (*UH*, 83).

It is quite possible that Borges' taste for this figure stems from his fondness for Anglo-Saxon. Litotes appears in *Beowulf* and Old English poetry with such frequency that together with kennings, or *kenningar*, it became a distinguishing mark of that literature. Borges wrote his essay "The Kenningar" in 1932 and included it in *Historia de la eternidad* (1936). It is evident that his stories of infamy, written and published during those years, are contaminated, as far as the prose is concerned, by those verbal games used and abused by kennings. In the story "The Widow Ching, Lady Pirate," the subchapter "The Dragon and the Fox" mentions "shiftless flocks of airy dragons" that "rose each evening from the ships of the imperial squadron and came gently to rest on the enemy decks and surrounding waters" (*UH*, 47). We are told nothing about those "airy dragons" except that they were constructions of paper and strips of reeds and that when their number increased the Widow Pirate surrendered. But in the catalog of *kenningar,* compiled by Borges himself, the dragon is the kenning for sword and for spear. The same text refers to blood as "reddish water," a variant of the kenning "sword's water," and describes the clouds as "yellow dragons." In the last section of the same story, it is said that "from that day, ships regained peace. The four seas and the innumerable rivers became safe and happy *roads*" (*UH,* 48). Two kennings for the sea are "road of the sails" and "the whale's road."

In his essay on *kenningar,* included in *Historia de la eternidad,* Borges defined them as "deceiving and languishing exercises" (*HE,* 64). They are often defined as implied similes in circumlocution for nouns not named. He has also said that "the dead *ultraist* whose ghost still haunts him delights in these verbal games" (*HE,* 66). In the stories of infamy, he has left a testimony of that pleasure through the evocation of a few kennings and the convoluted manner that underlies litotes, thus conveying at the level of style the same playful and parodic approach adopted at the level of vision.

Coda and conclusion

The style of the code of rules drawn up by the Widow Ching, in "The Lady Pirate," is described as "laconic and straightforward, utterly lacking in the faded flowers of rhetoric that lend a rather absurd loftiness to the style of Chinese officialdom" (*UH,* 44). It is the style that Borges himself was striving to find and that he had, to a certain extent, achieved in the stories of infamy. The reference to the "faded flowers of rhetoric" is a clear allusion to the fierce battle he waged against the baroque excess of his time and against his own early abuses of that mannerist style. Remnants of those abuses appear scattered in this first collection – the portrait of Monk Eastman, for example:

> Era un hombre ruinoso y monumental. El pescuezo era corto, como de toro, el pecho inexpugnable, los brazos peleadores y largos, la nariz rota, la cara aunque historiada de cicatrices menos importante que el cuerpo, las piernas chuecas como jinete o de marinero. Podía prescindir de camisa como también de saco, pero no de una galerita rabona sobre la cíclopea cabeza.

> He was a battered, colossal man. He had a short bull neck; a barrel chest; long, scrappy arms; a broken nose; a face, although plentifully scarred, less striking than his frame; and legs bowed

like a cowboy's or a sailor's. He could usually be found without
a shirt or coat, but not without a derby hat several sizes too small
perched on his bullet-shaped head. (*UH*, 54)

Other examples of this overloaded style: "A hunchbacked house by the
water" (*HU*, 66) (translated as "a waterfront dive" [*UH*, 62]); criminals
"pullulate" over their victim (*HU*, 67) (translated as "swarm him" [*UH*,
62]); "Mitford's account leaves out the continuous distractions of local
color" (*UH*, 69); "El incivil maestro de ceremonias le dijo que, en ver-
dad, era incorregible, y que sólo un patán era capaz de frangollar un nudo
tan torpe" (*HU*, 75) (translated as "The rude master of etiquette told him
that, in truth, he was unteachable and that only a boor could tie a knot so
clumsily" [*UH*, 70]).

Yet these few excesses stem more from the excessive nature of the
subjects than from an unruly or merely self-indulgent style. The proof
that this is indeed so is given in the translated pieces included in the last
section of the same volume under the title "Etcetera." Here is a prose
that in its straightforwardness and exactness, its tightness and conciseness, reminds us very much – and strangely – of the "invisible"
prose style of his last two collections: *Doctor Brodie's Report* (1970) and
The Book of Sand (1975).

A Universal History of Infamy not only represents Borges' first attempt
at writing fiction but also anticipates some of the major stylistic features
that will typify his later prose. The changes in ratio and frequency of
those stylistic devices, from this early collection to the later ones, respond to changes in theme and narrative vision: caricature yields to
metaphysical ponderings, laughter to intellectual ruminations. What the
stories of infamy tell us at the level of theme, these figures – metonymy,
oxymoron, and litotes – perform at the level of style. The story as the
summary of another story defines the modus operandi of metonymy;
plot is organized as hyperbole or litotes; characterization is oxymoronic.
Thus, theme and style are just different manifestations of the same literary vision; poetic diction and semantics have been closely intertwined.

NOTES

1 I have paraphrased the passage in which Borges concludes his survey of
   Kafka's precursors: "Kafka's idiosyncrasy, in greater or lesser degree, is present in each of these writings, but if Kafka had not written we would not
   perceive it; that is to say, it would not exist" (*OI*, 113).
2 Scholem, *Major Trends in Jewish Mysticism* (New York: Schocken, 1961), p.
   268.

3 Alonso, *Materia y forma en poesía* (Madrid: Gredos, 1960), p. 345.
4 "Encuentro con Borges" [with James E. Irby], *Vida universitaria* (Monterrey, Mexico), April 12, 1964, pp. 7–16.
5 In addition to the quoted examples, I have found the following ones: "Algunos cometían la ingratitud de enfermarse y morir" (20); "coraje borracho" (7); "una respuesta donde lo criminal se exaltaba hasta la redención y la historia" (27); "miseria insípida" (31); "color rosa tiznado," "Era persona de una sosegada idiotez," "su confusa jovialidad," "pudoroso temor" (32); "insensata ingeniosidad," "inmejorable ignorancia," "Sabía también que todas las similitudes logrades no harían otra cosa que destacar ciertas diferencias inevitables" (35); "plácido fantasma" (37); "Desprovistos de lágrimas y de soledad, pero no de codicia" (38); "[Bogle cruzó] las decorosas calles de Londres [en las que los cascos de un vehículo] la partieron el cráneo" (39); "Para ejercer con dignidad la profesión de pirata" (41); "La golosina fue fatal" (43); "la metódica aventura," "una majestad más bien irrisoria" (44); "y convidan a su víctima a la ruina, a la mutiliación o a la muerte" (47); "fiestas espantosas" (48); "ineptitud gigantesca," "asesinos precoces" (54); "era un hombre ruinoso y monumental"; "el epiceno Capone" (57); "terneras degolladas con rectitud" (56); "los honorarios del malevo: 25 dólares un balazo en una pierna, 25 una puñalada" (58); "la errónea seguridad" (60); "los dos ilustres malevos," "mujeres de frágil peinado monumental" (61); "un gato, desconocedor feliz de la muerte" (63); "el hombre que para el terror y la gloria sería Billy the Kid" (66); "Ve a los hombres *tremendos, felices, odiosamente sabios*" (69; emphasis added); "de esa feliz detonación [que mata a un hombre]" (70); "el hombre más temido (y quizá más nadie y más solo)," "practicó ese lujo, el coraje" (71); "incivil maestro de ceremonias" (73); "espías incorruptibles" (76); "esa pesadilla tan lúcida," "la razón ignominiosa de esas lealtades" (78); "El asco es la virtud fundamental," "Dos disciplinas: la abstinencia y el desenfreno" (90); "Basura venerable" (91).
6 Borges, "Elementos de preceptiva," *Sur* (Buenos Aires), April 7, 1933, pp. 158–61.
7 In addition to the quoted examples, the following appear in the same collection: "río de aguas mulatas" (18); "miedos africanos," "el sórdido Jordán," "cultura impaciente" (for "cultivos de los blancos impacientes"), "el desierto confuso" (20); "efusiones sagradas" (for "efusiones pronunciadas en el lugar sagrado") (22); "calles decorosas de Londres" (for "calles de vida decorosa") (38); "Ciento veinte mujeres que solicitaron el *confuso amparo*" (for "ciento veinte mujeres confundidas"), "las miserables lágrimas" (for "lágrimas de las mujeres miserables"), "Lo cierto es que organizó una segunda expedición *terrible*" becomes "Lo cierto es que organizó una segunda, *terrible* en estandartes, en marineros, en soldados, en pertrechos de guerra, en provisiones, en augures y astrólogos"; "pesada muchedumbre de naves" (for "las naves con esa muchedumbre") (48); "cubiertas enemigas" ("cubiertas de los barcos enemigos") (49); "felices caminos" ("caminos de viajeros felices") (50); "dos compadritos en *seria* ropa negra" ("dos compadritos serios en ropa negra") (53); "el brutal garrote" ("el garrote del malevo brutal") (58); "la brutal

convicción" ("la convicción de los brutales protagonistas"), "el estrépito insensato de cien revólveres" ("el estrépito de cien revólveres disparados por los insensatos protagonistas"), "el combate obsceno o espectral" ("el combate que tiene lugar a esa hora asociada con la abscenidad o los espectros") (60); "su vigilante nube de pistoleros" ("su nube de vigilantes pistoleros") (61); "a la menor impuntualidad del telón" ("la impuntualidad de los que levantaban el telón") (67); "el muerto lujoso" ("el muerto vestido lujosamente") (69); "Aprendió el arte vagabundo de los troperos" ("Aprendió el arte de los troperos vagabundos") (71).

8 I have studied those functions in *La prosa narrativa de Jorge Luis Borges* (Madrid: Gredos, 1974). See the subchapters devoted to metonymy (239–68), oxymoron (223–33), and hypallage (215–23).

PART III
Poetry

8 Outside and inside the mirror in Borges' poetry

In the Preface to his fifth book of poetry – *In Praise of Darkness* – Borges writes: "To the mirrors, mazes, and swords which my resigned reader already foresees, two new themes have been added: old age and ethics."[1] Mirrors are a constant in Borges' poetry, but long before becoming a major theme or motif in his works, mirrors had been for Borges an obsession that goes back to his childhood years. To his friends he has told that as a child he feared that the images reflected on his bedroom mirror would stay there even after darkness had effaced them. For the boy, the images inhabiting mirrors were like the ghosts haunting the castle of a gothic novel – constantly lurking and threatening through ominous darkness.

In the brief piece entitled "The Draped Mirrors" from *Dreamtigers* he reminisces upon those fears: "As a child, I felt before large mirrors that same horror of a spectral duplication or multiplication of reality. Their infallible and continuous functioning, their pursuit of my actions, their cosmic pantomime, were uncanny then, whenever it began to grow dark. One of my persistent prayers to God and my guardian angel was that I not dream about mirrors. I know I watched them with misgivings. Sometimes I feared they might begin to deviate from reality; other times I was afraid of seeing there my own face, disfigured by strange calamities" (*DT,* 27).

One of the earliest references to mirrors appears in the essay "After the Images" originally published in the journal *Proa* in 1924 and later included in his first book of essays, *Inquisiciones* (1925). There he says: "It is no longer enough to say, as most poets have, that mirrors look like water . . . We must overcome such games . . . There ought to be shown a person entering into the crystal and continuing in his illusory country, feeling the shame of not being but a simulacrum that night obliterate and daylight permits" (*I,* 29). This first use of mirrors as the country of simulacra appears also in his first poems. "La Recoleta," from *Fervor of Buenos Aires* (1923), opens with a series of images in which mirrors are just a simile, the vehicle of a comparison which is repeated with the frequency of a linguistic tic. In that poem he says that when "the soul goes out,"

> Space, time and death also go out,
> As when light is no more,
> And the simulacrum of mirrors fade . . .   (*OP*, 20)

In his first volume of poetry and in the next – *Moon Across the Way* (1925) – mirrors are referred to merely on account of their reflective function. The city is "false and crowded / like a garden copied on a mirror." In "El jardín botánico," "each tree is movingly lost / and their lives are confined and rugged / like mirrors that deepen different rooms." In "Ausencia," the reflection on the mirror represents the reflected object: "I shall raise life in its immensity / which even now is your mirror: / stone over stone I shall rebuild it." In other poems, some qualities associated with mirrors are mentioned: the silence of mirrors in "Atardeceres"; their capacity for repetition in "El Paseo de Julio," for multiplication in "Mateo, XXV, 30," and for memory in "El reloj de arena."

These random references meet in the poem "Mirrors" included in *Dreamtigers* (1960). In many ways this poem is a recapitulation of most of the previous motifs. Borges recalls his early fears of mirrors and asks: "What whim of fate / made me so fearful of a glancing mirror." The poem is an attempt to answer that question. A first explanation is its generative power: "They prolong this hollow, unstable world / in their dizzying spider's web." Here Borges reiterates an idea advanced earlier on "Tlön, Uqbar, Orbis Tertius." Facing a spying mirror, Bioy Casares "recalled that one of the heresiarchs of Uqbar had declared that mirrors and copulation are abominable, because they increase the number of men" (*L*, 3). And in the poem he writes:

> I see them as infinite, elemental
> Executors of an ancient pact,
> To multiply the world like the act
> Of begetting. Sleepless, Bringing doom.   (*DT*, 60)

A second answer to the same question defines mirrors as "a mute theater" of reflections where "everything happens and nothing is recorded," and where the Other breaks in:

> Claudius, king of an afternoon, a dreaming king,
> Did not feel he was a dream until the day

When an actor showed the world his crime
In a tableau, silently in mime.   (*DT*, 61)

This last stanza brings to mind that memorable idea formulated in the essay "Partial Enchantments of the *Quixote*," where Borges wrote:

> Why does it make us uneasy to know that the map is within the map and the thousand and one nights are within the book of *A Thousand and One Nights*? Why does it disquiet us to know that Don Quixote is a reader of the *Quixote*, and Hamlet is a spectator of *Hamlet*? I believe I have found the answer: those inversions suggest that if the characters in a story can be readers or spectators, then we, their readers or spectators, can be fictitious. (*OI*, 48)

In a similar fashion, the poem "Mirrors" concludes:

> God has created nighttime, which he arms
> With dreams, and mirrors, to make clear
> To man he is a reflection and a mere
> Vanity. Therefore these alarms.   (*DT*, 61)

Here we get much closer to the ultimate meaning of mirrors in Borges' poetry. That illusory reality that mirrors produce becomes in turn a profound mirror of our own universe since our image of the world is just a fabrication of the human mind. The world as we know it is that illusory image produced on the mirror of culture, "that artificial universe in which we live as members of a social group."[2] Mirrors, like the map within the map, like Don Quixote reader of the *Quixote*, and like Hamlet spectator of *Hamlet*, suggest that our intellectual version of reality is not different from that "ungraspable architecture / reared by every dawn from the gleam / of a mirror, by darkness from a dream."

Mirrors and dreams have for Borges an interchangeable value. In the poem "Spinoza," for instance, the lens grinder "dreams up a clear labyrinth – / undisturbed by fame, that reflection / of dreams in the dream of another / mirror . . .", and more explicitly in the poem "Sarmiento" where dreaming is tantamount to "looking at a magic crystal." Borges has pointed out that "according to the doctrine of the Idealists, the verbs *to live* and *to dream* are strictly synonyms" (*L*, 164). A more transcendental significance of mirrors in Borges' poetry should emerge, thus, from a syllogistic transposition of the terms *life*, *dream* and *mirror*. If *life* is a *dream* Somebody is dreaming, and dreams are, as stated in the poem "The Dream," "reflections of the shadow / that daylight deforms in its *mirrors*," life is, consequently, not less illusory than the images reflected on the surface of the mirrors. In the poem "The Golem," the dummy is the dream of a Rabbi who in turn is the dream of a god who in turn is the dream of another god and so on *ad infinitum* as suggested in "The Circular Ruins." Yet, it should be noted that the Rabbi's golem is described as "a simulacrum," as "a distressing son" and as "a symbol," and that all these terms have been used before in relation to mirrors. In the Rabbi's lamentations as he gazes on his imperfect son – "To an infinite series why was it for me / to add another symbol? To the vain / hank that is spun out in Eternity / another cause and effect, another pain?" – there is an unequivocal echo of the "multiplying and abdominable power of mirrors." On the other hand, in the poem "Everness" the universe is but the mirror of a total memory: God. God, in another poem entitled "He," "is each of the creatures of His strange world: / the stubborn roots of the profound / cedar and the mutations of the moon." God is, in addition, "the eyes that examine / a reflection (man) and the mirror's eyes." Also Emmanuel Swedenborg knew, according to the poem so entitled, "like the Greek, that the days / of time are Eternity's mirrors."

The notion that the whole of Creation is but a reflection of a Divine power is more clearly defined in the short stories. In "The Aleph," for example, Borges writes that "for the Kabbalah, the Aleph stands for the *En Soph,* the pure and boundless godhead; it is also said that it takes the shape of a man pointing to both heaven and earth, in order to show that the lower world is the map and mirror of the higher." And, in a more condensed manner, in "The Theologians": "In the *Zohar,* it is written that the higher world is a reflection of the lower," and once again in "the Zahir": "The Kabbalists understood that man is a microcosm, a symbolic mirror of the universe; according to Tennyson, everything would be." The pertinence of these quotations to our subject lies in the value conceded to reality as a reflection and the notion that such reflections contains a secret order inaccessible to men. Our reality, says Borges (our reality as codified by culture), is made of mirror images, appearances that reflect vaguely the Other, or, more precisely, as the sect of the Histrionics sustains in "The Theologians":

> To demonstrate that the earth influences heaven they invoked Matthew, and I Corinthians 13:12 ("for now we see through a glass, darkly") to demonstrate that everything we see is false. Perhaps contaminated by the Monotones, they imagined that all men are two men and that the real one is *the other,* the one in heaven. They also imagined that our acts project an inverted reflection, in such a way that if we are awake, the other sleeps, if we fornicate, the other is chaste, if we steal, the other is generous. When we die, we shall join *the other* and be him. (*L,* 123)

Borges' short stories and poems are full of characters and people searching for *the other*, for the source of the inverted reflection. Laprida, in "Conjectural Poem," "who longed to be someone else" finds *the other* "in one night's mirror" when he can finally "comprehend his unsuspected true face." The idea of this life as a composite of reflections whose source is *the other* appears even more clearly in the poem devoted to López Merino's suicide included in the collection *In Praise of Darkness* (1969). There he says:

> The mirror awaits him.
> He will smooth back his hair, adjust his tie (as fits a
> young poet, he was always a bit of a dandy), and
> try to imagine that the other man – the one in the
> mirror – performs the actions and that he, the double,
> repeats them. . .   (*PD*, 41-3)

Even about himself Borges has written in the poem "Junín": "I am myself but I am also the other, the dead one" (*SP*, 211).

Mirrors are thus defined as the residence of the other. Life outside the mirror, by contrast, surfaces as a reflection, as a dream, and as a theater. Sometimes the reader witnesses a dialogue between the simulacrum outside the mirror and the other inside the glass. Among those poems, none has dramatized in such a definite manner that old dialogue between the two Borgeses that reverberates throughout his work as "El centinela" (The Sentry) included in *El oro de los tigres* (1972):

> Light comes in and I remember: he's there.
> He begins by telling me his name which is (clearly) mine.
> I come back to a slavery that has lasted more than seven times
>   ten years.
> He imposes his memory on me.
> He imposes the everyday miseries, the human condition on me.
> I am his old male nurse; he forces me to wash his feet.
> He lies in wait for me in mirrors, in the mahogony, in store
>   windows.
> One or two women have rejected him and I must share his grief.
> Now he is dictating this poem to me, which I don't like.
> He requires me to undertake the hazy apprenticeship of stubborn
>   Anglo-Saxon.
> He has converted me to the idolatrous cult of military dead men,
>   with whom I could perhaps not exchange a single word.
> On the last step of the staircase I feel that he is by my side.

He is in my steps, in my voice.
I hate him thoroughly.
I notice with pleasure that he can barely see.
I am in a circular cell and the infinite wall gets tighter.
Neither of us fools the other, but we both lie.
We know each other too well, inseparable brother.
You drink water from my cup and you devour my bread.
The door of suicide is open, but the theologians affirm that in
    the ulterior shadow of the other kingdom, I will be there,
    waiting for myself.[3]

The reader notices without much effort that "The Sentry" is a reenactment of the piece "Borges and Myself" from *Dreamtigers*. Both texts are part of an exchange between Borges the writer and Borges the man, between "a man who lives and lets himself live" and "the other who weaves his tales and poems," between one condemned to his inexorable destiny as writer and one who from the depth of a mirror paces equally inexorably toward his "secret center." In both texts the voice comes from an intimate Borges who watches the other as though one were the audience in a theater and the other an actor on stage, but whereas in the prose the exchange takes place between Borges the writer and the other who simply lives, in the poem the exchange is much less symmetric. The confrontation is not between the writer and the man. There is no confrontation, but rather reflections voiced by a person who has reached seventy and contemplates, in the manner of Kohelet, his life and the miseries of the human condition. This Borges, profoundly intimate, looks at the other as a sentry and examines this sentry's visible and public life as a fiction or a theatrical representation. To define life as a dream presupposes the notion that with death we shall wake up from that dream; to define the world as a stage implies the idea of a spectator who will applaud or boo when the show is over. Likewise, there is an obverse of the mirror that reproduces and multiplies, that dreams and gesticulates, and there is reverse from whose depths the other – the awake one and the spectator – watches us. The ultimate meaning of mirrors in Borges' poetry lies in that reverse, dwelling of the other, house of the self. "Ars Poetica" has masterfully expressed this meaning:

At times in the evening a face
Looks at us out of the depths of a mirror;
Art should be like that mirror
Which reveals to us our own face.   (*SP*, 143)

Of the various significations that mirrors propose throughout Borges' poetry this is, beyond any doubt, the most transcending and the richest in suggestions. In a strict sense, we are dealing with the mirror of poetry as a road of access to the other, with literature as a bridge between the visible side of the mirror and the other side which poets of all times have always tried to reach. There is a mirror that "melts away, just like a bright silvery mist" so that the poet, like Lewis Carroll's Alice, may go through the glass and jump into the other side – the looking-glass room of fantasy; and to such a mirror Borges refers in the poem devoted to Edgar Allan Poe:

> As if on the wrong side of the mirror,
> He yielded, solitary, to his rich
> Fate of fabricating nightmares. . .   (*SP*, 173)

But the mirror that in the last analysis Borges vindicates as a vehicle of art is the one "which reveals to us our own face." In the context of *Dreamtiger's* Epilogue, it is clear that the face he alludes to is a symbolic face which, like a cipher, encodes the destiny of the writer. It is this writer who "shortly before his death discovers that that patient labyrinth of lines (his writings) traces the image of his face" (*DT*, 93).

The poem "Oedipus and the Riddle" also adheres to this same meaning. Borges had already reviewed the myth of Oedipus and the Sphinx in *The Book of Imaginary Beings*. There he explains:

> It is told that the Sphinx depopulated the Theban countryside asking riddles and making a meal of any man who could not give the answer. Of Oedipus the Sphinx asked: "What has four legs, two legs, and three legs, and the more legs it has the weaker it is?" Oedipus answered that it was a man who as an infant crawls on all four, when he grows up walks on two legs, and in old age leans on a staff. (*BIB*, 211–12)

With these materials Borges makes his poem:

> At dawn four-footed, at midday erect,
> And wandering on three legs in the deserted
> Spaces of afternoon, thus the eternal
> Sphinx had envisioned her changing brother
> Man, and with afternoon there came a person
> Deciphering, appalled at the monstrous other
> Presence in the mirror, the reflection
> Of his decay and of his destiny.
> We are Oedipus; in some eternal way
> We are the long and threefold beast as well—
> All that we will be, all that we have been.
> It would annihilate us all to see

> The huge shape of our being; mercifully
> God offers us issue and oblivion.   (*SP*, 191)

In the monstrous image of the Sphinx, Oedipus recognizes his own destiny and that of all man, and Borges adds: "It would annihilate us all to see / the huge shape of our being." But the poet inevitably looks for "the shape of his being," and his written work is but the mirror where he will see his face, and in it the total image of his fate. But such a moment, similar to a revelation, comes "shortly before death." One of Borges' most personal and intense poems, "In Praise of Darkness," celebrates old age and darkness as forms of happiness; in the last lines he returns to the same idea presented in "Oedipus and the Riddle" but now in order to tell us that if art is "the imminence of a revelation that is not yet produced" (*OI*, 4) it is so because that last line to be traced by a hand stronger than any destiny (Death) is still missing:

> From south and east and west and north,
> roads coming together have led me
> to my secret center.
> These roads were footsteps and echoes,
> women, men, agonies, rebirths,
> days and nights,
> daydreams and dreams,
> each single moment of my yesterdays
> and the world's yesterdays,
> the firm sword of the Dane and the moon
>   of the Persian,
> the deeds of the dead,
> shared love, words,
> Emerson, and snow, and so many things.
> Now I can forget them. I reach my center,
> my algebra and my key,
> my mirror.
> Soon I shall know who I am.   (*PD*, 125–7)

Only with death the patient labyrinth of lines that represents the writer's work is completed; only with death the labryinth yields its key and reveals its center; and only with death it becomes possible to cross and jump into the mirror and join the other, a way of saying that only then a revelation finally occurs as the outer image from this side of the mirror encounters its counterpart on the other side, looks at the shape of his being, and discovers who he is.

NOTES

1 J. L. Borges, *In Praise of Darkness* (Tr. by Norman Thomas di Giovanni). New York, Dutton, 1974, p. 10.
2 Claude Lévi-Strauss, *Arte, lenguaje, etnología* (Entrevistas de Georges Charbonnier), México, Siglo Veintiuno, 1968, pp. 131–132.
3 I thank my friend and colleague Willis Barnstone for having produced under rather unfavorable conditions this English translation of "El centinela."

9 Enumerations as evocations: on the use of a device in Borges' late poetry

Enumerations in literature are as old as the Old Testament, but in modern times they have achieved the status of an established rhetorical device only since the writings of Walt Whitman. Such are the conclusions of Detlev W. Schumann and Leo Spitzer, two critics who have studied enumerations in contemporary poetry. Spitzer summarized his findings in a well known essay entitled "Chaotic Enumerations in Modern Poetry."[1] There he says: "All seems to indicate that we owe chaotic enumerations as a poetic device to Whitman."[2] In a different essay devoted to Whitman, Spitzer defines the device as "consisting of lumping together things spiritual and physical, as the raw material of our rich, but unordered modern civilization which is made to resemble an oriental bazaar. . . ."[3] If enumerations have been, until Whitman, one of the most effective means of describing the perfection of the created world in praise of its Creator, it was Whitman's task to render that same perfection and unity into attributes of our chaotic modern world."[4] Whitman did not invent the device, but he used it with such intensity and skill that his poetry became a showcase of the rich possibilities offered by the device for poets who succeeded him. In Spanish America, Darío and Neruda were deeply influenced by Whitman and his enumerative style. So was Borges, who wrote about Whitman and on enumerations as early as 1929.

In a short note entitled "The Other Whitman," he argued that Europeans misread Whitman: "They turned him into the forerunner of many provincial inventors of free verse. The French aped the most vulnerable part of his diction: the complaisant geographic, historic, and circumstantial enumerations strung by Whitman to fulfill Emerson's prophecy about a poet worthy of America."[5] Borges viewed enumerations and free verse – at that time – as foundations of European avant-garde poet-

116

ry. "Those imitations," he concluded caustically, "were and are the whole of today's French poetry."[6] He then added, on the subject of enumerations, "many of them didn't even realize that enumeration is one of the oldest poetic devices – think of the Psalms in the Scriptures, and of the first chorus of *The Persians,* and the Homeric catalogue of the ships –, and that its intrinsic merit it not its length but its delicate verbal balance. Walt Whitman didn't ignore that."[7]

Almost fifty years later, in a footnote to his latest collection of poems, *La cifra,* Borges restated the same notion. Referring to the poem "A-quél," he wrote, "this composition, like almost all the others, abuses chaotic enumerations. Of this figure, in which Walt Whitman abounded with so much felicity, I can only say that it should impress us as chaos, as disorder, and be, at the same time, a cosmos, an order."[8] There are three elements here that need to be emphasized. The first is that Borges adopts in 1981 the term coined, or rather divulged, by Spitzer as it was used earlier by Schumann. Raimundo Lida translated Spitzer's article into Spanish and it was published in Buenos Aires in 1945. It is presumable that Borges read it, but he didn't have to, since the term has become part of our literary jargon and we use it familiarly, unaware of our debt to either Schumann or Spitzer. What matters is that this is the first reference Borges makes to the device under the name of "chaotic enumerations."

The second point is that Borges emphasizes the idea of order in the guise of chaos underlying the effectiveness of chaotic enumerations in Whitman. This is the very core of Spitzer's definition: "Whitman's catalogues," he says, "present a mass of heterogeneous things integrated, however, in a majestic and grand vision of All-One."[9]

The third and last point is Borges' explicit recognition that his last collection, *La cifra,* abuses chaotic enumerations. He is right. Although enumerations appear already in his early collections, and reappear throughout his entire poetic work, the device is considerably more frequent in his latest book. Following is an attempt to track the course of enumerations in Borges' poetry, and an effort to define the implications of the device in the development of his art.

For a writer who has been an early reader and admirer of Whitman, who has written several essays on him, who has acknowledged his debt to Whitman in numerous texts, early and late, and who has (more recently) translated *Leaves of Grass* into Spanish, it is not at all surprising to find in Borges' own poetry the use and abuse of enumerations. They appear as early as 1925 in his collection *Luna de enfrente,* in such poems as "Los Llanos," "Dualidá en una despedida," "Al coronel Francisco Borges," "La promisión en alta mar," "Mi vida entera," and "Versos de catorce." With the exception of "Mi vida entera" ("My Whole Life"), these poems use enumerations either partially or for the rhythmic element performed by a repeated word or anaphora. What sets "My Whole Life" aside from the others in his early poetry is the use of enumerations in a manner that will become characteristic of his later work. Note the poem in a translation by W. S. Merwin:

> Here once again the memorable lips, unique and like yours.
> I am this groping intensity that is a soul.
> I have got near to happiness and have stood in the shadow
>   of suffering.
> I have crossed the sea.
> I have known many lands; I have seen one woman and two
>   or three men.
> I have loved a girl who was fair and proud, and bore a
>   Spanish quietness.
> I have seen the city's edge, an endless sprawl where the
>   sun goes down tirelessly, over and over.
> I have relished many words.
> I believe deeply that this is all, and that I will neither see
>   nor accomplish new things.
> I believe that my days and my nights, in their poverty and
>   their riches, are the equal of God's and of all men's.[10]

With the years, the list will become longer, the lines shorter, the voice deeper, the tone calmer, but the effort to survey his whole life through enumerations will remain the same.

But what exactly do enumerations enumerate in poetry? In the case of Whitman, they list the diversity or even chaos of a country, time, or people, in order to cluster that diversity into a unity: the poem renders that oriental bazaar of our unordered civilization – in the words of Spitzer – into "the powerful Ego, the 'I' of the poet, who has extricated himself from the chaos."[11] This is not the use Borges makes of enumerations. In his second essay on Whitman, he comments on this use of enumerations reminiscent of the holy texts found in most religions: "Pantheism," he writes, "has disseminated a variety of phrases which declare that God is several contradictory or (even better) miscellaneous things." He then brings up examples from the *Gita,* Heraclitus, Plotinus, and the Sufi poet Attar, and concludes: "Whitman renovated that device. He did not use it, as others had, to define the divinity or to play with the 'sympathies and differences' of words; he wanted to identify himself, in a sort of ferocious tenderness, with all men."[12] Borges himself has employed this particular type of enumeration, proper to pantheism, in his fiction, in the description of divine visions or theophanies in stories like

"The Aleph," "The Zahir," and "The God's Script," but not in his poetry.

There is another use of enumerations. It is best summarized by Whitman himself toward the end of his essay "A Backward Glance Over Traveled Roads" when he writes, "*Leaves of Grass* indeed has mainly been the outcropping of my own emotional and personal nature – an attempt from first to last, to put a *Person,* a human being (myself, in the latter half of the 19th Cent., in America) freely, fully and truly *on record.*"[13] But for Whitman to put a human being on record was to write about Humanity and Nature, History and Politics, America and Sex, or, as he says elsewhere, "to sing the land, the people and the circumstances of the United States, to express their autochtonous song and to define their material and political success."[14]

Borges shares this task of poetry ("to articulate in poetic form my own physical, emotional, moral, intellectual and aesthetic Personality," in Whitman's words), but in a much more modest and restricted way. Compared to the cosmic world of Whitman, Borges' poetry is an intimate environment inhabited by sunsets and cityscapes, streets and outskirts, authors and books, branches of his family tree, Argentine heroes and counter-heroes, obsessions and mythologies, metaphysical and literary reflections, Old English and Germanic sagas, time, blindness, memory, oblivion, old age, love, friendship and death. There is no need to reconcile these two different perceptions of poetry belonging to Whitman and Borges, the question is rather how to explain the latter's admiration for the former.

In the preface to *Elogio de la sombra* he wrote, "I once strove after the vast breath of the psalms and of Walt Whitman."[15] And in his poem "Buenos Aires," from the same collection, he writes: "Buenos Aires is a tall house in the South of the city, where my wife and I translated Whitman whose great echo, I hope, reverberates in this page."[16] And again in the preface to *El otro, el mismo* he insisted, "In some of these poems, Whitman's influence will be – I hope – noticed."[17] That Whitmanesque "vast breath" is present, paradoxically, in poems where enumerations convey intimate evocations of the poet's personal past, as in his early poem "My Whole Life," written in 1925. Another example, chronologically, of this type of intimate evocation is the second of the "Two English Poems" written in 1934. Like the previous one, this too is a sort of family album in which the most significant experiences and events of the poet's personal life are recorded: desperate sunsets, lean streets, ragged suburbs, a lonely moon, his grandfather killed on the frontier of Buenos Aires, his great-grandfather heading a charge of three hundred men in Peru, the memory of a yellow rose, books, explanations, theories, the poet's loneliness, darkness, and his heart. The poem can be read, indeed, as a microcosm of his entire poetic work; most of his major themes and motifs are spun in this early cocoon.

What needs to be pointed out, though, is that this poem typifies the kind of enumerations that will be predominant in later poetry. There is no chaos here, in the sense used by Spitzer, as an expression of modern world disorder. There is a random survey of experiences we call chaotic enumerations, but the chaos refers mainly to the nature of the presentation rather than to the disorder of the representation (be that a country, a civilization, or the world). Borges too strives "to put a person on record," but not, as in Whitman's case, in the crucial latter half of the nineteenth century, during the rise of America as a world power, but in a very familiar time and in a place that is perceived more in personal than in historical terms.

Enumerations in which the specified material belongs to a strictly intimate space and a highly personal time may be illustrated by this passage:

> Stars, bread, libraries of East and West,
> Playing cards, chessboards, galleries, skylights, cellars,
> A human body to walk with on the earth,
> Fingernails, growing at nighttime and in death,
> Shadows for forgetting, mirrors busily multiplying,
> Cascades in music, gentlest of all time's shapes,
> Borders of Brazil, Uruguay, horses and mornings,
> A bronze weight, a copy of the Grettir Saga,
> Algebra and fire, the charge at Junín in your blood,
> Days more crowded than Balzac, scent of the honeysuckle,
> Love and the imminence of love and intolerable remembering,
> Dreams like buried treasure, generous luck,
> And memory itself. . . All this was given to you. . .[18]

This scrutiny of things past and present comes from "Matthew XXV:30" written in 1953. It is a recasting, slightly modified, of the enumeration put forth in the second "English Poem" of 1934, which in turn rewrites the earlier inventory recorded in "My Whole Life" of 1925. They are not the same poem: each one has a different intent and a different tone suitable to that intent. In the first, the emphasis is on the admission that, as the poem declares, "this is all, and I will neither see nor accomplish new things," a lucid anticipation, in 1925, of Borges' basic approach to writing as rewriting. The second is a love poem, and in it the poet's life is inscribed through its most memorable assets to be offered, as a trophy, to the beloved one: "I am trying to bribe you with uncertainty, with danger, with defeat."[19] The third poem recounts those same items, concluding: "You have used up the years and they have used up you / And still, and still, you have not written the poem."[20]

The evocation of those chosen moments or things or people will be repeated throughout Borges' entire poetic work, although never in quite the same way. Specifically it will appear in the poems "Somebody," "Elegy," and "Another Poem of Gifts." In some cases, the poem enumerates not the things that life gave the poet but those it didn't – poems about gifts not received, like "Limits," expanded into "An Elegy of the Impossible Memory," and tried once again in "Things That Might Have Been." In other poems, there are just inventories of things dear to the poet's memory, like "The Things," reenacted in "Things," and repeated once again in "Inventory." In poems like "The Threatened One" and "To the Sad One," personal things and interests are listed together. There are also poems whose enumerations are intended to give not a portrayal of the poet but of somebody else, or of animals, places, countries, cultures, books, or questions, such as "Descartes," "The Righteous Ones," "The Orient," "Israel," "Buenos Aires," "Iceland," "The Islam," "England," "A Thousand and One Nights," and "Insomnia." Finally, in a poem like "John I:4" the enumeration foregoes the particulars and concentrates on the abstract side of gifts from life.

But the more interesting and the more relevant to this study are those instances of enumeration addressed to a survey of the poet's life. In addition to those already mentioned, the following should be added: "I," "I Am," "Talismans," "The Thing I Am," "A Saturday," "The Causes," "The Maker," "Yesterdays," and "Fame." What pertains to the first three poems applies to these also; each has its own focus, its own inflection and tone. Yet all share the condition of enumeration as a means of evoking the poet's past and reflecting upon his present. The theme is recast, again and again, each time to strike a different chord, a different poem. The method was essentially set forth in that early poem of 1925; time completed it, skill refined it. The early hesitant and elementary lyrics evolved into the perfection and complexity of Borges' later poetry in which we hear the same intrinsic melody, but the music now has the balance, the harmony and serenity that befit a master.

A final and concluding remark. Borges' penchant for summaries is proverbial. He has insisted that "to write vast books is a laborious nonsense" and suggested that "a better course is to pretend that those books already exist and then offer a summary, a commentary."[21] Such a tendency applies to his poetry as well. The poems mentioned as examples of enumerations are summaries of the poet's major themes and motifs, indexes of his poetic production, or metonymies of his main subjects. His ancestors' battles and deaths, splendidly sung in numerous poems, are now resolved in a single and slim line: "I am the memory of a sword." His entire poetic endeavor is compressed into a single verse: "I have woven a certain hendecasyllable," and the plots and counter-plots of his fiction are encapsulated in a terse line from the poem "Fame": "I have only retold ancient stories." There is no need for more. Borges, the master of metonymy, understands that having constructed a literary world of his own, an artful intimation suffices.

I also believe that this type of enumeration expresses his long held notion that "memory is best fulfilled through oblivion." Everything must be forgotten so that a few words remain. But those few words, in turn, condense and contain everything – personal Alephs, indeed. Oblivion thus becomes the ultimate realization of memory: "Viviré de olvidarme": "I shall live out of forgetting about myself," he says. What is left is an echo, a trace, a single line, the wake of a long journey that the poem proceeds to compile.

NOTES

1 Leo Spitzer, *Lingüística e historia literaria* (Madrid: Gredos, 1961): 245–291. Second edition.
2 Spitzer, *Lingüística*, 258.
3 Leo Spitzer, "Explication de Text." Applied to Walt Whitman's poem "Out of the Cradle Endlessly Rocking." Included in *Essays on English and American Literature* (Princeton University Press, 1962): 23.
4 Spitzer, *Lingüística*, 261.
5 Jorge Luis Borges, "El otro Whitman." Included in *Discusión* (Buenos Aires: Emecé, 1957): 52. My own translation.
6 Borges, "El otro Whitman," 52.
7 Borges, "El otro Whitman," 52.
8 Jorge Luis Borges, *La cifra* (Buenos Aires: Emecé, 1981): 105.
9 Spitzer, *Lingüística*, 258.
10 Jorge Luis Borges, *Selected Poems 1923–1967*. Edited by Norman Thomas di Giovanni. (New York: Delacorte Press, 1972): 43.
11 Spitzer, "Explication de Text," 22.
12 Jorge Luis Borges, "Note on Walt Whitman." Included in *OI*, 73–4.
13 Walt Whitman, "A Backward Glance o'er Travel'd Roads." Included in *Leaves of Grass, Authoritative Texts, Prefaces, Whitman on His Art, Criticism* (New York: A Norton Critical Edition, 1973): 573–4.
14 Whitman, "Backward Glance," 574.
15 Borges, *ES*, 11.
16 Borges, *ES*, 128.

17 Borges, *OM*, 11.
18 Borges, *SP*, 93.
19 Borges, *OM*, 18.
20 Borges, *SP*, 93.
21 Borges, *F*, 11.

10 Language as a musical organism: Borges' later poetry

From his early poems of the twenties to his later collection *Historia de la noche* (A History of the Night, 1977), Borges' poetry has traveled a long way. It first moved from a nostalgic rediscovery of his birthplace, Buenos Aires, to a cult of his ancestors and an intimate history of his country: heroes, anti-heroes, counter-heroes. He then found that metaphysical subjects, literary artifacts, and religious myths were not unworthy material for poetry: "The Cyclical Night," "Poem Written in a Copy of Beowulf," and "The Golem" are samples which illustrate this later period. His perception of poetry in those years could be defined, in T. S. Eliot's dictum, "not as a turning loose of emotions, but as an escape from emotion: not as the expression of personality, but as an escape from personality." A reflective and ruminative poetry. His ruminations were not about the fortunes or misfortunes of the heart, or existential angst, or the conundrum of life, but about the monuments of the imagination, and particularly those of literature: intellect as passion, culture as the true adventure, knowledge as invention. A rather selfless poetry, a poetry in which the most powerful presence of the self is found in its absence.

A grandson and great-grandson of military heroes, Borges turned his poetry into an epic exploration by evoking everything poetry can possibly evoke other than his own personal drama. In his more recent poetry this drama is defined as a lack of personal drama. Borges muses relentlessly and painfully about his life devoid of heroic violence: "Soy . . . el que no fue una espada en la guerra" (I am that who did not wield a sword in battle) "Yo, que padecí la vergüenza / de no haber sido aquel Fransisco Borges que murió en 1874" (I, who suffered the shame / of not having been that Francisco Borges who died in 1874) (*RP,* 83).

124

Estoy ciego. He cumplido los setenta;
No soy el oriental Francisco Borges
Que murió con dos balas en el pecho,
Entre las agonías de los hombres,
En el hedor de un hospital de sangre. . .   (*RP*, 107)

I am blind, and I have lived out seventy years.
I am not Francisco Borges the Uruguayan
who died with a brace of bullets in his breast
among the final agonies of men
in the death-stench of a hospital of blood. . .   (*GT*, 79)

Soy también la memoria de una espada   (*RP*, 13)

I am also the memory of a sword   (*GT*, 49)

Since he is denied a sword, he turns poetry into a sword; since epic action
has been ruled out of his life, he converts poetry into an epic exercise:

Déjame, espada, usar contigo el arte;
Yo, que no he merecido manejarte.   (*RP*, 45)

Let me, sword, render you in art;
I, who did not deserve to wield you.

How did he accomplish this? By effacing himself from his own poetry,
by speaking of everybody but forgetting about himself. Borges has said
of Bernard Shaw that "he is the only writer of our time who has imagined and presented heroes to his readers," and he explains further:

> On the whole, modern writers tend to reveal men's weaknesses
> and seem to delight in their unhappiness; in Shaw's case, howev-
> er, we have characters who are heroic and whom one can ad-
> mire. Contemporary literature since Dostoevsky – and even
> earlier – since Byron – seems to delight in man's guilt and
> weaknesses. In Shaw's work the greatest human virtues are ex-
> tolled. For example, that a man can forget his own fate, that a
> man may not value his own happiness, that he may say like our
> Almafuerte: "I am not interested in my own life," because he is
> interested in something beyond personal circumstances.[2]

Here we find a first explanation of the seemingly impersonal quality of
his poetry; yet what Borges defends is not impersonality but an epic
sense of life. The poet disregards his own tribulations to become the
singer of virtues, values, people, and literary works dear to him. Haunted by the memories of his ancestors' "romantic death," Borges cele-

brates the courage of heroes and knife fighters ready to die in defense of a cause or belief more precious than their own life. Since he is denied an epic destiny on the battlefield, he will turn literature into his own battlefield by refusing to speak about himself, by lending his voice to others. This epic attitude has been deliberate, and it stems from his family background as well as from the fact that, as he put it, "my father's library has been the capital event in my life":[3] books as events, intellection as life, past as present, literature as passion.

Until 1964. That year Borges published a sonnet entitled "1964" with which he inaugurated a new theme in his poetry. To what he has called his "habits" – "Buenos Aires, the cult of my ancestors, the study of old Germanic languages, the contradiction of time"[4] – he now adds his broodings over what can be called a vocation for unhappiness. The sonnet opens with the line "Ya no seré feliz. Tal vez no importa" (I shall no longer be happy. Perhaps it doesn't matter) (*OM*, 175), a motif that appears and reappears in his last four collections between 1969 and 1976,[5] and culminates in the 1976 sonnet "Remordimiento" (Remorse), included in *La moneda de hierro* (The Iron Coin):

> He cometido el peor de los pecados
> Que un hombre puede cometer. No he sido
> Feliz. Que los glaciares del olvido
> Me arrastren y me pierdan, despiadados.
> Mis padres me engendraron para el juego
> Arriesgado y hermoso de la vida,
> Para la tierra, el agua, el aire, el fuego.
> Los defruadé. No fui feliz. Cumplida
> No fue su joven voluntad. Mi mente
> Se aplicó a las simétricas porfías
> Del arte, que entreteje naderías.
> Me legaron su valor. No fui valiente.
> No me abandona. Siempre está a mi lado
> La sombra de haber sido un desdichado.　　　　　(*MH*, 89)

> I have committed the worst sin of all
> That a man can commit. I have not been
> Happy. Let the glaciers of oblivion
> Drag me and mercilessly let me fall.
> My parents bred and bore me for a higher
> Faith in the human game of nights and days:
> For earth, for air, for water, and for fire.
> I let them down. I wasn't happy. My ways
> Have not fulfilled their youthful hope. I gave
> My mind to the symmetric stubbornness

Of art, and all its webs of pettiness.
They willed me bravery. I wasn't brave.
It never leaves my side, since I began:
This shadow of having been a brooding man.   (*MEP*, 607)

I have dealt with and elaborated on this subject,[6] and I won't repeat myself. It will suffice to say that Borges' treatment of this intimate side of his life has little to do with romantic confessionalism, or with yielding to the same weakness he earlier condemned in modern literature. If he now breaks the silence about himself and tells us about his unhappiness, he does so without self-pity, without tears or pathos, simply by acknowledging it as a fact, or rather, as a sin. The poem represents the acceptance of that sin as guilt, and throughout the poem he assumes this sin of unhappiness with the same poise and endurance with which epic heroes accept defeat. He breaks the diffidence of his previous poetry without outcries, almost restating his early selflessness, since his misfortune, his having been unhappy, is not a torment one mourns over but a sin one must accept quietly or even expiate, or perhaps sublimate in the silence of a verse. "One destiny," he wrote in "The Life of Tadeo Isidoro Cruz," "is no better than another, but every man must obey the one he carries within him" (*A*, 85). Such is the spirit of his own acceptance: a heroic stamina that welcomes triumph and adversity with equal courage.

His later collection of poems – *Historia de la noche* – adds yet new paths into the elusive territory of his intimacy. The accomplished writer, the celebrated poet, the man who welcomes love and death with equal resignation and joy, feels now that decorum could also be an expression of vanity, that modesty in the face of death is but another form of pettiness blocking total reconciliation. The circle of life closes in, unhappiness no longer matters, and a mundane virtue matters even less. Borges seeks oblivion, but since oblivion is a privilege denied to his memory, he backtracks through its meanders, paths, and deep chambers:

A veces me da miedo la memoria.
En sus cóncavas grutas y palacios
(Dijo San Agustín) hay tantas cosas.
El infierno y el cielo están en ellas.   (*HN*, 87)

Sometimes I fear memory.
In its concave grottoes and palaces
(Said Saint Augustine) there are so many things.
Hell and Heaven lie there.

There is no way out of memory but death:

Soy el que sabe que no es más que un eco,
El que quiere morir enteramente.   (*HN*, 120)

I am he who knows he is but an echo,
The one who wants to die completely.

Two elements set *Historia de la noche* apart from his previous collections: a restrained celebration of love, and a serene acceptance of everything life brings, for better or for worse, including the imminence of death. Not that the old motifs or "habits" are missing here; they are present but in a different way. They are part of his indefatigable memory, and as such they inevitably reappear: tigers, mirrors, books, dreams, time, ancestors, friends, authors, knives, cities, and countries. The manner in which these motifs enter into the poem has changed. "El tigre" (The Tiger), for example, is an evocation of the animal that fascinates Borges as an obsession of his childhood, for its beauty, and because it brings reverberations of Blake, Hugo, and Share Kahn. Yet the last line reads: "We thought it was bloody and beautiful. Norah, a girl, said: It is made for love" (HN, 35). This last line makes the difference, and gives the poem an unexpected twist. The recalled anecdote – a visit to the Palermo Zoo – was an old strand in his memory, but only now has its true momentum been recaptured, only now does the tiger's face of love surface and overshadow all previous faces to mirror the author's own. In no other book of poems has Borges allowed himself to deal with love with such freedom and with a distance which ultimately is the condition of love's magic. "Un escolio" (A Scholium) offers a second example of this new theme. Borges returns to the world of Homer, and here too, as in previous poems, he chooses Ulysses' homecoming to Ithaca as one of the four stories that, he believes, comprise everything literature could ever tell. It appears in the brief prose piece "Los cuatro ciclos" (The Four Cycles) from *The Gold of the Tigers,* where Borges comments: "Four are the stories. During the time left to us, we'll keep telling them, transformed" (*OT,* 130). The story first appears in one of his most successful early poems, "Ars Poetica," as a metaphor for art:

> They say that Ulysses, sated with marvels,
> Wept tears of love at the sight of his Ithaca,
> Green and humble. Art is that Ithaca
> Of green eternity, not of marvels.   (*SP,* 143)

Four years later, in the collection *El otro, el mismo* (The Self and the Other, 1964), Borges turned the episode into a sonnet, "Odyssey, Book Twenty-Three," but the emphasis is now on the unpredictability of fate. In "A Scholium," on the other hand, the story becomes a love poem. Borges chooses the moment when the queen "saw herself in his eyes, when she felt in her love that she was met by Ulysses' love" (*HN,* 47). In each of the four versions of the story, one witnesses a switch of emphasis and preference: in the first, the focus is on the notion that literature is "the history of the diverse intonations of a few metaphors" (*OI*, 8); in the second, Ulysses' return to Ithaca is seen as a metaphor for art; the third captures the idea that "any life, no matter how long or complex it may be, is made up essentially of a *single moment* – the moment in which a man finds out, once and for all, who he is" (*A*, 83); and in the fourth, the accent is on love as an inviolable common secret. But the last version reveals also that the old metaphor has become Borges' own metaphor, because what the last poem underlines is the nature of love as a secret bond, as an unwritten pact expressing itself through its own code: "Penelope does not dare to recognize him, and to test him she alludes to a secret they alone share: their common thalamus that no mortal can move, because the olive tree from which it was carved ties it down to earth" (*HN*, 47). Borges chooses allusion as the language of love, but allusion also as the literary language he prefers. In the same prose poem, he adds: "Homer did not ignore that things should be said in an indirect manner. Neither did the Greeks, whose natural language was myth." What we have here, therefore, is a double metaphor. Penelope resorts to allusion to communicate with Ulysses; Borges, in turn, alludes to Homer's story to communicate his own perception of love. The thalamus as the metaphor for Penelope's love becomes the metaphor Borges conjures up to convey his own feelings about love. It is worth pausing on this aspect of his art. Not only because this example, dramatizes an all too well known device of his writing – the Chinese box structure to which he subjects much of his fiction and poetry – but because this last volume of poems further refines that device to the point of perfection. In the epilogue to *Historia de la noche,* he offers a possible definition of this literary artifice:

> Any event – an observation, a farewell, an encounter, one of those curious arabesques in which chance delights – can stir esthetic emotions. The poet's task is to project that emotion, which was intimate, in a fable or in a cadence. The material at his disposal, language, is, as Stevenson remarks, absurdly inadequate. What can we do with worn out words – with Francis Bacon's *Idola Fori* –, and with a few rhetorical artifices found in the manuals? On first sight, nothing or very little. And yet, a page by Stevenson himself or a line by Seneca is sufficient to prove that the undertaking is not always impossible. (*HN*, 139)

Borges, who in his early writings held that "unreality is the necessary condition of art," knows only too well that literature, and art in general, as Paul Klee once said, "is different from external life, and it must be organized differently." What Borges restates in the epilogue is his old belief that "since Homer all valid metaphors have been written down," and the writer's task is not to write new ones but to rewrite the old ones, or rather to translate them into his own language, time, and circumstance, very much in the way the nineteenth-century symbolist writer, Pierre Menard, undertook the rewriting of the *Quixote*. The creative act lies, then, not so much in the invention of new fables as in their transformation into vehicles of new content, in the conversion of an old language into a new one. Borges retells Ulysses' story of his return to Ithaca, but in each of his four versions a new perception has been conveyed.

The same principle can be applied to his other "fables." He keeps repeating them, as he himself has acknowledged, but it is a repetition of the materials, not of their substance. There is no escape from that "absurdly inadequate" tool – language – yet with those same trite words the poet shapes the uniqueness of his emotion. "Gunnar Thorgilsson" offers a third example of this outlook on literature which sees in the new a derivation from the old: Iceland, which appears and reappears in Borges' poetry, is evoked once more, but now the focus is not on the ship or the sword of the sagas, but on the wake and the wound of love. The poem concludes simply: "I want to remember that kiss / You gave me in Iceland" (HN, 59). "El enamorado" (The Lover) and "La espera" (The Waiting) are also love poems in which Borges tersely reviews some of his literary habits – moons. roses, numbers, seas, time, tigers, swords – but they are now shadows which vanish to uncover the only presence that truly counts:

> Debo fingir que hay otros. Es mentira.
> Sólo tú eres. Tú, mi desventura
> Y mi ventura, inagotable y pura.   (*HN*, 95)

> I should feign that there are others. It's a lie.
> Only you exist. You, my misfortune
> And my fortune, inexhaustible and pure.

If literature is, as Borges once wrote, "essentially a syntactic fact," it is clear that his latest volume of poetry should be assessed not for whatever is new at the level of theme (love being the thematic novelty), but by how he succeeds in bestowing on old subjects a new intensity and a rekindled poetic strength. The reader of his last collection can find here the vertex of his new achievement.

Those of us who have been closely following Borges' poetry of the last ten years have witnessed several changes in his voice. His earliest poems strove to convey a conversational tone. They were a dialogue with the familiar city, its myths and landscapes, sometimes bearing Whitman-esque overtones. To emphasize that intimate and nostalgic accent, he often used free verse, local words, and Argentine slang. Then when he "went from myths of the outlying slums of the city to games with time and infinity" (*A,* 152), he opted for more traditional meters and stanzaic forms. This alone conferred a certain stilted inflection on his poetic voice. Rhymes were strong and at times even a bit hammering (Scholem was made to rhyme with Golem). He brought the hendecasyllable and the sonnet to new heights, stimulated undoubtedly by his advanced blindness. In spite of this sculptural perfection, there was still a declama-tory falsetto in his voice that was particularly apparent when we read (or rather recited) aloud his own poetry. It goes without saying that this stiffness, however slight, disappeared in his best poems. In 1969, five years after his previous collection *El otro, el mismo,* he published *In Praise of Darkness.* With this volume Borges freed his verse from any linguistic slag. The sonnet, the form he has been using most frequently since, bordered on perfection: these sonnets are masterfully carved, with chis-eled smoothness and a quiet flow that turns them into verbal music.

Poetry as music has always been to Borges a crystallizing point at which language succeeds in bringing forth its melodic core. This is not a music produced by sound; the poem turns words into a transparent surface which reveals a certain cadence, a harmony buried under the opacities of language, much in the same manner as music rescues a privileged order of sound and silence from a chaotic mass of sounds. In the prologue to the collection *El otro, el mismo,* he has explained this understanding of poetry:

> On occasion, I have been tempted into trying to adapt to Span-ish the music of English or of German: had I been able to carry out that perhaps impossible adventure, I would be a great poet, like Garcilaso, who gave us the music of Italy, or like the anony-mous Sevillian poet who gave us the music of Rome, or like Dario, who gave us that of Verlaine and Hugo. I never went beyond rough drafts, woven of words of few syllables, which very wisely I destroyed. (*SP,* 279)

My contention is that Borges, whose "destiny" – as he put it – "is in the Spanish language" (*GT,* 31), has found in his most recent poetry not the music of English or German or of any other poet, but his own voice, and through it a music the Spanish language did not know before him. Not that Spanish did not produce great poets. It certainly did, and each of them represents an effort to strike a different chord of that musical instrument language becomes at the best moments of its poetry. One has only to think of Jorge Guillén as a definite virtuoso of that instrument, as a poet whose voice has given to Spanish some of the most luminous and joyous movements of its hidden music. Like Borges, Jorge Guillén has sought through his work to touch that musical kernel contained in language very much the way brandy is contained in the residual marc. For Borges, as for Guillén, poetry is a form of linguistic distillation.[7]

In *Historia de la noche,* there is hardly a subject or motif that has not been dealt with in his previous collections, love being the exception. "Ni siquiera soy polvo" (I Am Not Even Dust), which deals with the trinity Cervantes-Alonso-Don-Quixote as a dream-within-a-dream-within-a-dream, is a variation on a theme previously treated in "Parable of Cervantes and Don Quixote" (*Dreamtigers*) and in "Alonso Quijano Dreams" (The Unending Rose). "The Mirror" returns to his old obsession with mirrors first recorded in the short piece "The Draped Mirrors" (*Dreamtigers*), and then meticulously explored in the thirteen quatrains of "The Mirrors" (*El otro, el mismo*). The same could be said of "Lions" vis à vis "The Other Tiger," "Dreamtigers," and "The Gold of the Tigers." Or "Iceland" as a new avatar of "To Iceland" (*The Gold of the Tigers*). Or "Milonga del forastero," which is a sort of Platonic summation of all his other *milongas*. But precisely because Borges returns to his old subjects (he once stated: "A poet does not write about what he wants but about what he can"), the subject matters less than the voice. Furthermore: the voice is the subject.

In this last collection Borges further refines a device first developed in "Another Poem of Gifts": the poem as a long list, listing as a poetic exercise. "Metaphors of the Arabian Nights," "Lions," "Things That Might Have Been," "The Lover," and "The Causes" follow this pattern. The device accentuates the magic character of poetry as a voice speaking in the dark, words reaching out for meanings that are beyond words. What is left is a music that speaks from its innumerable variations, but the variations are not repetitions. They are, as in the art of the fugue, new versions of the same tune, and in each variation the theme is further explored, condensed, and simplified, until it becomes so transparent that one sees the bottom, the poet's deepest voice, a face free of masks, a certain essence that more than saying, sings. It is as if Borges had put behind him his old habits as themes to focus on the tones and inflections of his own voice; and what that voice expresses is a serenity, a calm not heard in the Spanish language since Juan de la Cruz or Luis de León. Borges must have felt that he was nearing that shore of harmony glimpsed by the mystical poets. In the last poem of the collection, "A History of the Night," he wrote referring to the night: "Luis de León saw it in the country / of his staggered soul." Yet the soul that surfaces from Borges' last poems is not one pierced by divine emotion, but a fulfilled and resigned soul that can see life as a river of "invulnerable water," an earthy soul anchored in life and yet unfearful of death, one that can look upon life from a timeless island against whose shores time breaks and recedes like sea waves:

Adán es tu ceniza

La espada morirá como el racimo.
El cristal no es más frágil que la roca.
Las cosas son su porvenir de polvo.
El hierro es el orín. La voz, el eco.
Adán, el joven padre, es tu ceniza.
El último jardín será el primero.
El ruiseñor y Píndaro son voces.
La aurora es el reflejo del ocaso.
El micenio, la máscara del oro.
El alto muro, la ultrajada ruina.
Urquiza, lo que dejan los puñales.
El rostro que se mira en el espejo
No es el de ayer. La noche lo ha gastado.
El delicado tiempo nos modela.

Qué dicha ser el agua invulnerable
Que corre en la parábola de Heraclito
O el intrincado fuego, pero ahora,
En este largo día que no pasa,
Me siento duradero y desvalido.   (*HN*, 131)

Adam Is Your Ash

The sword will die like the vine.
Crystal is no weaker than rock.
Things are their own future in dust.
Iron is rust, the voice an echo.
Adam, the young father, is your ash.
The last garden will be the first.
The nightingale and Pindar are voices.
Dawn is the reflection of sunset.
The Mycenaean is the gold mask.
The high wall, the plundered ruin.
Urquiza, what daggers leave behind.
The face looking at itself in the mirror

Is not yesterday's. Night has wasted it.
Delicate time is shaping us.

What joy to be the invulnerable water
Flowing in Heraclitus's parable
Or intricate fire, but now, midway
Through this long day that does not end,
I feel enduring and helpless.   (trans. Willis Barnstone)

A restatement of his famous line "Time is the substance I am made of. It
is a river that carries me away, but I am the river" (*OI*, 197). Now,
however, the same idea flows without the lapidary sententiousness of the
essay; simply, with ease and resolution, unconcerned with rejections or
acceptances, free of outcomes or outcries, a meditative voice reconciled
with life, accepting its gifts and losses with the same acquiescent gesture.

In the poem "The Causes," Borges goes through an inventory of
mementoes from history, literature, and life. The list encompasses some
of the most memorable moments of his own poetry and becomes a sort
of miniature of his poetic *oeuvre*. The poem closes with two equally
compressed lines: "All those things were needed / so that our hands
could meet" (*HN,* 128), a masterful coda that renders his tight survey of
motifs into a love poem. This is the surface, however impeccable, of the
text, its outer meaning. But what the text also says, between the lines, is
that its laconic eloquence, terse to the point of diaphaneity, is sustained
by sixty long years of poetic creation, the understated notion being: all
those poems were needed so that this one could be written. The idea
appears at the end of one of his most relaxed and subtly personal short
stories, "Averroes' Search" (1947): "I felt, on the last page, that my
narration was a symbol of the man I was as I wrote it and that, in order to
compose that narration, I had to be that man and, in order to be that
man, I had to compose that narration, and so on to infinity" (*L,* 155).
Literature, as well as life, as an inexorable concatenation of causes and
effects; each poem as a stepping stone toward the poem; the poem as a
symbol of the poet: in order to write this poem I had to write all the
others; in order to write this poem I had to be the man I was. But this last
poem does not form a circle with the others, it is rather the answer to the
others, a sort of prism that reintegrates the dispersed shades of his
poetry into one text, and this text gleams like a single beam of white light
with a radiant simplicity that none of the individual texts had. With
Historia de la noche Borges' poetry has found an equilibrium that undoubtedly conveys his own inner serenity; but this serenity, being a
linguistic externalization, is also a song through which the Spanish lan-

guage voices a music unheard before: an austere, poised, dignified, and quiet music:

> Soy el que no conoce otro consuelo
> Que recordar el tiempo de la dicha.
> Soy a veces la dicha inmerecida.
> Soy el que sabe que no es más que un eco,
> El que quiere morir enteramente.   (*HN*, 119–20)

> I am one who knows no other consolation
> Than remembering the time of joy,
> I am at times unmerited joy,
> I am one who knows he is only an echo,
> One who wants to die totally.   (trans. Willis Barnstone)

The young poet who once delighted in the exhilaration of his own performance has been left far behind. The voice we hear now is that of a consummate musician who has achieved total mastery over his medium. The music we hear now is that of the Spanish language attuned to its own registers, and that of a poet skillfully true to his own perceptions.

NOTES

1 Jorge Luis Borges, *La rosa profunda* (Buenos Aires: Emecé, 1975), p. 53; *The Gold of the Tigers; Selected Later Poems* trans. A. Reid (New York: E. P. Dutton, 1977), p. 63. When English translations have been available, I have indicated the source; when unavailable, I have provided my own.
2 Rita Guibert, *Seven Voices* (New York: Vintage, 1973), p. 98.
3 J. L. B., Epilogue to *Historia de la noche*, p. 140.
4 J. L. B., *Selected Poems*, p. 278.
5 They are *Elogio de la sombra (In Praise of Darkness)*, 1969; *El oro de los tigres (The Gold of the Tigers)*, 1972; *La rosa profunda* (The Unending Rose), 1975; and *La moneda de hierro* (The Iron Coin), 1976.
6 In my essay "Borges o el difícil oficio de la intimidad: reflexiones sobre su poesía más reciente", *Revista Iberoamericana*, XLIII, 100–101 (julio-diciembre 1977), pp. 449–463.
7 Borges has written on this subject:
   Pater wrote that all arts aspire to the condition of music, perhaps because in music meaning is form, since we are unable to recount a melody the way we can recount the plot of a story. Poetry, if we accept this statement, would be a hybrid art – the reduction of a set of abstract symbols, language, to musical ends. Dictionaries are to blame for this erroneous idea, for, as we seem to forget, they are artificial repositories, evolved long after the languages they

explain. The roots of language are irrational and of a magical nature. The Dane who uttered the name of Thor or the Saxon who uttered the name of Thunor did not know whether these words stood for the gods of thunder or for the noise that follows the lightning. Poetry tries to recapture that ancient magic. Without set rules, it works in a hesitant, daring manner, as if advancing in darkness. (*SP*, 279–80)

PART IV
Essays and other questions

11 Oxymoronic structure in Borges' essays

Borges the fiction writer and poet has been a subject of greater appeal and interest for critics than Borges the essayist. Among the twenty-odd books dealing with his work, and throughout extensive periodical criticism, his essays are presented and discussed not as a separate genre but rather as "a necessary complement to the stories of *Ficciones* and *El Aleph*,"[1] or as "fundamental reading for the full understanding of his creative works."[2] They most certainly could be considered complementary to his narrative, but it is clear that they are a separate creative endeavor and should be studied accordingly. Yet we don't have critical work devoted to the essayist. A few explanations for such an anomaly can be suggested: (a) the overpowering success of his short stories, which have earned Borges the reputation he enjoys as a writer; (b) the misleading tendency, on the part of some critics, to exclude the essays from his creative oeuvre; (c) the error of viewing the essay not as an entity in itself but rather as exegesis or supplement to poem or short story (an almost inevitable heresy when the essayist is also a poet and a short story writer); (d) the thin borderline between Borges' essay and short story and the consequent need to study one in conjunction with the other. Other reasons could be added. They might help to explain the void, but not to justify it. Just as Borges' short stories have been included in universal anthologies of this genre (*The Contemporary Short Story*, Columbia University Press), so his essays are now finding their way into similar collections. In the anthology entitled *50 Great Essays* (Bantam), next to the all-time masters of the genre, Borges is represented with four essays. There can be no doubt that Borges is as much a master of the essay as he is of the short story.

Borges has produced excellent studies on Lugones, Evaristo Carriego, and *Martín Fierro*. While his views and evaluations may be debatable, no serious student of Spanish American literature can overlook them – they represent definite contributions to criticism of the three poets' works. Yet it is not these lengthy essays (more than sixty pages) which lend full stature to Borges as an essayist. His contribution to the genre stems from the short essays collected in *Discusión* and *Otras inquisiciones* (Other Inquisitions, 1964). The originality of these essays arises not from the manifold and erudite scope of their themes: the work of at least two well-established Latin American essayists – Alfonso Reyes and Ezequiel Martínez Estrada – are equally as manifold and erudite. Reading the essays of Martínez Estrada and those of Borges, the reader immediately perceives a similar intention; both deny the efficacy of photographic realism and both mistrust Aristotelian logic. Speaking of Kafka, Martínez Estrada states: "He is not a writer of the fantastic except in respect to naive realism that accepts an order based on God, on reason, or on the logical happening of historical events. The world of the primitive has a greater functional resemblance to his. There, God is an inscrutable constellation; logic is a system of inferences based on observable analogies; and the organic process of events is filled with wonder, always open to the unforeseen. In short, a magic world . . ."[3] And Borges: "It is venturesome to think that a coordination of words (philosophies are nothing more than that) can resemble the universe very much" (*L,* 207). And again: "A philosophical doctrine begins as a plausible description of the universe; as the years pass it becomes a mere chapter – if not a paragraph or a name – in the history of philosophy" (*L,* 43). Like Borges, Martínez Estrada seeks to transcend an image of the world invented by "the deductive logic of Aristotle and Descartes" in order to draw near to a world which no longer can be categorized, a world perceived by intuition rather than thought by reason, a world closer to Lao Tzu than to Socratic Greece. But while Martínez Estrada seeks cognitive alternatives, because essentially he believes in the possibility of grasping "the true order of the world" (hence his enthusiasm for Kafka as a return to myth and the language of myth), Borges does not polarize Western reason and Oriental myth. He sees in Buddhism a form of idealism, and Schopenhauer – who had in his study a bust of Kant and a bronze Buddha – represents for Borges more than just a doctrine; it is a veritable reality or, as he puts it: "few things have happened to me more worth remembering than Schopenhauer's thought or the music of England's words" (*DT,* 93). In opposition to Martínez Estrada's enthusiasm – an enthusiasm for a true order – Borges expresses a flat skepticism: if there is an order in the world, that order is not accessible to man. In both writers we find rejection of philosophical idealism, but in Borges this rejection is also a form of acceptance. Borges rejects the validity of philosophical idealism as an image or sketch of the world, but accepts its value as "a branch of fantastic literature." Borges' fiction is nurtured by the failure of philosophical theories or, as he says, by the "aesthetic worth [of those theories] and what is singular and marvelous about them" (*OI*, 201). By making them function as the coordinates of his short stories, Borges evinces their fallacy and their condition of being not "a mirror of the world, but rather [of] one thing more added to the world." Yet, despite differences (a transcendental faith in Martínez Estrada and a radical skepticism in Borges), in both authors the reader perceives a genuine effort to overcome the narrowness that Western tradition has imposed as master and measure of reality.

It is in the element of form that Borges' essay outweighs Marínez Estrada's. The essays of Estrada fall, with regard to form, within the rational orthodoxy they seek to refute. One might claim that such rationality is the distinctive mark of the essay, and that even when dealing with the most abstruse and least malleable of themes, the essayist is bound to elucidate in accordance with a system of reasoning that, in the final analysis, frames and defines the very essence of the essay. But it is precisely in this aspect that Borges offers an alternative. In his *Inquisitions* there is an imaginative dimension which is new to the Spanish American essay. Borges uses a technique similar to that of his fiction: the material of his essays is in some way subjected to metaphysical and theological ideas which make up, to a certain degree, our context of culture. Bearing this in mind one finds that his poems, short stories, and essays share certain constants which could be considered recurrent motifs or, as they have been called, Borgesian *topoi*. For example, the theme of order and chaos, basic to the short stories "The Library of Babel," "The Lottery in Babylonia," and "Tlön, Uqbar, Orbis Tertius," is set forth fully in the essay dedicated to "The Analytical Language of John Wilkins." The invention of John Wilkins receives precisely the same treatment as the short stories: "we do not know what the universe is. This world is perhaps the first rude essay of some infant deity who afterwards abandoned it, ashamed of his own performance. . . . But the impossibility of penetrating the divine scheme of the universe cannot dissuade us from outlining human schemes, even though we are aware that they are provisional. Wilkins's analytical language is not the least admirable of those schemes" (*OI*, 109). The same idea that forms the frame on which the stories are woven also constitutes the backbone of the essay: the analytical language of John Wilkins is just as powerless to penetrate reality as the efforts of the librarians to decipher the illegible books of the library of

Babel. The analytical language of Wilkins and the ordered world of Tlön are both expressions of the same yearning for an order that is unattainable to human intelligence.

The *topos* of the universe as a dream or book of God, a central theme in the stories "The Circular Ruins," "The Dead Man," and "Death and the Compass," is also presented in all its perplexities in the essay "Forms of a Legend." Borges attempts to elucidate "the defects of logic" in the legend of Buddha, following an expositive order characteristic of many of his essays: (a) presentation of the subject or the question the essay intends to answer, (b) a summary of various theories which propound an explanation of the subject or an answer to the question, (c) Borges' own solution, and (d) a conclusion, which generally dismisses both (b) and (c) as inevitably fallible. In (c) Borges explains that for the solution of the problem (the defects of logic in the legend) "It suffices to remember that all the religions of India and in particular Buddhism teach that the world is illusory. 'The minute narration of a game' [of a Buddha] is what Lalitavistara means . . .; a game or a dream is, for Mahayana, the life of the Buddha on earth, which is another dream" (*OI*, 160–61). Once again short story and essay share the same premise. This basic idea renders to the story a generic value that explains and intensifies the events of the fable, and to the essay a perspective that overcomes the "accidental errors" and converts them into "substantial truth." Even in a short story so apparently close to the realistic model as "Emma Zunz," Borges interprets the events of the narrative by the same principle. In the last paragraph he says: "Actually the story *was* incredible, but it impressed everyone because substantially it was true" (*L*, 137). In the essay he asserts: "The chronology of India is uncertain; my erudition is even more unreliable. Koeppen and Hermann Beckh are perhaps as fallible as the compiler who has hazarded this article. It would not surprise me if my story of the legend turned out to be legendary, formed of substantial truth and accidental errors" (*OI*, 162). The "accidental errors" of the essay and the "false circumstances" of the short story represent the contingent immediacy of reality, the limits of a province where Aristotelian logic prevails. In the essay as well as in the short story, Borges attempts to cross these logical limits to explore a reality that can no longer be translated into facile syllogisms, because the postulates of the essay are erroneous, yet true, and the events of the story of Emma Zunz are false, but substantially true.

Numerous examples of this correlation between the essay and the short story could be cited. But since the real concern here is to define Borges' contribution to the essay, the above examples will have to suffice. What Martínez Estrada suggests for a more thorough understanding of Kafka's message will also help us, to a certain extent, to define the mechanics of Borges' essays. In the one on "Literal Meaning of Myth in Kafka" the author of *Radiografía de la Pampa* observes that "in order to understand Kafka's message, his stupendous revelation of a reality previously glimpsed only in flashes, it must be recognized that all that truly occurs does so in conformity with the language of myth, because it is pure myth (mathematics is also a mythical system). Therefore the most meaningful way of expressing that reality is through its logical connotation, that is: myth and allegory."[4] Martínez Estrada understands myth as "a logical system of better understanding the inexpressible."[5] In the case of Kafka, myth represents a form of "not accepting the hideous and conventional order of a reality conditioned by norm and factitious law."[6] We previously stated that in both essay and short story Borges draws upon metaphysics and theology. These two disciplines make up, in essence, the antithesis of myth: the first attempts to substitute myth with reason; the second, exorcism with doctrine. To attribute to Borges, then, the use of myth would be an obvious contradiction. It is not so, though, if we recall his tendency "to evaluate religious or philosophical ideas on the basis of their aesthetic worth and even for what is singular and marvelous about them" (*OI*, 201). Thus Borges reduces philosophical and theological ideas to mere creations of the imagination, to intuitions that differ little from any other mythical form. This modus operandi brings several of his narratives to mind: a two or three centimeter disc that encompasses the universe in "The Zahir"; Averroes defining the Greek words "comedy" and "tragedy" without ever knowing what a theater was; a library of undecipherable books; Pierre Menard composing *Don Quixote* in the twentieth century; a pursuer being pursued in "Death and the Compass." This oxymoronic treatment is found with equal success in Borges' essays. Having reduced the products of philosophy and theology to myths, there is no reason not to perform the same operation with other phenomena of culture. Thus the myths of intelligence would be restored to the only reality that befits them: not to the labyrinth created by the gods but to the labyrinth invented by man. Borges approaches cultural values to understand them not in the context of reality but in the only context open to man – his own created culture. John Donne's "Biathanatos" is understood according to the law of causality. The essays "Pascal's Sphere" and "The Flower of Coleridge" are examples which show that "perhaps universal history is the history of the diverse intonation of a few metaphors" (*OI*, 8). And the avatars of Zeno's tortoise, as well as the solutions of Aristotle, Agrippa, St. Thomas, Bradley, William James, Descartes, Leibniz, Bergson, Bertrand Russell, and others, are explained in the lapidary phrase: "the world is a fabrication of the will" (*OI, 120*), a paraphrase from a book very dear to Borges, *The World as Will and Idea*.[7] The enigma of Omar Khayyám's *Rubáiyát* and the later Fitzgerald version is resolved with the assistance of a pantheistic concept: "the Englishman could have recreated the Persian, because both were, essentially, God – or momentary faces of God" (*OI, 82*). A similar solution is applied to the problem of Kubla Khan – a palace built by a thirteenth-century Mongolian emperor in a dream narrated in Samuel Coleridge's poem of the same name – in Borges' essay "The Dream of Coleridge."

Thus, the treatment of themes in the essays does not differ, basically, from that employed in the narratives. There are some instances in which the short story is merely a variation or an elaboration of material contained in the essay, as exemplified in "The Library of Babel" with regard to "The Total Library" (essay). This first conclusion reveals in itself the outlook of culture manifest in the Borgesian essay: the various expressions of the human spirit with which his essays deal are understood not as attempts to comprehend or interpret the historical universe, but rather as schemes of a world "constructed by means of logic, with little or no appeal to concrete experience."[8] In essence, this prognosis is the same as that posited by Martínez Estrada for the study of Kafka: "reason first shaped the world, and then enjoyed understanding and explaining it rationally."[9] The originality of Borges, then, does not lie in the premise. He has coined one of the most ingenious and fertile formulations of it – "the impossibility of penetrating the divine scheme of the universe cannot dissuade us from outlining human schemes, even though we are aware that they are provisional" (*OI, 109*), or "metaphysics is a branch of fantastic literature" – but he is far from being the first to express such disbelief. Already Kant, "half seriously and half in jest, suggested that Swedenborg's mystical system. which he calls 'fantastic,' is perhaps no more so than orthodox metaphysics."[10] Lévi-Strauss has shown that history as we read it in books has little to do with reality; he later explains that "the historian and the agent of history choose, sever and carve the historical facts, for a truly total history would confront them with chaos, and so 'the French Revolution,' as it is known, never took place."[11] Mathematicians tell us that "the characteristic of mathematical thought is that it does not convey truth about the external world."[12] But the reference that bears closest affinity to Borges' spirit of the metaphor, and also the closest in formulation, is a paragraph from Cassirer's essay *Language and Myth*:

> Consequently all schemata which science evolves in order to classify, organize, and summarize the phenomena of the real

world turn out to be nothing but arbitrary schemes – airy fabrics of the mind, which express not the nature of things, but the nature of mind. So knowledge, as well as myth, language, and art, has been reduced to a kind of fiction – to a fiction that recommends itself by its usefulness, but must not be measured by any strict standard of truth, if it is not to melt away into nothingness.[13]

Why not make fiction out of theories and doctrines that are fictional anyhow? Borges seems to have persuaded himself that "Parmenides, Plato, John Scotus Erigena, Spinoza, Leibniz, Kant, and Francis Bradley are the unsuspected and greatest masters of fantastic literature" (*D*, 172). The themes of his stories often find their inspiration in metaphysical hypotheses accumulated through many centuries of the history of philosophy, and in theological systems that are the scaffoldings of several religions. His originality stems from the creative use of this material in his narratives, as much as in his essays. The results in the latter are no less fruitful than in the former. With Borges the essay attains a new quality in which structure becomes an effective expressive vehicle for the intended theme. As with oxymora, where a word is modified by an epithet which seems to contradict it, in his essays Borges studies a subject by applying theories that he has previously condemned as fallible and fallacious. Oxymoron is an attempt to overcome the inherent narrowness that reason has imposed on language; it is a "no" to a reality conceptually ruled by words. This stylistic device best defines the technique of Borges' essay because the ideas being dealt with are evaluated or modified by theories which contradict those ideas, stripping them of all transcendent value in historical reality.[14] At the same time those theories function as oxymoronic modifiers in a different way – they restore the ideas, the subject matter of the essay, to a level where they regain their validity, not as a description of the world but as marvels of human imagination. Thus the seeming contradiction between the two terms (a theory acting as modifier and an idea standing as a noun) is in essence a form of conciliation. The incongruity, then, is only illusory. The two components of the oxymoron clash on a conventional level only to reach a deeper and richer level of reality. Like any other literary trope, it represents an effort to correct through language the deficiencies of language itself. The oxymoronic structure of Borges' essay is likewise an attempt to bring theories and ideas to a plane where their shortcomings find an adequate corrective within the realm of those same theories and ideas. The two terms may often seem to contradict each other. It is only so because we insist on seeing them in the context of reality, where they no longer belong. In their new context – human imagination and fantasy – Borges establishes a new set of values by means of which metaphysics and theology, and for that matter any product of the human mind, is no less fantastic than, say, the Ptolemaic system. Hence Borges' assertion with reference to Donne's theory of time: "With such a splendid thesis as that, any fallacy committed by the author becomes insignificant" (*OI*, 21).

Borges' essays would not have reached their high degree of originality if he had merely followed the discursive patterns of structure traditionally accepted in the essay form. Martínez Estrada saw in Kafka and in myth in general the use of magic to perceive a magical world. Borges has renounced that possibility with respect to the world but not with respect to intellectual culture. He has given up the labyrinth of the gods but not the labyrinth of man.[15] His way of perceiving this human labyrinth is based on illustrious ideas: cyclical time, pantheism, the law of causality, the world as dream or idea, and some others. But for Borges they are no longer absolute truths, as once claimed, but marvels, intuitions, myths. Myths by which man attempts to understand not that magic reality unattainable for feeble human intelligence, but rather that other reality woven by laborious undertakings and painstaking endeavors of the human mind in an effort to penetrate the impenetrable. In spite of their rational nature they are myths, because they function in the essay for the creation of oxymoronic relationships that not only challenge traditional order, but open the possibility of a completely new understanding of the subject. According to this understanding, man has been denied access to the world. He is confronted with the only alternative left at his disposal: to sublimate his impotence toward reality by creating another reality; and this man-made reality is the only one accessible to man. One could indeed say, with Borges the world has become Tlön. The poet "makes or invents himself in his poetry," according to Octavio Paz; the writer, in Borges' own words, "sets himself the task of portraying the world . . ., to discover, shortly before his death, that the patient labyrinth of lines traces the image of his face" (*DT*, 93). Man, powerless to know the world, has invented through the products of culture his own image of the world. Thus he lives in a reality designed by his own fragile architecture. He knows that there is another "irreversible and iron-clad" reality which constantly besieges him and forces him to feel the enormousness of its presence, and between these two realities, between these two dreams, between these two stories (one imagined by God and another invented by man) flows the conflictive history of humanity. There is a moment in Borges' essay in which he captures this tragic condition of man in a memorable sentence which epitomizes man's plight as both dream and dreamer; it occurs at the end of "A New Refutation of Time," one of his most remarkable essays: "The world, unfortunately, is real; I, unfortunately, am Borges."

NOTES

1 James Irby, Introduction to *Other Inquisitions,* New York, 1965, p. vii.
2 Emir Rodríguez Monegal, "Borges, essayiste," *L'Herne,* Paris, 1964, p. 345.
3 Ezequiel Martínez Estrada, *En torno a Kafka y otros ensayos,* Barcelona, 1967, p. 30.
4 *Ibid.,* p. 35.
5 *Ibid.,* p. 34.
6 *Ibid.*
7 For a more detailed discussion of Borges' contacts with Schopenhauer see notes 13 (chapter I) and 9 (chapter VI) of my study, *La prosa narrativa de J. L. Borges,* Madrid, 1968, pp. 29–30, 82.
8 Bertrand Russell, *Our Knowledge of the External World,* New York, 1960, p. 15.
9 Martínez Estrada, p. 24.
10 Bertrand Russell, *A History of Western Philosophy,* New York, 1965, pp. 705–706.
11 Claude Lévi-Strauss, *The Savage Mind,* Chicago, 1966, p. 258.
12 *Ibid.,* p. 248.
13 Ernest Cassirer, *Language and Myth,* New York, 1946, pp. 7–8.
14 On the use of oxymoron in Borges' style see the chapter "Adjetivación" in my *La prosa narrativa de J. L. Borges,* pp. 186–95.
15 The reference is to a widely quoted passage from the story "Tlön, Uqbar, Orbis Tertius." There Borges says: "It is useless to answer that reality is also orderly. Perhaps it is, but in accordance with divine laws – I translate: inhuman laws – which we never quite grasp. Tlön is surely a labyrinth, but it is a labyrinth devised by men, a labyrinth destined to be deciphered by men" (*L,* 17–18).

12 Borges and the new Latin American novel

> Hence the final meaning of Borges' prose – without which there
> simply would not be a modern Spanish-American novel – is to attest
> that Latin America lacks a language and, consequently, must create it.
> To do so, Borges confounds all genres, rescues all traditions, kills all
> bad habits, creates a new order of exigency and rigor over which there
> may rise irony, humor, play – indeed – but also a profound revolution
> that matches freedom with imagination, and with both he constitutes
> a new Latin-American language which, by sheer contrast, reveals the
> lie, the submission and the deceit of what traditionally was taken for
> "language" among us.
> – Carlos Fuentes, *La nueva novela hispanoamericana*

At a time when Borges' work is being acknowledged as a driving force in what has been called "the Borgesian phase"[1] of recent American fiction, little or nothing has been said about his impact on contemporary Latin American fiction. One reason for this anomaly is that Spanish American students and critics take Borges so much for granted that the extent of his influence has been deluged in vague generalities. While Fuentes' statement that "without Borges there simply would not be a modern Latin-American novel" is sweeping enough to supply an epigraph, it is time to move from a notion which is accepted as axiomatic to the specifics of its verification: "technicalities," warns Harry Levin, "help us more than generalities."

In Ernesto Sábato's novel *Sobre héroes y tumbas* (On Heroes and Tombs), two of the characters, Bruno and Martín, walking down a Buenos Aires street, meet a man moving cautiously aided by a cane. "Borges," says one to the other. Bruno engages in a short conversation with Borges, and Sábato reproduces some of Borges' habits of speech. This fictional Borges seems also to be acquainted with Alejandra, one of the novel's axial characters. After this encounter, Bruno and Martín discuss various aspects

148

of Borges' writings and Argentine literature in general. To one's question as to whether Borges, as a writer, is more European than Argentine, the other replies: "What else can he be but an Argentine? He is a typical national by-product. Even his Europeanism is national. A European is not a Europeanist but simply a European."[2] In explaining the non-Argentine traits of Borges' writings as only another true manifestation of Argentine temperament, Sábato paraphrases a belief long held and defended by Borges himself. In his essay "The Argentine Writer and Tradition," Borges maintains that *La urna,* a book of sonnets by Enrique Banchs, is no less Argentine than *Martín Fierro,* which is, by definition, *the* Argentine poem. Borges goes on to explain that in lines like "The sun shines on the slanting roofs / and on the windows. Nightingales / try to say they are in love . . .," from a poem written in a suburb of Buenos Aires, where there are neither slanting roofs nor nightingales, "Argentine architecture and ornithology are of course absent, but we find [in these lines] the Argentine's reticence and constraint."[3] The conversation between Bruno and Martín, in Sábato's novel, is a critique of Borges' work in the context of Argentine literature. Here Sábato airs opinions on Borges he has previously cast in essay form,[4] mixing his great admiration for the author of *Ficciones* with a relentless aversion to the formal rigor (he calls it "Byzantinism") which has always characterized Borges' prose. Sábato gets his point across through Bruno:

> Can you imagine Tolstoy trying to dazzle the reader with an adverb when one of his characters' life or death is at stake?[5]

> Yet, not everything in Borges is Byzantine, really. There is something very Argentine in his best pages – a certain nostalgia, a certain metaphysical sadness. . . . Actually, many stupidities are said about what Argentine literature *should* be like. The important thing is that it should be profound. All the rest is derivative. And if it is not profound it will not help to display *gauchos* or *compradritos* [Argentine hoodlums]. The most representative writer in Elizabethan England was Shakespeare. However, many of his plays do not even take place in England.[6]

This attack on Borges is strange on two accounts. First, Sábato accuses Borges of local color when it was Borges himself who fought the decisive battle against local color in Argentina;[7] Borges was also the first Argentine writer to achieve genuine universality in spite of the *gauchos* and *compadritos* one finds in his stories. Second, the arguments Sábato uses to remedy a nonexistent evil (since one can safely say that the most representative writer of contemporary Argentina *is* Borges, although many of his stories are set in such places as Tlön, Babylon, the land of the troglodytes, and similar extraterritorial territories) are, oddly enough, of pure Borgesian extraction. Consciously or unconsciously, Sábato is repeating one of the arguments Borges uses in his fight against local color: "I think," Borges writes, "Shakespeare would have been amazed if people had tried to limit him to English themes, and if they had told him that, as an Englishman, he had no right to compose *Hamlet,* whose theme is Scandinavian, or *Macbeth,* whose theme is Scottish" (*L,* 180–81). Sábato, along with other Latin American writers, accepts Borges even when attacking him.[8]

The very device of mixing real beings (Borges) with fictional characters (Bruno and Martín) is of unquestionable Borgesian lineage. It could be argued that the reference to Borges in a novel that aims to portray all the features that shape the face of Buenos Aires is only natural, in the same degree that the references to Gardel, Firpo, or Roberto Arlt give expression to some of the myths which are part of that city. Yet the difference between these and other figures mentioned or commented upon throughout the novel, and the allusion to Borges, lies in the fact that the latter is presented not just nominally but as a living presence. The reader sees Borges walking through the streets of Buenos Aires and stopping casually to chat, as no doubt has occurred many times in the life of the town. It is this experience that Sábato probably strove to capture: Borges, the author of a mythical Buenos Aires, now strolling the streets of a real Buenos Aires. A novel that seeks to re-create the very pulse of Beunos Aires cannot afford to miss such a ponderable dimension. The result, however, goes far beyond Sábato's intention. Borges appears in the novel not only as one more reality among the many that cluster under the roofs of the city, but also as a symbol of the impact produced by his work on contemporary Latin American fiction. Borges' passage through the pages of one of its fairly representative novels becomes a symbol – a *lapsus linguae* through which Latin American fiction of the last three decades acknowledges its debt to Borges.

Let us now ask the obvious question: "What is the nature of Borges' impact, and what is the extent of his influence?" I have already pointed out how the very fact that fictional characters in Sábato's novel intermingle with real ones responds to an imaginative freedom which – although it is already found in Spanish American fiction since *modernismo* and its first explorations into the realm of the fantastic – only gained momentum with the publication of Borges' first *ficciones* from the forties on. The concept of the fantastic as found in modernist short stories – Lugones being the exception – is one of overrefinement and virtuosity. The point of departure in their stories is the split between the real and the unreal, and also the assumption that the story moves within the limits of the latter, where everything is permissible, however whimsical. This fracture between the real and the unreal ends by producing estrangement: the former seems to be ruled by laws and norms identical to those which govern historical life, while the latter appears to repudiate and break those very laws and norms. In the fantastic stories of the modernists, one finds a flat acceptance of this break, and no bridge is provided to cross from one territory to the other. Thus, these stories are closer to a supernatural and marvelous world – a mixture of Poe and H. G. Wells with the lyricism of a Maeterlinck. Their sole purpose seems to be to re-create our imagination, and the difference between this type of fancy and the fantasy that nourishes a wide area of children's books is only one of degree.[9] Not only does Borges move freely between the literature of the real and the unreal, but he has gone so far as to blur the borderline between the two. The fantastic in his stories springs less from the subject than from the treatment of it. His premise is that "unreality is the necessary condition of art." His *ficciones* are not only a way of freeing imagination but also a form of suggesting a new understanding of the world. Borges seems to be saying that we cannot de-realize the world we have so neatly constructed and that to grasp the reality that lies on the other side of our obedient mirror is a privilege of gods, not a task of men. His treatment of the fantastic therefore differs intrinsically from the stories of marvel and astonishment of his modernist predecessors, and this approach to the fantastic has opened a wide road in Latin American fiction.

Among those who have followed that road, Julio Cortázar is the most obvious and distinguished example. Although his short stories go their own way, responding to a fictional outlook quite different from Borges', it is clear that Cortázar found the way to fantastic literature under the stimulus of Borges' achievements.[10] Cortázar's poem in prose *Los reyes* (The Kings) was first published in *Los anales de Buenos Aires,* a magazine edited by Borges. Its subject – like Borges' "The House of Asterion" – is a re-creation of the myth of the Minotaur. Cortázar's choice of a motif (the labyrinth), already so clearly dominant in Borges' work, is in itself indicative of close affinities. Other examples of this osmotic influence are Cortázar's stories "Las puertas del cielo" (The Gates of Heaven) and particularly "El móvil" (The Motive). The reader immediately associates the latter with Borges' "Streetcorner Man."[11] There are no knife fights in Cortázar's stories, but the vindication of the literary worth of low life out on the raw edges of Buenos Aires deepens a trend in Argentine letters which, if not initiated by Borges, was certainly updated and renewed by him from the thirties on. In addition to stories like "Streetcorner Man," "The Dead Man," and "The South," which deal directly with old-time

Argentine hoodlums (*compadritos*), Borges published in 1945 an anthology whose title alone is informative – *El compadrito: su destino, sus barrios, su música* (The *Compadrito:* His Destiny, His Barrios, His Music). It was an invitation to write the poem that would do for the *compadrito* what Martín Fierro did for the gaucho. It seems unlikely that a poet as Mallarméan as Cortázar was at the time he wrote the narratives of *Bestiario* (Bestiary) would have chosen characters from the *compadrito's* underworld as the protagonists for his stories without the incentive of Borges' early efforts to vindicate the literary potential of this segment of Argentine society.

Other instances of Borges' influential presence in contemporary Spanish American fiction can easily be singled out. Traces of this presence are found in works far removed from the Borgesian scope of theme and genre. His influence resonates through the novel *One Hundred Years of Solitude* by Gabriel García Márquez, whose story of an imaginary family, the Buendías, in a fictitious community, Macondo, is so skillfully told that it becomes a microcosm of all Latin America – with the legends, myths, history, and magic of a whole continent. While it is true that one of its themes is "the wonder and strangeness of a continent in which *the fantastic* is the normative"[12] (a face of Latin America that has nurtured much of Miguel Angel Asturias' fiction), it is equally true that the magic of the book stems not from a reality historically chronicled but from a view of life imaginatively and fantastically elaborated. To explain the nature of this alchemy, García Márquez has, in an interview, told the story of a Colombian girl who eloped. To avoid the shame, the family declared that the last time they saw her she was folding linen sheets in the garden, but then she rose to heaven. In the novel, this experience goes through a Borgesian transmutation. ("Funes the Memorious," as the literary sublimation of Borges' own insomnia, and "The South," as the metaphor of an unhappy experience, are obvious examples at hand.) One of the characters – Remedios, *la bella* – is asked to help Fernanda fold her linen sheets in the garden, and when a mild wind begins to blow, Remedios rises with the sheets until she and they vanish into heaven. The naive excuse becomes a literary reality which now functions not as a metaphor nor as an allegory but according to a strength of its own. Imagination blends fantasy and experience into an autonomous world, with loyalties to both.

But where one most distinctly sees the traces of a Borgesian mode that delights in assembling and disassembling narrative components, as if they were pieces of a Chinese box, is in the treatment of one of García Márquez's most puzzling characters – Melquíades. He is a gypsy who spends the last years of his life in Macondo with the Buendías, writing enigmatic books on sheets of parchment which nobody can decipher. After Melquíades' death, his ghost appears to one of the Buendías' descendants, who struggles unsuccessfully to read the parchments. Melquíades tells him that he is willing to convey to him his wisdom but he refuses to translate the manuscripts because "no one must know their meaning until one hundred years have elapsed."[13] And indeed, the mysterious contents of the book are revealed only when the reader reaches the novel's last two pages, which not only conclude the story but also complete the one hundred years predicted by Melquíades. Only then does the impenetrable language, which turns out to be Sanskrit, yield its meaning to the last offspring of the Buendías. Thus Aureliano reads the parchments, "as if they had been written in Spanish," to discover that they contain the history of the family down to the most trivial details by Melquíades one hundred years ahead of time. Fascinated, Aureliano reads what the reader has been reading through the novel from the first page on, finally reaching the very sheet which describes what he is doing at that moment: "he began to decipher the instant that he was living, deciphering it as he lived it, prophesying it to himself in the act of deciphering the last page of the parchments, as if he were looking at himself in a talking mirror."[14]

The artifice reminds us of *Don Quixote*'s Chapter IX, in which Don Quixote learns that the whole novel has been translated from the Arabic and that Cervantes acquired the manuscript in the Toledo marketplace. In his essay "Partial Enchantments of the *Quixote*," Borges has surveyed the most illustrious examples of this artifice. Along with the *Quixote*, he mentions *A Thousand and One Nights*, and particularly night DCII, "magic among the nights, when the Sultan hears his own story from the Sultana's mouth." But the example from which García Márquez seemed to have benefited most is the third one, the *Ramayana*. "In the last book," comments Borges, "Rama's children, not knowing who their father is, seek refuge in a forest, where a hermit teaches them to read. That teacher, strangely enough, is Valmiki; the book they study is the *Ramayana* [epic poem by Valmiki]. Rama orders a sacrifice of horses; Valmiki comes to the ceremony with his pupils. They sing the *Ramayana* to the accompaniment of the lute. Rama hears his own story, recognizes his children, and then rewards the poet" (*OI*, 45). As if the idea of a minor character – Melquíades – writing the story that the novel unfolds, and of a main character – Aureliano – reading it up to the point where both texts overlap, were not close enough to the device used by Valmiki in the great Sanskrit epic of India, García Márquez makes Melquíades write the history of Macondo in Sanskrit – a kind of mischievous wink signaling the remote source. But the existence of a book within a book, of a fictional book which already contains what the actual book tells, page after page, reminds us most of all of that Borgesian artifice which suggests that "if the characters in a story can be readers or spectators, then we, their readers or spectators, can be fictitious" (*OI*, 46). Such inversions, by means of which reality and fiction seem to exchange domains, are, of course, one of the constants of Borges' fiction. In his story "Theme of the Traitor and the Hero," for example, Ryan, the great-grandson of Fergus Kilpatrick, engages in writing a biography of the assassinated hero, but he realizes at the end of the tale that he too forms part of the assassin's plot. Like García Márquez's hero in the act of deciphering the last page of the parchments, Ryan discovers that in the plan of the assassins he is but one ingredient more, and that even the book he publishes, dedicated to the hero's glory, was perhaps also foreseen in the assassins' work.

The device of turning characters from other works into characters of his own fiction, so common in Borges' narratives that the reader is inclined to think of Don Quixote ("A Problem"), Auguste Dupin ("Death and the Compass"), Martín Fierro ("The End"), Leopold Bloom ("The Zahir"), Cruz ("The Life of Tadeo Isidoro Cruz"), John H. Watson ("The Approach to al-Mu'tasim"), and others as real beings interpolated in a fictitious world, is a device also found in *One Hundred Years of Solitude*. García Márquez himself has spotted for us the guest characters he intermixed with his own fictional beings:

> Victor Hughes, a character from Alejo Carpentier's *Explosion in a Cathedral;* Colonel Lorenzo Gavilán, from Carlos Fuentes' *The Death of Artemio Cruz.* There is also another character in my novel who goes to Paris and lives in a hotel on the Rue Dauphine, in the same room where Rocamadur, a character from Julio Cortázar's *Hopscotch,* died. I am also convinced that the nun who carries the last of the Aurelianos in a small basket is Mother Patrocinio from Mario Vargas Llosa's *The Green House.*[15]

When, in García Márquez's novel, Aureliano finally verifies that in the manuscript "Melquíades had not put events in the order of man's conventional time, but had concentrated a century of daily episodes in such a way that *they all coexisted in one instant,*"[16] it is hard not to recall Borges' speculations with time, and particularly the infinite and iridescent Aleph, which Borges introduces with these words: "In that single gigantic instant I saw millions of acts both delightful and awful; not one of them amazed me more than the fact that *all of them occupied the same point* in space, without overlapping or transparency" (*A*, 26; italics added).

Still, these and other analogies[17] are far from sufficient to define the role of Borges' writings as a catalyst for the new Spanish American literature. They do, however, suggest on the part of the Latin American writer a great fascination for another Latin American writer – a rather unusual phenomenon in a literature that has consistently sought its models in foreign letters. The full strength of Borges' impact lies in his having produced for Spanish American fiction what Rubén Darío produced for its poetry at the turn of the century: namely, the forging of a linguistic instrument, exact, effective, authentic, capable of revealing an undiscovered Latin America. This is not to say that in this quest Borges was alone. Neither was Darío alone in that poetic revolution which brought forth a whole generation of brilliant poets; however, it is generally agreed that it was Darío who not only capitalized on all the achievements and innovations of modernism, but also brought them to their highest accomplishment in his own poetry. Today we accept as a truism that before Darío and the modernists Spanish was a lifeless, inflated language incapable of giving poetic expression to the nuances of modern perception. The poets who came after modernism and who produced the best poetry ever written in Latin America have all acknowledged their indebtedness to Rubén Darío. Poets like Vallejo, Neruda, Borges, and Paz have left some form of testimony of this admiration and recognition. Neruda, for one, has clearly stated: "Many believe that they have nothing to do with Darío, and yet, if they write the way they do it is owing to Rubén's brilliance, which so radically modified the Spanish language."[18] And Paz has written in similar terms:

> Spanish poetry had its muscles numbed by dint of solemnity and pathos; with Rubén Darío the language begins to move. Darío's place is central. He is not a living influence but a term of reference: a point of departure or arrival. To be or not to be like him: in both ways Darío is present in the spirit of contemporary poets. He is the founder. He is the origin.[19]

Borges himself has referred to Darío as "a great master and poet," and he has pointed out that Darío created with the Spanish language a kind of music which did not exist before him. Says Borges:

> I think that when a great poet passes through the language it matters not if we like or dislike him. Something has happened to the language and that will not be forgotten. We may like or dislike Chaucer but, of course, after *Troilus and Criseyde* and the *Canterbury Tales* the English language is not what it was before. The same thing, I think, might be said of Darío.[20]

Similarly, I believe, contemporary Spanish American fiction, consciously or unconsciously, willingly or unwillingly, is marked by a prose that did not exist in Spanish before Borges. Shuffling a few words in

Paz's statement, one can safely say: "To be or not to be like Borges: in both ways he is present in the spirit of contemporary Spanish American fiction." A writer like Sábato, who, as we have seen, has branded Borges' writings with labels like "evasion" and "Byzantinism," has openly stated through his character Bruno: "What I am sure about is that Borges' prose is the most remarkable being written today in the Spanish language." And writers like García Márquez and Vargas Llosa have made similar statements. At the invitation of a Peruvian university, these two young novelists engaged in a dialogue on the Latin American novel, in which Borges became the inevitable subject:

> *Vargas Llosa:* . . . I have always had problems in justifying my admiration for Borges.
> *García Márquez:* Ah, I have no problem at all, I have a great admiration for him, I read him every night. I just came from Buenos Aires and the only thing I bought there was Borges' *Complete Works.* I carry them in my suitcase; I am going to read them every day, and he is a writer I detest. . . . But, on the other hand, I am fascinated by the violin he uses to express his things. . . . I think that Borges' writings are a literature of evasion. Something strange happens to me with Borges: he is one of the authors I read most and have read most and perhaps the one I like least. I read Borges because of his extraordinary capacity for verbal artifice. I mean that he teaches you how to tune up your instrument for saying things.[21]

From García Márquez's view of literature, one can learn about the understated difficulties that the Latin American writer must face. What becomes particularly clear is that a linguistic vacuum confronts him, the lack of a literary tradition in his own language, forcing him to resort to foreign literatures, most in bad translations. Cortázar has pointed out the differences separating the European writer from the Argentine, and presents the case for the Latin American at large:

> European novelists (genius aside) waged a war with weapons sharpened collectively through centuries of intellectual, esthetic, and literary tradition, while we are forced to create for ourselves a language which may rid us of *Don Ramiro*[22] and other mummies with Hispanic bandages, a language which may rediscover the Spanish that produced Quevedo or Cervantes and that produced for us *Martín Fierro* and *Recuerdos de Provincia.*[23]

For Cortázar, then, and for the new novelist in general, the quest in the Latin American novel is "the unavoidable battle for the conquest of a language."[24] "Radical in facing his own past," wrote Carlos Fuentes, "the new Latin American writer undertakes a revision starting from a self-evident fact – the lack of a language."[25] If the problem of the language represents one of the central preoccupations of today's Latin American novelists (and it does), one begins to understand their attraction to Borges. Borges was the first (after Sarmiento, one must add) to undertake that revision of the Spanish language which contemporary novelists find indispensable if Latin America is to speak with a voice of its own. This is not to say that there were no prose writers in Latin America. There were, and excellent ones: Sarmiento, Martí, Rodó, Alfonso Reyes, to mention just a few. But their prose was written in the mold of the essay. When a powerful essayist like Martí wrote a novel – *Amistad funesta* – he produced the same overrefined prose, consecrated by modernism, which on the one hand created the seminal "new" poetic language but on the other forced fiction writing into a prose of preciosity whose ideal was "the eternal beauty of art." Modernist novels and stories were written in a prose full of color and melody which became ornate for its own sake; the themes of those narratives were either overburdened by color or deafened by the rhythm of the prose. For the modernists, narration was a pretext – although a beautiful pretext – which allowed the author to create a world of sensory impressions, artistic transpositions, and verbal rhythms where all things were valued for their esthetic potential and their capacity for generating beauty.[26]

The regionalist novel, which came after modernism, described the exuberances of Spanish America – the pampa, the *llano* (of Venezuela), the jungle – in the luxuriant language inherited from Rubén Darío. Borges represents a double renovation in Latin American fiction: he abandoned the realistic mode that had traditionally prevailed in the regionalist narratives, and sought in the fantastic a more creative treatment of his themes; and with regard to language, he sought a new concept of style. For the modernists, the color and rhythm of language were the most admired characteristics of good prose. A stylist was, consequently, a writer who handled language with the greatest splendor, who showed the greatest display of verbal wealth and achieved the most talented rhythms. In contrast to this external understanding of style, Borges concentrated on the inner effectiveness of language. "Those who labor under that superstition [of style as an end in itself]," he wrote in 1930, "give no thought to the effectiveness or ineffectiveness of a page, but are merely conscious of a writer's supposed skills: his metaphors, his ear, the circumstances of his punctuation and word order."[27] Borges understands style not as ornamentation but as function. The adjective or adverb which in some way is not a living, functioning cell is a dead and useless body that only obstructs the healthy physiology of the text. In opposition to the verbal profusion of modernism, Borges proposed a definition of style which constitutes a veritable turning point: *"Plena eficiencia y plena invisibilidad serían las dos perfecciones de cualquier estilo."* ("Total effectiveness and total invisibility should be the twin aims of any style.")[28] Here, as early as 1928, Borges had enunciated a theory of style that only two and a half decades later found a similar formulation in so-called "writing degree zero."

In contemporary French fiction, Roland Barthes' dictum came to define a whole trend against the tradition of stylistic artistry; the intention was to replace estheticist language by a bare, simple, colorless one. "This neutral writing," according to Barthes, "rediscovers the primary condition of classical art: instrumentality. . . . Initiated by Camus' *Outsider,* it achieves a style of absence which is almost an ideal absence of style . . .; it deliberately forgoes any elegance or ornament; it is the mode of a new situation of the writer, the way a certain silence has of existing."[29] But if Barthes found a felicitous designation for this new outlook of style, the style itself was not only, as Barthes himself acknowledges, "a phenomenon invented by authors like Camus,"[30] it was also clearly and keenly defined by Camus himself two years earlier. "If," writes Camus in *The Rebel,* "stylization must necessarily be rather exaggerated, since it sums up the intervention of man and the desire for rectification which the artist brings to his reproduction of reality, it is nevertheless desirable that it should remain *invisible* so that the demand which gives birth to art should be expressed in its most extreme tension. *Great style is invisible stylization, or rather stylization incarnate.*"[31] This is identical to Borges' formula of invisibility of style. What is even more surprising than the coincidence, however, is its implication. Camus published his essay in 1951. By then, Borges had already published most of his narrative work; back when he formulated his concept of style, Camus was only fourteen. My point is that if it is true that the tradition of a highly wrought language came to Latin America primarily from France,[32] it is no less true that through Borges Spanish American novelists rid themselves of estheticism much earlier than the French, who only did so, led by Camus, in the late forties. This is certainly a new phenomenon for a literature like that of Latin America, which has traditionally depended on foreign models.

As a theorist of the new language the Latin American writer was searching for, Borges did not abound in slogans or manifestoes. Instead, he diligently applied himself to the difficult task of dissecting the deadened language in an effort to establish the causes of its long disease. One has only to look into his half-dozen books of essays to realize the extent of this undertaking. As early as 1927, Borges saw the wealth of words about which the Royal Spanish Academy boasts as "a necrological spectacle" and "a statistical superstition," since "what counts is not the number of symbols but the number of ideas," and he adds that the Spanish language cannot claim "great thoughts or great feelings, that is to say, great poetry or great philosophy."[33] He further assails the Academy for having "always used the Spanish language for purposes of death, of discouragement, of advice, of remorse, of scruples, of misgivings, or – in too many cases – for puns and plays on words, which in themselves are a form of death." Borges finally offers his own program: ". . . we would prefer a pliant and hopeful Spanish which would be in harmony with our landscape and our own ways and our professed faith."[34] In search of this language, Borges resorted to style analysis long before stylistics became a practiced method in Spanish criticism. Disregarding conventions and canons, he treated established writers with the same rigor as he did his contemporaries. In the close examination of a sonnet by Góngora or Quevedo, in the minute analysis of a line from *Martín Fierro,* in the meticulous "inquisitions" into the expressive possibilities and limitations of the adjective and the metaphor, Borges explored and studied the mechanics of a text. He did not hesitate to disparage established work in an effort to destroy the myths that had stiffened literary language. Thus, for example, in distinguished pieces by Ortega, Lugones, or Gabriel Miró he found that the language was euphoniously beautiful but expressively superfluous. Overwhelmed by the exigencies of studying a writer through close examination, Borges has pessimistically concluded that a consistent esthetic is altogether impossible:

> If no word is useless, if even a common *milonga* is a whole network of stylistic successes and failures, how can anyone hope to explain that "tide of pomp that beats upon the high shore of this world" – the 1056 quarto pages attributed to Shakespeare? How can we take seriously those who judge these pages en masse, with no method other than a wondrous flow of awe-stricken praise, and never looking into a single line?[35]

Borges was also among the first in Latin America to stimulate and advise the use of colloquial language in a literature where, as Cortázar jests, the writer "wears a stiff collar and climbs the highest mountain whenever he decides to write." Borges defended the legitimacy of colloquial language in literature, thus anticipating the wide use of it in the present Spanish American novel, where it has become a significant asset. As far back as 1927, Borges posed the question:

> What unbridgeable gap lies between the Spanish of the Spaniards and that of the Argentines? I say none, luckily for the mutual

understanding of our speech. There is, though, a nuance of difference: a nuance so slight as not to hamper the full circulation of the language, and yet clear enough to make us fully aware of an Argentine consciousness. I am not thinking here of the many thousands of local colloquialisms that Spaniards hardly understand. I think of the different tone of our voice, of the ironic or kindly coloring we give to certain words. . . . We have not varied the intrinsic meaning of words, but we have varied their connotation.[36]

Among the new Latin American novelists, it is Cortázar who has best echoed Borges' efforts on behalf of a more expressive and living Spanish and has most brilliantly taken over "the battle of language." While acknowledging that he is neither critic nor essayist, Cortázar has created an original and highly successful type of essay entirely appropriate to his search for naturalness, humor, and anti-solemnity in language. A close reading of his essays immediately shows that his revision of Spanish in the framework of Argentine letters is a renewal of Borges' earlier undertaking. In one of his central essays on this subject, Cortázar urges "the revision of our literary impossibilities as Borges once did."[37] Cortázar renews the attacks against "the pseudo-style of surface," "the verbose Spain of *tertulias,*" "inflated language," and "the lavish adjective"; like Borges, he praises the Spanish of Cervantes and Quevedo and the prose of Sarmiento. And again like Borges, Cortázar formulates his own concept of style, one "born out of a patient and arduous meditation on our reality and our language,"[38] which could well be the complement of Borges' "total effectiveness and total invisibility."

The alternative to an invisible style has come from the Cuban novelist Alejo Carpentier. He holds that "our art has always been baroque," and that "the legitimate style of today's Latin American novelist is the baroque."[39] Thus Carpentier belabors a point that is hardly acceptable, for when he says "today's Latin American novelist" he is thinking primarily of himself. In his novels he has adopted an Olympian, baroque style which stands at the opposite extreme of Borges' dictum – a style so *visible* that it ends by distracting the reader and even annoying him. Just as Borges struggles to avoid uncouth, archaic, or astonishing words, Carpentier wrestles to display all the treasures of the dictionary – in fact, he has advocated a return to "the forgotten part of the dictionary." The prose of the new Spanish American novel has carefully avoided this lavish language. The reason is clear: while the baroque style preached and practiced by Carpentier flaunts a bookishness that alienates the reader, the new novel seeks – conversely – to involve him deeply. What Carpentier's dazzling style creates is an estranging distance between author and reader, while in the new novel the effort is toward producing a "reader-accomplice" who, according to Cortázar's explanation, becomes "a coparticipant and cosufferer of the experience through which the novelist is passing."[40] As for stylistic artistry, the same text points out that to reach this reader "artistic tricks are of no use: the only worthwhile thing is the material in gestation . . . transmitted through words, of course, but the least esthetic words possible."[41] Hence the presence of colloquial and informal language in the new novels. Even in the works of younger novelists where language seems to become a reality in itself, style is straightforward and masterfully plain rather than ostentatiously baroque. It would be accurate to conclude that the new Latin American novel, instead of choosing the road of baroque language, has followed Borges' formula of invisibility, which in its latest version reads:

> I lay no claim to any particular theories. Time has led me to the use of certain devices: to shun synonyms, which labor under the disadvantage of suggesting imaginary differences; to shun Hispanisms, Argentinisms, archaisms, and neologisms; to employ common words rather than unusual ones; to work into a story circumstantial details, which readers now insist on; to feign slight uncertainties, for, although reality is exact, memory is not; to narrate events (this I got from Kipling and the Icelandic sagas) as if I did not wholly understand them; to bear in mind that the rules I have just set down need not always be followed, and that in time they will have to be changed. Such devices, or habits, hardly make up a theory of literature. Besides, I am skeptical of aesthetic theories.[42]

If one considers that the prose of his early essays suffered the same ills he intended to cure,[43] it was not Borges' patient laboratory of "inquisitions" into the language that truly set a model for the new novelists, but the prose of his short stories. There Borges has created a language that, to use Cortázar's words, "can invent and can open the door to the game; a language that has produced a style born out of a patient and arduous meditation of our reality and our word." The novelists who came after Borges are now writing a prose different from that written by the author of *Dreamtigers*, but before leaving Borges they had first come to him. In both ways, he is present in the spirit and the flesh of the contemporary novel.

NOTES

1   I quote Morris Dickstein, *The New York Times Book Review*, April 26, 1970: ". . . in the last three years an important segment of American fiction has

entered a new and more unexpected phase, a more deliberately experimental one, far less likely to issue in best-sellerdom and *succès de scandale*. Call this the Borgesian phase, though Borges has not been the only model for the short, sometimes dazzlingly short, and multi-layered fiction that is involved. (Interestingly, Borges' example has served to release the influence of others, including his own master, Kafka, and even such different writers as Beckett and Robbe-Grillet.)" I should add that American writers such as John Barth and John Updike have dedicated enthusiastic and lucid essays to Borges' work. See also Tony Tanner's remarks on Borges in his *City of Words: American Fiction 1950–1970* (London, 1971).

2 Ernesto Sábato, *Sobre héroes y tumbas* (Buenos Aires, 1969), p. 164.

3 Borges concludes as follows: ·"The fact that Banchs, when speaking of his great suffering which overwhelms him, when speaking of this woman who has left him and has left the world empty for him, should have recourse to foreign and conventional images like slanted roofs and nightingales, is significant: significant of Argentine reserve, distrust and reticence, of the difficulty we have in making confessions, in revealing our intimate nature" (*L*, 180).

4 See Sábato's articles "En torno de Bores," *Casa de las Américas* (Havana, 1963), III, No. 17–18, pp. 7–12; "Los dos Borges," *Indice* (Madrid, 1961), XV, No. 150–151, pp. 6–7; "Borges y Borges el argentino y la metafísica," *Vida Universitaria* (Monterrey, Mexico, April 12, 1964), pp. 3–18; and, particularly, "Borges y el destino de nuestra dicción," in his book of essays *El escritor y sus fantasmas* (Buenos Aires, 1964), pp. 245–57.

5 What Sábato does not seem to realize is that Tolstoy (like any other writer) deals with his characters' lives or deaths by means of words, and that in a reality constructed with words (literature), one adverb too many or too few is often decisive. Also, if one takes Sábato's irony at its face value, the importance of one adverb varies in degree according to the genre. In poetry, for example, or in the short story, one word (even an adverb) may sometimes be the key to its success. Finally, as Borges has not written any novel, Sábato's example of Tolstoy is, to say the least, rather imprecise.

6 Sábato, *Sobre Héroes y tumbas*, p. 174.

7 On this aspect of his work, see "The Argentine Writer and Tradition," L, 177–85.

8 In the case of Sábato, it should be pointed out that he worked with Borges on the editorial board of the magazine *Sur* during the years when Borges published most of his prose writings. Many of his stories and essays appeared in the same magazine, and the least one can assume is that Sábato read them and discussed them thoroughly with friends and colleagues.

Obviously the question of what is Argentine and what is not was a problem that troubled most Argentine writers who, from the twenties on, engaged in a search for alternatives to the regionalist themes that dominated Argentine fiction. Borges was not alone in that quest, but undoubtedly the flourishing of fantastic and detective literature that followed can hardly be explained without bearing in mind Borges' efforts in that direction. Cortázar, another Argentine writer deeply preoccupied by this question, has said of this matter: "Like Borges and a few others, I seem to have understood that the best way to be an Argentine is not to run around broadcasting the fact all the time, especially not in the stentorian tones used by the so-called autochthonous writers. . . . I think there's a deeper way of being an Argentine, which might make itself felt, for instance, in a book where Argentina is never mentioned." L. Harss and B. Dohmann, *Into the Mainstream* (New York, 1967), p. 238.

9 In this regard, Roger Caillois distinguishes between marvelous (*merveilleux*) and fantastic art; while the marvelous encompasses "*les oeuvres d'art créés expressément pour surprendre, pour dérouter le spectateur par l'invention d'un univers imaginaire, féerique, où rien ne se présente ni se passe comme dans le monde réel,*" the fantastic is a more permanent and universal art: "*le fantastique me parut venir, plutôt que du sujet, de la manière de le traiter.*" *Au coeur du fantastique* (Paris, 1965), pp. 8–9. For further discussion on the differences between the two concepts, see Roger Caillois' preface to *Anthologie du fantastique* (Paris, 1958) and also his *Images, images* . . . (Paris, 1966).

10 In a 1970 interview, Cortázar said: "Borges nous a beaucoup marqués, nous les écrivains de ma génération. Il nous a montré les possibilités inouïes du fantastique. En Argentine, on écrivait plutôt une littérature romantique, réaliste, un peu populaire parfois, le fantastique est né vraiment à haut niveau avec Borges." C. G. Bjurström, "Entretien avec J. Cortázar," *La quinzaine littéraire*, 100 (August 1970), 16.

11 Elsewhere, I have studied these two stories in an attempt to show how the same theme is resolved differently at the levels of structure and style. See "Dos soluciones estilísticas al tema del *compadre* en Borges y Cortázar" in *La prosa narrativa de J. L. Borges*, apéndice II (Madrid: Gredos, 1983).

12 Jean Franco, *An Introduction to Spanish-American Literature* (Oxford, 1969), p. 346.

13 Gabriel García Márquez, *Cien años de soledad* (Buenos Aires, 1967), p. 161.

14 *Ibid.*, p. 350.

15 G. Márquez–V. Llosa, *La novela en América Latina: diálogo* (Lima, 1969).

16 G. Márquez, *op. cit.*, p. 350. Italics added.

17 In one of Octavio Paz's most ambitious poems, "Blanco," I found these verses in which, much as they reflect Paz's own metaphysical preoccupations, no reader of Borges will fail to sense familiar vibrations:

El espíritu
Es una invención del cuerpo
El cuerpo
Es una invención del mundo
El mundo
Es una invención del espíritu

For the unfamiliar reader, I quote the following lines with which Borges closes his essay "Avatars of the Tortoise": "We . . . have dreamed the world. We have dreamed it strong, mysterious, visible, ubiquitous in space and secure in time; but we have allowed tenuous, eternal interstices of injustice in its structure so we may know that it is false" (*OI*, 115).

18 G. Castañeda Aragón, "P. Neruda habla para Colombia," interview published in *Repertorio Americano* (Costa Rica, August 9, 1941). This statement was later elaborated in Neruda's book *Viajes*. There he has written: "Martí has said of Quevedo: 'He penetrated so deeply into what was coming that those who live today speak with his tongue.' Speak with his tongue. . . . What is Martí referring to here? To Quevedo's status as father of the language – a situation similar to Rubén Darío's, whom we will spend half of our lives disowning, to understand later that without him we would not speak our own tongue, that is, that without him we would be still talking a hardened, pasteboard, tasteless language." *Viajes* (Santiago, 1955), pp. 12–13.

19 Octavio Paz, "Rubén Darío," in *Cuadrivio* (Mexico, 1965), pp. 11–65.

20 J. L. Borges, "Leopoldo Lugones," unpublished lecture given at Princeton University, 1967. (The passage is a transcription from the recorded version.)

21 García Márquez–Vargas Llosa, *La novela en América Latina: diálogo* (Lima, 1969), pp. 36, 40.

Undoubtedly, García Márquez's admiration for Borges' "extraordinary capacity for verbal artifice" has left deep imprints on his own prose. In a recent article on this subject, Suzanne J. Levine traces some possible influences on García Márquez's approach to biography. She mentions Marcel Schwob's *Vies imaginaires* and Borges' *Historia universal de la infamia*. She also points out that there are reasons to believe that Virginia Woolf's *Orlando* had a strong impact on García Márquez's novel, and that in all probability he read *Orlando* in the Spanish translation by Borges, "thus assimilating the style and the art of the English writer through the language of Borges in a translation that, in many cases, is more concise and imaginative than the original itself." ("*Cien años de soledad* y la tradición de la biografía imaginaria," in *Revista Iberoamericana* XXXVI, 72 [July–Sept., 1970], 453–63.)

22 An Argentine novel, written in 1908 by Enrique Larreta, which typifies the archaic and inflated Spanish that Cortázar deprecates.

23 Julio Cortázar, *La vuelta al día en ochenta mundos* (México, 1967), p. 100.

24 *Ibid.*

25 Carlos Fuentes, *La nueva novela hispanoamericana* (México, 1969), p. 30.

26 Juan Ramón Jiménez, theorist and practitioner of this esthetic, has defined modernism as "a movement towards beauty."

27 Borges, "La supersticiosa ética del lector," in *Discusión* (Buenos Aires, 1957), p. 45.

28 Borges, "Eduardo Wilde," in *El idioma de los argentinos* (Buenos Aires, 1928), p. 158.

29 Roland Barthes, *Writing Degree Zero* (London, 1967), pp. 83–84. (First published in 1953 as *Le degré zéro de l'écriture*.)

30 *Ibid.*, p. 73.

31 Albert Camus, *The Rebel* (New York, 1961), pp. 271–72. Italics added.

32 Although modernism borrowed from many sources, it is generally accepted

that it primarily derived from French symbolism and the Parnassian trend, bringing for the French much blessing as well as much evil (for *afrancesamiento* and other ills in Spanish literature, see Unamuno).

33 *El idioma de los argentinos* (Buenos Aires, 1928), pp. 170–74.

34 *Ibid.,* pp. 182–83.

35 Borges, "Elementos de preceptiva," *Sur,* III, 7 (April 1933), 161.

36 Borges, *El idioma de los argentinos,* pp. 178–79.

37 Cortázar, *La vuelta al dia en ochenta mundos,* p. 96.

38 *Ibid.,* p. 100.

39 Alejo Carpentier, *Tientos y diferencias* (México, 1964), pp. 42–43.

40 Cortázar, *Hopscotch* (New York, 1966), p. 397.

41 *Ibid.*

42 Borges, Preface to *Elogio de la sombra* (In Praise of Darkness) (Buenos Aires, 1969), pp. 9–10. Translated by Norman Thomas di Giovanni in collaboration with the author.

43 One can easily understand Borges' adamant refusal to republish those "forgotten and forgettable" early volumes of essays.

13 Borges' modernism and the new critical idiom

In his essay on modern man, Jung has observed that although "many people call themselves modern – especially the pseudo-moderns – the really modern man is often to be found among those who call themselves *old-fashioned*."[1] I doubt very much if Jung's category of modern man befits Borges. Writers like Musil, Beckett and Cortázar come much closer to this definition, even to the point of providing an illustration for Jung's profile of modern man. But I cannot think of anyone who has more strongly claimed to be old-fashioned and who has more consistently defended his right to be so than Borges. When asked about contemporary authors or more fashionable trends of thought, he has invariably replied that he "is not to blame if he was born in this century," adding: "Why should one pick his literary preferences from twentieth-century writers when one has thirty centuries of literature to choose." Supporting this seeming eccentricity, André Maurois has pointed out, rather hyperbolically, that "Borges has read everything, and especially what nobody reads anymore."[2] More recently, in William Buckley's interview, Borges has been held responsible for "reintroducing Americans to American writers," but to nineteenth-century American writers. "Borges reminds me" – writes Alfred Kazin – "not of contemporaries, not of any novelists, but of Poe and Melville, of Emerson and Thoreau, even to their 'immaturity'."[3] Being old-fashioned in an age that worships contemporaneity is an expression of modernity, because, according to Jung, "to be 'unhistorical' is the Promethean sin, and in this sense the modern man is sinful."[4]

As for Borges, only when he stopped aping seventeenth-century Spanish writers, from Saavedra Fajardo to Quevedo and Gracián, did he begin to write the prose for which he is now known. He refers to those early years as his baroque period: "I used to write in a very baroque and

166

ostentatious style. Out of timidity, I believed that if I wrote in a simple way, people would think that I did not know how to write. I felt then the need to prove that I knew many rare words and that I was able to combine them in a very startling fashion."[5] Borges was then playing the role of being a modern writer, and by so doing he was, at most, a pseudo-modern. He was honoring a Spanish tradition against which he would eventually wage a fierce war, but even this was a form of attitudinizing. If "an honest admission of modernity means voluntarily declaring oneself bankrupt, taking the vows of poverty and chastity in a new sense, and – what is still more painful – renouncing the halo of sanctity which history bestows," as Jung has asserted, Borges' modernity as a writer begins with his own admission of the bankruptcy of the Spanish language (in his 1927 essay "The Language of Argentines"), with his acceptance of the poverty of literature as a whole, and with his acknowledgment that "perhaps universal history is the history of the diverse intonation of a few metaphors."[6] The consequence of the first admission is the notion of style as "total efficiency and total invisibility," and the conclusion of the second, the idea that the writer's task is less to invent new metaphors than to rewrite old ones.

Borges was able to derive these two fundamental tenets only after he moved from a limited and provincial outlook on literature to a more cosmopolitan one. He remained old-fashioned in the sense that while reading Joyce he thought of Góngora, as he wrote in an essay of 1925,[7] and while reading Kafka he was able to trace his precursors back to Zeno, Kierkegaard, Lord Dunsany, and Robert Browning.[8] Borges resisted the dazzling and bewildering impressions that modern writers leave us with. Instead, he read them as updated versions of those few metaphors Homer coined once and for all. Raymond Queneau has said that "all literary work is either an *Iliad* or an *Odyssey*."[9] Much earlier, Borges advanced a similar thesis: "The *Iliad*" – he wrote in *A History of Eternity* – "was composed some three thousand years ago; during this vast lapse of time every familiar and necessary affinity has been noted and recorded. This does not mean, of course, that the number of metaphors has been exhausted; the ways of stating or hinting at these hidden sympathies are, in fact, limitless."[10] Later, he will arrive at a conclusion which is a direct result of this early finding: "Perhaps it is a mistake to suppose that metaphors can be invented: the real ones, those that formulate intimate connections between one image and another, have always existed; those we can still invent are the false ones, which are not worth inventing."[11] Borges reads literature not as an archipelago of isolated texts, but as a written continent that comprises one single text. This holistic approach led him to the views of literature that form the backbone of his essay

"The Flower of Coleridge," in which he quotes Valéry as saying that "the history of literature should not be the history of the authors and their work but rather the history of the Spirit," and refers to Shelley, who said that "all the poems of the past, present, and future are fragments of a single infinite poem."[12] The ultimate inference of this reasoning is the statement that "one literature differs from another not so much because of the text as for the manner in which it is read."[13] The writer's task is therefore to read anew those few metaphors, to rewrite, as Pierre Menard did, the *Quixote*, or as John Barth put it, referring to that story, "to write an original work of literature, the implicit theme of which is the difficulty, perhaps the unnecessity, of writing original works of literature."[14] Literature as a formal game? Literature as a verbal algebra? Literature as a mere syntax? Yes. Such is the sweeping conclusion that closes his short piece "Elementos de preceptiva": "Literature is fundamentally a syntactic fact."

That article was published in *Sur* in April 1933, the same year that most of the stories later to be collected in *A Universal History of Infamy* (1935) appeared in *Crítica*. The two conclusions presented in the short note defined two basic elements of Borges' more mature concept of literature: first, the place and function of each word or group of words as the unit that conditions the effective or ineffective performance of a text, and therefore "the validity of rhetoric as a discipline of literary analysis"; and second, the formulation, in a nutshell, of a theory of literature which views writing as rewriting. I believe that Borges' modernity stems from these two main assumptions; one deals with language, and the other with syntax or structure as the text's basic raison d'être.

As early as 1927, Borges defined "total efficiency and total invisibility as the twin perfections of any style."[15] At the time he pronounced this dictum, it was only a desideratum, since he was still writing in the very Mannerist style he was castigating and rejecting. Only with the narratives of *A Universal History of Infamy* did he put this theoretical machinery to work. There are, of course, some differences between the prose style of *Inquisitions* (1925) and the prose of *The Language of Argentines* published three years later: fewer pompous words, showy neologisms, and tortuous constructions, but still a rather heavy and obtrusive prose. The last essay in the collection, the one that gives the title to the book, approaches the prose of the first essays of *Discusión* (1932), written in the late 1920s. It is not yet the compressed and free-flowing style of his more mature prose; there are still residues of the old style,[16] but one can easily notice a gradual cleansing of the baroque arabesques of his early writing. By 1933, the year of publication of the first stories of infamy, and in spite of what he later said in the preface to the collection

("The very title of these pages flaunts their baroque character"), he was able to write a more restrained, smooth, and balanced prose.[17]

The metaphysical perplexities of his later fiction are still missing in this collection, but one recognizes the basic traits of his masterful prose – a transparency one is tempted to call invisible, and, at the same time, the subtle use of a clockwork of stylistic devices. Five years after he defined what style ought to be, he produced a prose that was the skillful praxis of that earlier program.

The stories of infamy are also important on a different account. They represent the first instance in which Borges applied the literary strategy disclosed for the first time in the short note of 1933, namely that "literature is fundamentally a syntactic fact." In the preface to the 1954 edition of *A Universal History of Infamy*, he wrote: "These pages are the irresponsible game of a shy young man who dared not write stories and so amused himself by falsifying and distorting the tales of others."[18] Yet, the method of writing adopted in this first collection will become a permanent feature of his poetics of fiction in later collections. When he wrote the preface of 1954, he already knew, if one is to take his explanation at its face value, that he was going to remain *shy* for the rest of his literary career; but he turned his shyness into his most daring weapon. What he said about his tales of infamy applies to his entire narrative work. After *Ficciones* and *The Aleph,* he repeated, in the same apologetic tone of the 1954 preface, that he was rewriting what others had already written: "Everything I have written could be found in Poe, Stevenson, Wells, Chesterton, and some others."[19] One is tempted to dismiss this and similar declarations as sheer modesty, or perhaps false modesty. The truth is that the statement is neither literally accurate nor completely false; it is rather a casual formulation, with modesty as its dress, of what can be regarded as the cornerstone of his poetics. He is suggesting informally the same idea very carefully formulated in the essays quoted earlier, namely, writing as rewriting. Throughout prologues and comments, Borges will tirelessly restate this central notion. About the novel *The Approach to Almutasim,* that the story with the same title reviews, he said that it shows "the double tutelage of Wilkie Collins and of Farid uddin Attar"; about "The Library of Babel" he wrote: "I am not the author of this narrative; those curious to know its history and its prehistory may interrogate a certain page of the 59th issue of the journal *Sur,* which records the heterogeneous names of Leucippus and Lasswitz, of Lewis Carroll and Aristotle" (*F*, 15). Of the Circular Ruins," which is a recasting of the legend of the golem, he said: "Lewis Carroll gave me my epigraph, which may have been the story's seed" (*A*, 267). Of "Street-corner Man": "This story was written under the triple influence of Stevenson, G. K. Chesterton, and Josef von Sternberg's unforgettable gangster films" (*A*, 264). Of "Death and the Compass": "Should I add that the Hasidim included saints and that the sacrifice of four lives in order to obtain the four letters imposed by the Name is a fantasy which dictated the form of my story" (*F*, 105). Of "The Life of Tadeo Isidoro Cruz": "This tale is a gloss of the gaucho poem *Martín Fierro*, written by Hernández in 1872" (*A*, 270). Of "The End": "Apart from one character – Recabarren – nothing or almost nothing is an invention of mine; everything in it is implicit in a famous book, and I have merely been the first to reveal, or at least, to declare it" (*F*, 105). Of "Three Versions of Judas": "In this Christological fantasy I believe I perceive the remote influence of León Bloy" (*F*, 107). The postscript to "The Immortal" registers interpolations, intrusions or thefts from Pliny, De Quincey, Descartes, and Bernard Shaw, and Borges said of this story: "Blake wrote that if our senses did not work – if we were blind, deaf, etc. – we would see things as they are: infinite. "The Immortal" sprang from that strange idea and also from the verse by Rupert Brooke, "And see, no longer blinded by our eyes" (*A*, 279). Of "The Dead Man": "Azevedo Bandeira, in that story, is a coarse divinity, a wild and mulatto version of Chesterton's incomparable Sunday (Chapter 29 of *Decline and Fall of the Roman Empire* tells a destiny similar to Otálora's but by far greater and more incredible)" (*A*, 271). Of "The Other Dead": "The eleventh-century churchman Pier Damiano grants God the unimaginable power of undoing the past. This idea gave me the start for my story" (*A*, 272).

One can find similar acknowledgments for most of his stories. It will be wrong to take them as demonstrations of sheer intellectual probity or mere modesty. They are of a piece with his proposition that literature is "the diverse intonations of a few metaphors" stated in a sketchy yet unequivocal way in the short note of 1933. In the "Afterword" for the English translation of *Doctor Brodie's Report*, he reiterates: "William Morris thought that the essential stories of man's imagination had long since been told and that by now the storyteller's craft lay in rethinking and retelling them . . . I do not go as far as Morris went, but to me the writing of a story has more of a discovery about it than of deliberate invention." (*DBR*, 123)

Unknowingly, Borges was placing himself at the very center of one of the most modern approaches to literary theory. The Russian Formalists strove to define literature in terms similar to the ones enunciated by Borges. They believed that texts are not born in a vacuum, but evolve from other texts. What changes is less the ideas elicited by them than the new syntax that governs the rewriting of the old text. Eichenbaum, for instance, found that Tolstoy created the new Russian novel following the

direct legacy of the eighteenth-century novel; Osip Brik ascertained that
the vaudeville writer Belopiatkin was reborn in Nekrasov. They also
concluded that Blok canonized the themes and rhythms of the "Gypsy
Song," that Chekhov bestowed literary status to the *Budilnik,* a comic
newspaper in nineteenth-century Russia, and that Dostoevski brought to
his works the devices of the dime novel.[20] Their overall conclusion was
that "new forms come about not in order to express new contents but in
order to replace old forms."[21] Viktor Shklovsky, in his essay "Art as
Artifice," gives further and rather surprising support to Borges' own
outlook on literature as "the diverse intonations of a few metaphors."
Shklovsky's comment sounds like a paraphrase of Borges' notion: "Images" – he says – "originate nowhere, they belong to God. The more
one gets to know a period, the more one is persuaded that those images
that were considered as a creation of this or that poet, were taken by him
from another poet almost without any modification. The task of poetic
schools is no other than the accumulation and revelation of new devices
for *disposing* and elaborating the verbal material, and it consists in the
disposition of the images rather than in their creation. Images are there
once and for all, and in poetry they are remembered rather than utilized
for thinking."[22] Although Shklovsky's article was published as early as
1917, it is most unlikely that Borges knew it. The doctrine of the Formalists was not known in Western Europe until the 1940s, when Jakobson moved to the United States and one of his students, Victor Erlich,
published in 1955 the first book-length survey of the movement. One is
forced to conclude that Borges was working on his own, and that he
arrived independently at conclusions similar to those reached by the
Formalists. Besides, critical theory was for him a subsidiary undertaking
intended to sharpen his own awareness as a writer. He did what the
Formalists did not do: he incorporated some of his ideas about literature
into his creative writing, thus amalgamating theory and craft.

If one thinks of French structuralism as a consequence and derivation
of Russian Formalism – and Lévi-Strauss was the first to acknowledge
the debt of his anthropology to Vladimir Propp and the members of the
Opoiiaz – it is understandable that Borges' notion of literature as syntax
overlapped with the structuralist concept of literature as a system (Barthes). It is also understandable that a structuralist critic such as Gérard
Genette should read Borges with so much fascination and conviction.
Genette echoed Borges' enthusiasm for the idea of all literature constitut-
ing a single text, and relying on this assumption proposed the following
definition: "Literature is a coherent whole, a congruous space in whose
interior the works touch and penetrate each other."[23] He further sup-
ported his definition with the notion of writing as rewriting developed

by Borges in the essay "For Bernard Shaw" where he wrote: "If I were to read any contemporary page as it would be read in the year 2000, I would know what the literature would be like in the year 2000" (*OI*, 173). Genette quotes this sentence as the foundation for a structuralist theory of literature.

In the first part of "Elementos de preceptiva," Borges undertakes the stylistic examination of a *milonga* discovered "in a rural grocery store near Arapey, at the beginning of 1931." He leaves to Spitzer, he says, "las vivencias originales que la determinaron;" he simply seeks to explore its verbal effectiveness. What this example shows, Borges concludes, together with the analysis of two lines from the tango *Villa Crespo*, is that "a subtle interplay of changes, clever frustrations and supports defines the aesthetic artifact; those who neglect or ignore it, ignore literature's raison d'être."[24] Borges was showing in 1933 that poetic functions are not exclusive attributes of literary texts; they can appear in a *milonga* or a tango, or even in an anonymous inscription written on a street wall.

Roman Jakobson will say and do something similar in 1960. To prove that "the linguistic study of the poetic function must overstep the limits of poetry,"[25] he examined the various phonetic and morphological functions operating in the structural system of the election slogan, "I like Ike." For Jakobson, poetics, as the discipline that deals with problems of verbal structure, sees literature much as Borges did in 1933, as a syntactic construct. In the same essay, Jakobson warned that "the terminological confusion of 'literary studies' with 'criticism' tempts the student of literature to replace the description of intrinsic values of literary works by a subjective, censorious verdict."[26] Borges voiced, at the conclusion of his 1933 short note, a similar warning: "If there is no single word written in vain, if even a popular *milonga* is a world of attractions and rejections, how to elucidate the 1056 quarto-pages attributed to a Shakespeare? How to take seriously those who judge them as a whole, without any method other than a loud emission of terrifying praises, and without examining a single line?"[27]

Finally, I would like to add that when Borges postulated in 1927 "total invisibility and total effectiveness as the twin perfections of any style," he was anticipating Camus by twenty-four years. It was not until 1951 when the author of *The Rebel* wrote that "great style is invisible stylization, or rather stylization incarnate."[28] Two years later, Roland Barthes studied this trend against artistry in contemporary French fiction and coined the formula "writing degree zero." What he said in his essay was a restatement and a development of Camus' basic point: "This neutral writing achieves a style of absence which is almost an ideal absence of style . . .; it deliberately foregoes any elegance or ornament; it is the mode of a new situation of the writer, the way a certain silence has of existing."[29] More straightforward, more matter-of-fact, Borges had been saying the same in the 1920s, and had been putting this principle to work in his own writing since the 1930s. But Borges lived in Buenos Aires, not in Paris, and he was an Argentine who did not have the prestige and the weight of a literature which, like the French, had been dominating the European literary scene since the eighteenth century. Recognition came late, but the seed of Borges' modernity was already implanted in his early writing.

When Borges' work was translated into most European languages and became better known in Europe and the United States, his fiction and essays became a driving force in modern letters. Some critics have seen Borges' place in contemporary literature as a new example which "served to release the influence of others, including his own master, Kafka, and even such different writers as Beckett and Robbe-Grillet."[30] More germane to our topic is the fact that one of the most recent approaches to have appeared in the critical arena, after structuralism, found its spokesman in Borges. I am referring to intertextuality. Borges wrote the story that became the metaphor and the credo of the new method – "Pierre Menard, Author of the *Quixote*." In addition, at about the same time he wrote "Elements of Rhetoric" he published his first collection of short stories – *A Universal History of Infamy* (1935) – and in the preface strongly stated that he was not the author of those stories but merely their counterfeiter; he meant that he rewrote stories already written by others. Yet this "game of a shy man who dared not to write his own stories"[31] became his strongest asset. Borges turned his "shyness" into a powerful literary weapon by holding that writing is inevitably rewriting. Intertextuality is – in oversimplified terms – the study of the relationships between two or more texts, one that functions as a model or "hypotext" and a second or "hypertext" whose production is based on the first. The most important book on the method to have appeared so far is Gérard Genette's *Palimpsestes. La Littérature au second degré* (Paris, 1982). Genette borrowed the title from a passage in "Pierre Menard, Author of the *Quixote*,"[32] and there is even an indirect acknowledgment (p. 452). The debt to Borges is further recognized throughout Genette's book. Here he defines what the method owes to Borges:

> Attribuant à d'autres l'invention de ses contes, Borges présente au contraire son écriture comme une lecture considérée comme, ou déguisée en lecture son écriture. Ces deux conduites, faut-il le dire, sont complémentaires, elles s'unissent en une métaphore

des relations, complexes et ambiguës, de l'ecriture et de la lecture: relations qui sont bien évidemment – j'y reviendrai s'il le
faut – l'âme même de l'activité hypertextuelle.[33]

Borges always had a keen interest in and a strong attraction to the
classics.[34] After his brief participation in the Spanish brand of the avant-
garde – *ultraísmo* – and later in his more mature period, he gave blunt
signs of impatience toward modern writers. If as early as 1925 he translated into Spanish "the last page" of Joyce's *Ulysses,* from the late fifties
on – as his blindness became more advanced – he turned more and more
toward the past: he began the study of Old English and Old Norse,
returned to his favorite Victorian writers, kept rereading the classics, and
became disdainful and even vitriolic about the moderns. He did his best
to be seen and known as old-fashioned. Ironically, he became not only "a
classic of modern fiction," as John Barth defined him, but also the guru
of modern literary perception.

NOTES

1   Carl G. Jung, "The Spiritual Problem of Modern Man." *The Portable Jung,*
    edited by Joseph Campbell. New York, Viking, 1971, p. 459.
2   André Maurois, "Preface" to *Labyrinths; Selected Stories and Other Writings,*
    edited by D. A. Yates & J. E. Irby. New York, New Directions, 1964, p. ix.
3   Alfred Kazin, "Meeting Borges." *The New York Times Book Review,*May 2,
    1971, p. 5.
4   Carl G. Jung, *op.cit.,* p. 458.
5   James E. Irby, "Encuentro con Borges." *Vida universitaria,* Monterrey,
    Mexico, April 12, 1964, p. 14 (my translation).
6   Borges, *OI,* 8.
7   Borges, "El *Ulises* de Joyce," *I,* 25.
8   Borges, "Kafka and His Precursors." *OI,* 111–113.
9   Quoted by Gérard Genette in *Figuras; retórica y estructuralismo.* Córdoba
    (Argentina), Nagelkop, 1970, p. 187.
10 Borges, *HE,* 74.
11 Borges, *OI,* 47.
12 *Ibid.,* p. 9.
13 *Ibid.,* p. 173.
14 John Barth, "The Literature of Exhaustion." *The Atlantic,* August 1967, p.
    31.
15 Jorge Luis Borges, "Eduardo Wilde," *IA,* 158.
16 See the following paragraphs extracted from his essay "La penúltima versión
    de la realidad" of 1928 and included in *Discusión:* "Gaspar Marin, que ejerce
    la metafísica en Buenos Aires . . . Creo delusoria la oposición entre los dos
    conceptos incontrastables de espacio y de tiempo. Me consta que la ge-
    nealogía de esa equivocación es ilustre . . . Quiero complementar esas dos

imaginaciones ilustres con una mía, que es derivación y facilitación." (*D*, 42–44)

17 If those pages could be called Baroque they are so only in the sense defined by John Barth: "While his own work *is not* Baroque, except intellectually (the Baroque was never so terse, laconic, economical), it suggests the view that intellectual and literary history has been Baroque, and has pretty well exhausted the possibilities of novelty." (Barth, *op.cit.*, p. 34)

As an example of this new, more tempered prose, read this passage from "El espantoso redentor Lazarus Morell": "A principios del siglo diecinueve las vastas plantaciones de algodón que había en las orillas eran trabajadas por negros, de sol a sol. Dormían en cabañas de madera, sobre el piso de tierra. Fuera de la relación madre-hijo, los parentescos eran convencionales y turbios. Nombres tenían, pero podían prescindir de apellidos. No sabían leer." (*HU*, 19)

18 Borges, *Historia Universal*, p. 10 (translation by Norman T. di Giovanni, "Preface to *A Universal History of Infamy*" in *Prose for Borges*, by Mary Kinzie, *TriQuarterly*, No. 25, Fall 1972, p. 203).

19 J. Irby, N. Murat, & C. Peralta, *Encuentro con Borges*. Buenos Aires, Galerna, 1968, pp. 37–38.

20 See L. Matejka & K. Pomorska, eds., *Readings in Russian Poetics; Formalist and Structuralist Views*. MIT Press, 1971, p. 32.

21 *Ibid.*, p. 29.

22 Tzvetan Todorov, ed., *Teoría de la literatura de los formalistas rusos*. Buenos Aires, Signos, 1970, p. 56 (my translation).

23 Gérard Genette, *op.cit.*, p. 186 (my translation).

24 Jorge Luis Borges, "Elementos de preceptiva." *Sur*, año III, No. 7, abril de 1933, p. 159 (my translation).

25 Roman Jakobson, "Linguistics and Poetics." *Style in Language*, edited by Thomas A. Sebeok. MIT Press, 1960, p. 357.

26 *Ibid.*, pp. 351–352.

27 Borges, "Elementos de preceptiva", p. 161 (my translation).

28 Albert Camus, *The Rebel*. New York, 1961, pp. 271–272.

29 Roland Barthes, *Writing Degree Zero*. London, 1967, pp. 83–84. (First published in 1953 as *Le degré zéro de L'écriture*.)

30 Morris Dickstein, *The New York Times Book Review*, April 26, 1970.

31 Jorge Luis Borges, *A Universal History of Infamy*. New York, Dutton, 1979, p. 12 (*UH*, 12)

32 In that passage, Borges writes: "I have reflected that it is permissible to see in this 'final' *Quixote* a kind of palimpsest, through which the traces – tenuous but not indecipherable – of our friend's 'previous' writing should be translucently visible." *Labyrinths; Selected Stories and Other Writings*. New York, New Directions, 1964, p. 44. (*L*, 44)

33 Gérard Genette, *Palimpsestes. La littérature au second degré*. Paris, Seuil, 1982, p. 296.

34 See his essay "Sobre los clásicos" in *Sur* (Buenos Aires, Oct., 1941, No. 85), pp. 7–12.

Epilogue
On Borges' death:
some reflections

On June 14 of 1986, at about 4:30 in the afternoon, I was working on a long essay on Borges for the Charles Scribner Latin American
Encyclopedia in my home in Sarria, Barcelona, where I spent a year teach-
ing at the Universidad Autónoma. The telephone rang. It was María
Kodama. Her voice sounded faint but firm: "It's over. Borges is dead." I
thought of a dozen replies, but none reached my mouth. I mumbled a
few broken sentences, trivia, but I couldn't bring myself to ask her about
funeral or burial arrangements. Borges was too much of a living presence
to be thought of as a dead body. Besides, how do you go about sending
into the grave a man whose life had been a figment of his own literature,
the letter of his own spirit? I hung up more confused than disturbed. One
of those situations in which you don't know what it is that events expect
from you, how you fit into the scheme of things. And then, of course,
the regrets for not having found out the technical details about his burial.
While I was pondering these and other questions, I found myself calling
the Sants Railroad Station in Barcelona to get information about the first
train leaving for Geneva. There was one at 7:10 p.m. that Saturday. I had
barely two hours to pack a few clothes and head for the Station. By 7:15 I
was installed in my couchette on my way to Geneva. Induced by the
drumming of the train wheels rolling on the tracks, I let my mind
wander.

I had been with Borges only three weeks earlier. I knew he was in
Geneva because María Kodama had sent me a New Year's card to
Boston, which was then forwarded to Barcelona, and which I finally
received by the end of January. I answered her and eventually we established telephone communication, but it was not until May 14 that we
agreed on the timeliness of my visit. That Saturday I was returning to
Barcelona from Mannheim and made a stop in Geneva. By 10:30 in the

176

morning I was in the Hotel l'Arbalète, located in a very quiet corner of Geneva, knocking at the door of Borges' room. María opened. Borges was sitting on a chair, meticulously dressed, tie and suit, facing the door. I sat next to him, very close to his right side. His voice sounded husky and punctured with muffled blanks. It was very hard to follow his speech. At times, he had to repeat the same sentence a couple of times before I was able to understand. More disquieting still was the shape his head had taken. The last time I had seen Borges was at Dickinson College in April of 1983. During the sessions of that symposium, he had appeared lively and energetic, vigorous and tireless. The Borges I was sitting next to in Geneva, three years later, was a shadow of the other, a physical ruin. His head was deformed, as if the frontal bone had grown beyond proportion and was threatening to tear the skin through. It was not so much the ravages of time as the onslaught of disease, as if his mind kept growing while his body decayed. Publicly, Borges was suffering from a pulmonary emphysema. The cancer of the liver that eventually killed him was a secret known only to himself, his doctor, and María Kodama. Borges and María left Buenos Aires in November of 1985 after a biopsy revealed the terminal nature of his illness. They spent a short period in Italy and then settled in Geneva. When I visited them, three weeks before the final collapse, María told me that Borges was adamant about not returning to Argentina. Friends and relatives were pressing for his return, and María became the target of slanderous accusations. Borges' answer was his marriage by proxy in Paraguay to María Kodama.

After greeting him – I had met Borges for the first time back in 1969, in Norman, Oklahoma –, he received me kindly and with a warning: "No politics, please." "Borges," I replied, "I came to see you and wish you well." From then on the conversation was smooth, and at times intimate. Of that exchange, I have only the records of my memory, somewhat eroded by the moving circumstances of the encounter. I remember isolated phrases: "Argentine history is a work of fiction, that is, the official version of it." "The military have turned the country into a financial private business." "I am not loved in Argentina." "My nephews have robbed me and my friends have forsaken me." Then he added some details about his break with his closest friend and collaborator Adolfo Bioy Casares, about his refusal to return to Argentina, about the French edition of his complete works in the series "Bibliothèque de la Pléiade" of Gallimard (Cervantes and García Lorca being the only two Spanish authors included in that series). We reminisced about previous encounters in Oklahoma, San Diego, Los Angeles, Buenos Aires, Maine, Chicago, Pennsylvania, and Harvard, where he received an honorary degree in 1981. It was a rambling conversation, digressing from personal comments into literary matters, from food into the ways of the Swiss. But then, that has always been Borges' favorite way of chatting: going wherever the branching and winding corridors of his formidable memory would take him.

By noontime, a nurse showed up to bathe him, help him with daily physical exercises, and feed him lunch. Since Borges needed an afternoon nap, María suggested we go out for lunch, and so we did. The hotel was near the old city of Geneva, and as we strolled the meandering streets of that charming part of town, she showed me the exterior of a beautiful building near a magnificent church, with a stone foundation in one corner. Its falling water was the only sound breaking the deep and ancient silence of the area. She said that she was about to sign a lease on one of the apartments in that building. They had been living in that comfortable hotel since they arrived in Geneva close to six months ago, and they were eager to move to a homier place. She was very excited and filled with expectations about the move. Borges and María did move into that exquisite apartment, but only three days before his death.

We walked through town and headed to the John Calvin *Collège* where Borges had attended school between 1914 and 1919 while his family was living in Geneva. In that yard where we were standing, and under those same arches and galleries, Borges had spent a good chunk of his life learning Latin, German and French, and actually laying the foundations of his legendary erudition. "The city," he would say later of Geneva, "where I read all the great books, from Verlaine to Virgil."[1] Of those adolescent years, Borges wrote: "The first fall of 1914 I started school at the College of Geneva founded by John Calvin. It was a day school. In my class there were some forty of us; a good half were foreigners. The chief subject was Latin, and I soon found out that one could let other studies slide a bit as long as one's Latin was good . . . We lived in a flat on the southern, or old, side of town."[2] María and I were walking around that part of town, and she pointed to a new building on 17 Ferdinand Hodler Street that had been erected after the old one, where Borges and his family had lived, was demolished. But the memory of those years in Geneva, far from having been demolished by time or oblivion, was kept very much alive in Borges' mind and even grew to become the affectionate territory of a second country. In his "Auto-biographical Essay," back in 1970, he wrote: "I still know Geneva far better than I know Buenos Aires, which is easily explained by the fact that in Geneva no two street corners are alike and one quickly learns the differences. Every day, I walked along that green and icy river, the Rhône, which runs through the very heart of the city, spanned by seven quite different-looking bridges."³ Borges chose to die in Geneva. In his last published book – *Los conjurados* (The Conjurors), a 1985 collection of poems – he called Geneva one of his motherlands, and in its title composition he defines Switzerland as "a tower of reason and solid faith."⁴ Borges came to Geneva to search for a country which, through the years, had become very much his own. Argentina, his own country – he felt – had been lost to him, and Switzerland offered him a peace he could not find in his native land.

Argentina was, for Borges, a handful of friends, a few national and family myths, the Spanish language, intimate corners and wistful streets of Buenos Aires. But Argentina was far more than that: a nation that since Perón in the 1940s went through a period of profound changes in its social and political make-up. Borges refused to acknowledge and come to terms with those changes. Like Leopoldo Lugones in the 1920s, a leading Argentine writer who encouraged the military to intervene in the nation's political life and seize power by force so that the country could finally be run as an army barracks, so did Borges. He identified the generals with the fathers of Argentine independence and believed that the military were "the only gentlemen left capable of serving the country." Those gentlemen are now behind bars, tried by civilian courts and sentenced by Argentine laws. Borges could not find solace, let alone national recognition, in that tormented and soul-searching country. So he came to die in the country of his adolescence, in that "tower of reason" where life is as private as its aloof citizens and runs as serenely as the Rhône waters. That environment was much closer to his intellectual constructs and labyrinthine artifices. Perhaps Borges was mistakenly born in Buenos Aires. He wanted to believe – as he wrote – that "the Argentine tradition is all of Western culture." "And I also believe," he added, "we have a right to this tradition, greater than that which the inhabitants of one or another Western nation might have."⁵ He assumed that right and lived in a country that was very far from being European as if it were. History proved him wrong. Argentina is by its past and present, by its problems and dilemmas, an integral part of the Third World. Its future, like that of the rest of Latin America, has been mortgaged to American banks. Its present is still entangled in the hindrances of the past.

Of course I could not discuss this with Borges. I did not come to Geneva for that. Besides, I had no business doing that. I came to renew an old acquaintanceship and to pay homage to the artist. And there I was, with María, back from our stroll, standing by his side, taking photographs: Borges hugging María, clinging to her like a child, holding her as in a permanent farewell. The most vivid and moving impression of that last visit happened at the time of saying goodbye. Borges pressed my hand very hard, with a strength most unusual for him. For a person who has been so diffident, so distant and impersonal, this display of physical warmth and intimacy was an excess, or perhaps a tacit farewell, but I did not know it at the time.

Although back in 1980, in a poem entitled "Cuál será del caminante fatigado . . .", he wrote, "In which one of the various cities will I die? In Geneva, where I received the revelation, not of Calvin, certainly, but that of Virgil and Tacitus?",[6] Borges repeatedly stated that for him life was a burden and that he saw death as a welcome liberation. In a late interview, he said: "My existence is summed up by two illnesses: blindness and longevity," and in a prose poem of 1981 he explained: "What is longevity? It is the horror of being in a human body whose faculties are declining, it is a several decades long insomnia . . . It is not being able to ignore that I am condemned to wanting to sink in death without being able to sink in death, and therefore condemned to be and keep being."[7] In spite of this relentless call for death, most readers of Borges grew accustomed to his longevity, and to the assumption that if he had a mother who lived 99 years, and an aunt who was 100 when she died, he was going to follow suit and become a centenarian.

In a 1978 interview he said again: "If I was told that I would be dying tonight, I think I would feel very happy."[8] And now he was dying. Was he happy? I don't know, and I don't think anybody will ever know, simply because death is the most sealed of all human unknowns. Borges died with the same resignation with which he lived. In his sonnet "Remorse," published in 1976, he wrote: "I have committed the worst sin / That a man can commit. I have not been happy . . ."[9] Even during the peak of his literary success, in 1964, he wrote: "I shall not be happy. Perhaps it doesn't matter / . . . I am left only with the pleasure of being sad."[10] Between this first declaration about his unhappiness in 1964 up to the culmination of the motif in the sonnet "Remorse" of 1976, the topic lingers through this segment of his poetry written between those years. In a TV interview given to William Buckley in the 1970s, Borges said point blank: "I will welcome death, since I am very tired, since life has few pleasures left for me." His biggest pleasure was, of course, writing, and particularly writing poetry, but even the act of writing was viewed by him as a histrionic performance: "I like," he wrote memorably in "Borges and I," "hourglasses, maps, eighteenth-century typography, the taste of coffee, and Stevenson's prose. The other one shares these preferences with me, but in a vain way that converts them into the attributes of an actor . . . I live, I allow myself to live, so that Borges may contrive his literature and that literature justifies my existence."[11]

The act of writing appears here, if not as a duty, as something like a mission. In an earlier essay, I tried to show the epic overtones underlying his late poetry.[12] There are two lines which encapsulate this perception. In one he says: "I am the one who amidst the night counts the syllables," and in the other he defines himself as "A man who weaves hendecasyllabics."[13] Poetry – and literature for the case – are thus understood not so much as means of expressing experience, but as crafted artifacts. I will elaborate on this before returning to Borges the man.

Speaking about his father's unfulfilled literary aspirations, Borges wrote in his "Autobiographical Essay": "From the time I was a boy, when blindness came to my father, it was tacitly understood that I had to fulfill the literary destiny that circumstances had denied my father. This was something that was taken for granted. I was expected to be a writer."[14] In a later interview, he further commented on this assigned destiny:

> I thought I had been born a writer, but now I see that this was not the case. Today I know for sure that this vocation was fostered in me by my father because he himself wanted to be a writer but fate led him into a different direction: he became a lawyer and a psychology teacher . . . That is why I believe that this vocation of mine responds to a happy paternal *imposition*.

The son will carry out the frustrated aspirations of the father. But can literature – an endeavor intended to shape the inner perception of its creator – be passed over from father to son? Was the son's aspiration the same as the father's? And by carrying out the father's aspiration, isn't the son blocking his own? These questions sound futile, since we are dealing with a giant of modern letters, but they could shed some light on the subject of Borges' unhappiness as well as on the ultimate question of Borges' contribution to Hispanic and world literatures.

I recently ran across a psychology book in which I underlined the following remark: "Parents rob their children of their own identity when they demand that their children fulfill their own frustrated ambitions."[15] Even if the ambition was not "demanded" from or forced on Borges the child, it is nevertheless clear that the decision to become a writer was not Borges' own, but his father's. Furthermore, as "happy" as the decision was – in Borges' words – it was *imposed* upon him. I am not suggesting that Borges wrote just in order to please his father. In addition to sounding preposterous, that would be a gross oversimplification of a very complex problem. But I am trying to understand his notion of literature as "a syntactic fact" ("La literatura es fundamentalmente un hecho sintáctico")[16], and his widely quoted belief that "unreality is the necessary condition of art,"[17] coupled with his acknowledgment of unhappiness. I am also trying to understand his unbending refusal to deal with reality.

In an early essay of 1939, Borges was already charting the course that his fiction was eventually to follow: "Let us admit," he says, "what all idealists admit: the hallucinatory nature of the world. Let us do what no idealist has done: seek unrealities which confirm that nature. We shall find them, I believe, in the antinomies of Kant and the dialectic of Zeno."[18] Many of his short stories do precisely that: they present unrealities (a man who dreams a man and inserts him into reality, a library of unreadable books, a year contained in a minute) in which the reader recognizes the conceptualizations of metaphysics and the hypostases of theology. Yet they are stories, plots in whose sets of events and interplays of characters a resemblance of life as we know it from daily living has been conveyed. But it is only a resemblance, since the typical Borgesian story aims not so much – like conventional fiction – at capturing "a slice of life" as at advancing an *argumentum theologicum* or *philosophus*.

This strategy evolved from the conviction that "the inventions of philosophy are no less fantastic than those of art,"[19] and from a definite abhorrence of literary realism often equated with the trite, with the predictable, and even with the fastidious sides of life.[20] It also evolved from Borges' perception of his own life as lacking any drama worth recording or commenting on, at least for the purposes of fiction. As early as 1932 he wrote in the preface to his second most important volume of essays, *Discusión* (1932), this lapidary statement: "My life is devoid of life and death. From this poverty stems my laborious love for these minutiae."[21] Many years later, in his "Autobiographical Essay" of 1970, he reiterated his loyalty to the planet Tlön, that is, to the world of books: "If I were asked to name the chief event of my life, I should say my Father's library. In fact, I sometimes think I have never strayed outside that library."[22]

His story "The House of Asterion" can be read, without overinterpreting it, as Borges' own metaphor. In it, the Minotaur *chooses* to stay in the labyrinth where he has been imprisoned: "One afternoon," he confesses, "I did step into the street; if I returned before night, I did so because of the fear that faces of the common people inspired in me."[23] Confronted with the chaos of the world, Asterion the Minotaur chooses the orderly space he has found in a human construction, Daedalus' labyrinth. Borges has made a similar choice: confronted with the chaos of the world, he has chosen the order of the library, the safety of a decipherable labyrinth. His books grew out of other books. He wrote fiction based on theologies and philosophies, literature founded in literature. He knew that the hard face of reality lurks in every corner of life, but he renounced the world because, he said, of its impenetrable nature. Instead, he anchored his writings in the order of the intellect, in the chartable waters of the library. What he wrote about Paul Valéry is applicable to himself. "In a century that adores idols of blood, earth, and passion, he always preferred the lucid pleasures of thought and the secret adventures of order."[24] Any form of knowledge that challenged his skeptical understanding of the world met with his strong disapproval and even condemnation. In the same essay on Valéry, he wrote: "The meritorious mission that Valéry performed (and continues to perform) is that he proposed lucidity to men in a basely romantic age, in the melancholy age of . . . dialectical materialism, the age of the augurs of Freud's doctrine and traffickers in *surréalisme* . . ."[25] Borges indicts and harshly condemns literary movements (romanticism and surrealism) and forms of thought (Marxism and psychoanalysis) that deal not so much with sheer abstract reasoning (although *in* a highly abstract fashion) but with questions concerning life: distrust of and revolt against the abuses of rational order, class order, and ego order. Life as a subliminal realm, as chance, struggle or desire, seems to horrify him, and any effort addressed to exploring the depths of those waters has been met with resistance and frowns. Borges was an intellectual animal, a solipsist locked – like the Minotaur of his story – in a labyrinth of his own construction.

Because he saw writing as rewriting, and because he showed – in theory as well as in praxis – that "one literature differs from another, either before or after it, not so much because of the text as for the manner in which it is read,"[26] he fascinated structuralists as well as semioticians. Because he concluded in "Pierre Menard, Author of the *Quixote*" that "Cervantes' text and Menard's [version] are verbally identical, but the second is almost infinitely richer,"[27] he dazzled the followers of intertextuality. When he wrote, back in 1953, that since Homer all metaphor had been recorded, adding further, "this does not mean, of course, that the number of metaphors has been exhausted; the ways of stating or hinting at the terms of a given metaphor are, in fact, endless,"[28] he advanced a fundamental tenet in the theory of the Russian Formalists, and prompted John Barth to write his now-famous essay "The Literature of Exhaustion." Finally, because of his invisible and rigorous style, he became – as Carlos Fuentes put it – a sort of father figure of the contemporary Spanish American novel.

Yet his literary work is only the recasting of previous work. I recently unearthed an uncollected speech he gave back in 1945 to thank the Argentine Society of Writers for the Honorary Prize he was awarded as an apology for not having received the National Prize for Literature the year he published *Ficciones*. In that speech, he described the core of his creative laboratory. He said:

> For many years, I believed I had been raised in a suburb of Buenos Aires. The truth is that I was raised in a garden, behind a long iron fence, and in a library of endless English books. The Palermo of the knife-fights and of the guitar was roaming (I am told) about the streetcorners, but those who peopled my mornings and brought enjoyable horror to my nights were R. L. Stevenson's blind buccaneer, agonizing under the hoofs of horses, and the traitor who abandoned his friend in the moon, and the time traveler who brought from the future a withered flower, and the genie locked up in Solomon's jug for many centuries, and the Veiled Prophet from Khurasan who concealed his leprosy with a veil of white silk embossed with precious stones. Thirty years have gone by. The house where those fictions had been revealed to me was demolished. I have traveled through a number of European cities. I have forgotten thousands of pages and thousands of irreplaceable human faces, but I am inclined to think that, essentially, I have never stepped out from that library and from that garden. What I did since then, and what I will continue to do, is simply to weave and unweave stories derived from those early ones.[29]

In the poetry volume *The Gold of the Tigers* of 1972, he wrote an updated version of that early poetics. In the brief prose "The Four Cycles" he reviews four stories: one about a city sieged and defended by brave men (the Troy of the Homeric poems); another, the story of a return (Ulysses comes back to Ithaca); the third, a variation of the last, is about a search (Jason and the Golden Fleece, the thirty birds and the Simurg, Ahab and the whale, the heroes of James and Kafka); and the last one about a sacrifice of a god (Attis, Odin, Christ). Borges then concludes: "Four are the stories. During the time left to us we will continue telling them, transformed."[30]

I have shown elsewhere that his modus operandi is verifiable throughout most of his fiction. The narrative text becomes a reflecting mirror that either inverts or reverts a previous text.[31] Borges was not jesting when he posited the task of literature as that of rewriting old metaphors. What John Updike has said about Borges' essays is applicable to his fiction: "They are structured like mazes and, like mirrors, they reflect back and forth on one another . . . From his immense reading he has distilled a fervent narrowness. The same parables, the same quotations recur."[32]

Where then does Borges' originality lie? Does it amount – as John Barth has suggested – to his having written "original works of literature, the implicit theme of which is the difficulty, perhaps the unnecessity, of writing original works of literature"?[33] I believe that it was Paul de Man who, more than any other critic, came closest to an answer. De Man dismisses the philosophical component of his fiction as the possible explanation for his originality. "Borges," he writes, "should be read with expectations closer to those one brings to Voltaire's *conte philosophique* than to the nineteenth-century novel." And then he adds: "He differs, however, from his eighteenth-century antecedents in that the subject of the stories *is the creation of style itself . . . His stories are about the style in which they are written.*"[34]

Other critics have attested Borges' marriage not with the world of actual experience but with that of intellectual propositions. Alfred Kazin underscores the solipsistic nature of his writings. "Borges," he says, "has built his work, and I suspect his life itself, out of the same effort to make himself a home in his own mind . . . He certainly does not put us in close touch with his own country. His Argentina remains a place of dreams. Borges' mind is the realest thing in it."[35]

George Steiner, likewise, reminds us that "Borges is a curator at heart. He has built an *anti-world,* a perfect and coherent space in which his mind can conjure at will . . . His inventions move away from the active disarray of life."[36] And Patricia Merivale, who has compared Borges' work with Nabokov's, concludes with the following distinction: "While Nabokov usually dismisses his actors 'into thin air' and returns us to the real world, Borges takes the argument to its conclusion and perpetually reminds us that both, author and reader, 'are such stuff as dreams are made on'."[37] The conclusion is inescapable: Borges is a magician with words and a master of artifice. Such is Updike's stance: "Ironic and blasphemous as Borges' hidden message may seem," he writes, "the texture and method of his creations, though strictly inimitable, answer to a deep need in contemporary fiction – the need to confess the fact of artifice."[38]

Latin American writers such as García Márquez, Carlos Fuentes, Ernesto Sábato, Vargas Llosa and others have acknowledged their debt to Borges in terms of a language Spanish literature did not have before him. Julio Cortázar best summarized the extent of that debt: "The great lesson Borges taught us," he said "was neither a lesson in themes nor in contents or techniques. It was a lesson in writing, an attitude. The attitude of a man who, when writing a sentence, has very carefully thought not which adjective to add, but which one to suppress. Later on he fell into the trap of using, in a displayful way, a single adjective in order to dazzle the reader, turning sometimes the effective device into a defect. But originally, Borges' attitude towards the written page was the attitude of a Mallarmé, of extreme rigor and precision."[39]

Did Borges know that his legacy was going to be exactness and rigor in language, that is, a code rather than a message, a style rather than substance, aesthetic artifacts cut off from the world of experience? He not only knew it, he was inflexible in defending that view. In a 1968 interview, he put it squarely: "The 'Parable of the Palace' is a parable about art existing in its own place, but not being given to deal with reality. As far as I can recall it, if the poem is perfect then there's no need for the palace. I mean if art is perfect, then the world is superfluous. Besides, I think that the poet can never cope with reality. So I think of art and nature, well, nature as the world, as being two different worlds."[40] Alfred Kazin was right: the most real thing in Borges' work is his mind. And Borges knew it. Back in 1969, he closed his miscellaneous volume *Dreamtigers* with an epilogue in which he tersely confessed: "Few things have happened to me, and I have read a great many. Or rather, few things have happened to me more worth remembering than Schopenhauer's thought or the music of England's words."[41]

When I arrived in Geneva at seven-thirty in the morning of June 15, the day after Borges died, it was too early to look for María Kodama. I walked from the railroad station to the Hotel L'Arbalète at a slow pace. It was Sunday and the city was deserted. I eventually found an open coffee shop and had breakfast. Only then I crossed one of the seven bridges that span the Rhône and headed for the hotel. María was up, but she was swarmed by journalists and photographers and flooded with telegrams and phone calls from all over. When I finally got to talk to her I learned that there was no date for the funeral. Arrangements were being made to bury him in Plainpalais, the cemetery reserved for the Swiss notables, but that was not an easy undertaking. When at last the Swiss authorities approved the burial in Plainpalais, the funeral was scheduled for Wednesday, June 18. I had almost four days to kill in Geneva. Most of that time was spent with María, journalists, and publishers. We formed a small circle of close friends determined to protect María from cameramen, photographers, and intruders. Since there was no family present, we became her family surrogate. In addition to María and myself, the other people in the group included Carmen Criado, an editor from Alianza and a good friend of Borges and María, Jean Pierre Vernet, a French scholar who worked closely with Borges in the preparation of "La Pléiade" French edition of his complete works for Gallimard, and Héctor Bianchioti, an Argentine writer living in Paris and working for Gallimard, One day we went together to Plainpalais to help María choose the plot for Borges' grave. We were shown the few sites available in different areas of the small cemetery. María hesitated until she saw the last one under a mature and beautiful yew tree, which in French is called *if*, and only a few yards from a very modest grave that turned out to be John Calvin's. The tree, evoking Kipling's famous poem (Borges was a loyal admirer of Kipling), the closeness to Calvin's shadow, and the soothing peacefulness of that particular corner made the decision for María. Two days later Borges was buried in that spot, where he rests now.

The day of the funeral finally arrived. The religious services were conducted at the Saint Pierre Cathedral, a majestic church located in the highest and oldest part of town. There were two eulogies: one delivered by a Catholic priest and the other by a Protestant minister. The press rapidly explained that this was so because Borges' mother was a staunch Catholic, whereas his paternal grandmother was Protestant. What the press failed to explain, though, was that Borges had been, throughout his life, a committed agnostic. Furthermore, the Catholic priest disclosed in his oration that he had assisted Borges the night before his death, heard his confession and granted him absolution. Borges' agnosticism surfaced as another piece of fiction.

Borges' work is a prodigious artifice, an iridescent language, a self-contained form severed from historic reality. It was forged within the boundaries of that library he never, in his own words, ventured out of. The American poet John Ashbery has defined Borges' art as "the work of a metaphysical Fabergé," and in comparing him with Kafka, he added: "We read Kafka from something like necessity; we read Borges for enjoyment, our own indifference taking pleasure in the frightful but robust spectacle of a disinherited cosmos."[42] As Borges the man was being dispossessed of the world, the world was merciless in restating the terms of that old divorce he so much believed in – between himself, as the artist, and the world. With the exception of María Kodama – his old student and friend, his daughter figure and wife – Borges died in the most absolute solitude. One may say that he chose to die that way, but then the choice was the result of a slow and gradual losing of the world. First, by confining himself within the walls of the Library. Then, he lost the Argentine people by siding with the torturers and assassins of his own nation. This led to the loss of his native country. Eventually, for very complicated reasons and due to bitter feuds, he also lost the remaining part of his family. Finally, he lost his best friends, for obscure and controversial motives. All this was somewhat reflected in his funeral. All of Borges' most important publishers were there: Diego Hidalgo from Alianza Editorial, Claude Gallimard, who escorted María, Franco María Ricci, for whom Borges directed the series "The Library of Babel." There were a couple of official delegations from Spain and Argentina, a few local academicians, a handful of Argentine residents, and dozens of journalists, photographers, and cameramen preying on the piece of news. The most visible presence was the total absence of family, of personal friends, and of fellow writers. Loneliness at its best.

John Updike closes his essay "The Author as Librarian" with the following rumination: "We move, with Borges, beyond psychology, beyond the human, and confront, in his work, the world atomized and vacant. Perhaps not since Lucretius has a poet so definitely felt men as incidents in space."[43] His funeral at the Saint Pierre Cathedral and his death in Geneva were metaphors for that solipsistic existence: Borges' residence was not the world in constant disarray, but the tidy chambers of the Library.

NOTES

1   Borges, "An Autobiographical Essay," in *The Aleph and Other Stories 1933–1969* (New York: Bantam, 1971), p. 145.
2   *Ibid.*
3   *Ibid.*
4   Borges, *Los conjurados* (Madrid: Alianza Tres, 1985), p. 97.
5   Borges, "The Argentine Writer and Tradition," *L*, 184.
6   Borges, *La cifra* (Buenos Aires: Emecé, 1981), p. 77.
7   *Ibid.*, p. 29.
8   Joaquin Soler Serrano, *Escritores a fondo* (Barcelona: Planeta, 1986), p. 65.
9   "El remordimiento," *MH*, 89.
10 Borges, "1964," *OP*, 260.
11 Borges, *DT*, 51.
12 See my essay "Borges o el difícil oficio de la intimidad: reflexiones sobre su poesía más reciente," *Revista Iberoamericana* (julio–dic. de 1977), pp. 449–63.
13 Borges, *MH*, 140.
14 Borges, "An Autobiographical Essay," p. 142.
15 Willard Gaylin, *Rediscovering Love* (1986).
16 Borges, "Elementos de perceptiva," *Sur*, Año III, No. 7 (abril de 1933), pp. 158–61.
17 Borges, "El milagro secreto," in *Ficciones* (Buenos Aires: Emecé, 1956), p. 162.

18 Borges, "Avatares de la tortuga," *D*, 136.
19 Borges, "Magias parciales del *Quixote*," in *Otras inquisiciones* (Buenos Aires: Emecé, 1960), p. 68.
20 See Borges' review of José Bianco's *Las ratas* in which he refers sardonically to realism in the Argentine novel. Published in *Sur*, No. 111 (enero de 1944), p. 78.
21 Borges, *D*, 10.
22 Borges, "An Autobiographical Essay," p. 140.
23 Borges, *L*, 138.
24 Borges, *OI*, 78.
25 *Ibid.*
26 *Ibid.*, p. 173.
27 Borges, *L*, 42.
28 Borges, *Historia de la eternidad* (Buenos Aires: Emecé, 1953), p. 74.
29 See *Sur*, No. 129 (julio de 1945), pp. 120–21.
30 Borges, *OT*, 130.
31 See my *Versiones, inversiones, reversiones; el espejo como modelo estructural del relato en los cuentos de Borges* (Madrid: Gredos, 1977).
32 John Updike, "The Author As Librarian," in *Critical Essays on J. L. Borges*, ed. by Jaime Alazraki (Boston: G. K. Hall, 1987), p. 66.
33 John Barth, "The Literature of Exhaustion," in *Critical Essays*, p. 87.
34 Paul de Man, "A Modern Master," in *Critical Essays*, p. 57.
35 Alfred Kazin, "Meeting Borges," in *Critical Essays*, pp. 129–30.
36 George Steiner, "Tigers in the Mirror," in *Critical Essays*, p. 120.
37 Patricia Merivale, "The Flaunting of Artifice in Vladimir Nabokov and Jorge Luis Borges," in *Critical Essays*, p. 151.
38 Updike, in *Critical Essays*, p. 77.
39 Ernesto González Bermejo, *Conversaciones con Cortázar* (Barcelona: Edhasa, 1978), p. 21.
40 Richard Burgin, *Conversations with Jorge Luis Borges* (New York: Holt, Rinehart and Winston, 1969), p. 80.
41 Borges, *DT*, 93.
42 John Ashbery, "A Game with Shifting Mirrors," in *Critical Essays*, p. 96.
43 Updike, *op cit.*, p. 76.

Index

Abraham, 20
Acker, Kathy, xv
Adam:
  creation and makeup of, 21
  as golem, 21
Adam Kadmon:
  as archetype, 9
  God's relationship to, 24
  Sefiroth in composition of, 59
Aeneid, 57
aesthetics:
  Barthes' replacement of, 158
  impossibility of consistency in, 159
  style and, 80
"After the Images" (*I*), 107–108
Aggadah, de Leon's borrowing from, 30
Akhmatova, Anna, xi
"Al coronel Francisco Borges" (*OP*), 117
aleph, Borges' description of, 50
aleph (letter), 17, 50
"Aleph, The" (*A*), 17, 45–46, 49, 110, 119
Aleph, The, 82, 90, 98, 139, 169
  narrative devices in, 93–94
allegory, reality understood through, 143
Alonso, Amado, x, 81–82, 93
ambiguity, density of meaning and, 43
"Analytical Language of John Wilkins,
  The" (*OI*), 141–142
"Another Poem of Gifts" (*OP*), 121, 132
"Approach to al-Mu'tasim, The" (*F*), 25,
  41, 91, 154
  as detective story, 42–43
"Aquél" (*C*), 117
Aramaic, *Zohar* written in, 27–28
archetype,
  Adam Kadmon as, 9
  God as, 16

Argentina:
  civil war in, 70
  meaning to Borges of, 179
"Argentines' Language, The" (*IA*), 79
"Argentine Writer and Tradition, The"
  (*L*), 42, 149
Arjuna, 47, 48
"Ars Poetica" (*SP*), 112, 128
art:
  as different from life, 129–130
  symbols and, 33
  unreality as necessary condition of, 151
Ashbery, John, 187
Asturias, Miguel Angel, 152
"Atardeceres" (*OP*), 108
Atman, 44
  Brahman as, 43
Attar, Ferid ed-Din, 43
aura, body, 25
"Ausencia" (*OP*), 108
"Autobiographical Essay" (*A*), 19, 67–68,
  181
"Averroes' Search" (*L*), 134

"Backward Glance Over Traveled Roads,
  A" (Whitman), 119
Bahadur Ali, Mir, 28, 43
Bahir, 15
baroque style, definition of, 92–93
Barth, John, 14, 77, 168, 174, 183, 185
Barthes, Roland, xv, 158
  on style and "layeredness" of discourse,
  7–8
  writing degree zero concept of, 172–173
Beckett, Samuel, 173
Belopiatkin (writer), 171
Beowulf, 100

191